NO EXIT

AND

THREE

OTHER

PLAYS

NO EXIT
(Huis Clos)

&

THE FLIES
(Les Mouches)

*translated from the French
by Stuart Gilbert*

DIRTY HANDS
(Les Mains sales)

&

THE RESPECTFUL PROSTITUTE
(La Putain respectueuse)

*translated from the French
by Lionel Abel*

VINTAGE BOOKS
A Division of Random House

New York

NO EXIT

AND

THREE

OTHER

PLAYS

BY

JEAN-PAUL

SARTRE

Library of Congress Cataloging in Publication Data

Sartre, Jean Paul, 1905-
   No exit, and three other plays.
   CONTENTS: No exit (Huis clos) & The flies (Les mouches) translated from the French by S. Gilbert.—Dirty hands (Les mains sales) & The respectful prostitute (La putain respectueuse) translated from the French by L. Abel.
   I. Title.
[PQ2637.A82H82 1973]   842'.9'14   72-7484
ISBN 0-394-70016-3

Manufactured in the United States of America

Vintage Books Edition, September 1955

CONTENTS

NO EXIT
(*Huis Clos*)

A PLAY IN ONE ACT

CHARACTERS IN THE PLAY

VALET

GARCIN

ESTELLE

INEZ

Huis Clos (No Exit) was presented for the first time at the Théâtre du Vieux-Colombier, Paris, in May 1944.

SCENE

A drawing-room in Second Empire style. A massive bronze ornament stands on the mantelpiece.

GARCIN [*enters, accompanied by the* ROOM-VALET, *and glances around him*]: Hm! So here we are?

VALET: Yes, Mr. Garcin.

GARCIN: And this is what it looks like?

VALET: Yes.

GARCIN: Second Empire furniture, I observe. . . . Well, well, I dare say one gets used to it in time.

VALET: Some do. Some don't.

GARCIN: Are all the other rooms like this one?

VALET: How could they be? We cater for all sorts: Chinamen and Indians, for instance. What use would they have for a Second Empire chair?

GARCIN: And what use do you suppose I have for one? Do you know who I was? . . . Oh, well, it's no great matter. And, to tell the truth, I had quite a habit of living among furniture that I didn't relish, and in false positions. I'd even come to like it. A false position in a Louis-Philippe dining-room—you know the style? —well, that had its points, you know. Bogus in bogus, so to speak.

VALET: And you'll find that living in a Second Empire drawing-room has its points.

GARCIN: Really? . . . Yes, yes, I dare say. . . . [*He takes another look around.*] Still, I certainly didn't expect—this! You know what they tell us down there?

VALET: What about?

GARCIN: About [*makes a sweeping gesture*] this—er—residence.

VALET: Really, sir, how could you believe such cock-and-bull stories? Told by people who'd never set foot here. For, of course, if they had—

GARCIN: Quite so. [*Both laugh. Abruptly the laugh dies from* GARCIN's *face*.] But, I say, where are the instruments of torture?

VALET: The what?

GARCIN: The racks and red-hot pincers and all the other paraphernalia?

VALET: Ah, you must have your little joke, sir!

GARCIN: My little joke? Oh, I see. No, I wasn't joking. [*A short silence. He strolls round the room.*] No mirrors, I notice. No windows. Only to be expected. And nothing breakable. [*Bursts out angrily.*] But, damn it all, they might have left me my toothbrush!

VALET: That's good! So you haven't yet got over your—what-do-you-call-it?—sense of human dignity? Excuse me smiling.

GARCIN [*thumping ragefully the arm of an armchair*]: I'll ask you to be more polite. I quite realize the position I'm in, but I won't tolerate . . .

VALET: Sorry, sir. No offense meant. But all our guests ask me the same questions. Silly questions, if you'll pardon me saying so. Where's the torture-chamber? That's the first thing they ask, all of them. They don't bother their heads about the bathroom requisites, that I can assure you. But after a bit, when they've got their nerve back, they start in about their toothbrushes and what-not. Good heavens, Mr. Garcin, can't you use your brains? What, I ask you, would be the point of brushing your teeth?

GARCIN [*more calmly*]: Yes, of course you're right. [*He looks around again.*] And why should one want to see oneself in a looking-glass? But that bronze contraption on the mantelpiece, that's another story. I suppose there will be times when I stare my eyes out at it. Stare my eyes out—see what I mean? . . . All right, let's put our cards on the table. I assure you I'm quite conscious of my position. Shall I tell you what it feels like? A man's drowning, choking, sinking by inches, till only his eyes are just above water. And what does he see? A bronze atrocity by—what's the fellow's name?

—Barbedienne. A collector's piece. As in a nightmare. That's their idea, isn't it? . . . No, I suppose you're under orders not to answer questions; and I won't insist. But don't forget, my man, I've a good notion of what's coming to me, so don't you boast you've caught me off my guard. I'm facing the situation, facing it. [*He starts pacing the room again.*] So that's that; no toothbrush. And no bed, either. One never sleeps, I take it?

VALET: That's so.

GARCIN: Just as I expected. *Why* should one sleep? A sort of drowsiness steals on you, tickles you behind the ears, and you feel your eyes closing—but why sleep? You lie down on the sofa and—in a flash, sleep flies away. Miles and miles away. So you rub your eyes, get up, and it starts all over again.

VALET: Romantic, that's what you are.

GARCIN: Will you keep quiet, please! . . . I won't make a scene, I shan't be sorry for myself, I'll face the situation, as I said just now. Face it fairly and squarely. I won't have it springing at me from behind, before I've time to size it up. And you call that being "romantic"! . . . So it comes to this; one doesn't need rest. Why bother about sleep if one isn't sleepy? That stands to reason, doesn't it? Wait a minute, there's a snag somewhere; something disagreeable. Why, now, should it be disagreeable? . . . Ah, I see; it's life without a break.

VALET: What do you mean by that?

GARCIN: What do I mean? [*Eyes the* VALET *suspiciously.*] I thought as much. That's why there's something so beastly, so damn bad-mannered, in the way you stare at me. They're paralyzed.

VALET: What are you talking about?

GARCIN: Your eyelids. We move ours up and down. Blinking, we call it. It's like a small black shutter that clicks down and makes a break. Everything goes black; one's eyes are moistened. You can't imagine how restful, refreshing, it is. Four thousand little rests per hour.

Four thousand little respites—just think! . . . So that's the idea. I'm to live without eyelids. Don't act the fool, you know what I mean. No eyelids, no sleep; it follows, doesn't it? I shall never sleep again. But then —how shall I endure my own company? Try to understand. You see, I'm fond of teasing, it's a second nature with me—and I'm used to teasing myself. Plaguing myself, if you prefer; I don't tease nicely. But I can't go on doing that without a break. Down there I had my nights. I slept. I always had good nights. By way of compensation, I suppose. And happy little dreams. There was a green field. Just an ordinary field. I used to stroll in it. . . . Is it daytime now?

VALET: Can't you see? The lights are on.

GARCIN: Ah yes, I've got it. It's *your* daytime. And outside?

VALET: Outside?

GARCIN: Damn it, you know what I mean. Beyond that wall.

VALET: There's a passage.

GARCIN: And at the end of the passage?

VALET: There's more rooms, more passages, and stairs.

GARCIN: And what lies beyond them?

VALET: That's all.

GARCIN: But surely you have a day off sometimes. Where do you go?

VALET: To my uncle's place. He's the head valet here. He has a room on the third floor.

GARCIN: I should have guessed as much. Where's the light-switch?

VALET: There isn't any.

GARCIN: What? Can't one turn off the light?

VALET: Oh, the management can cut off the current if they want to. But I can't remember their having done so on this floor. We have all the electricity we want.

GARCIN: So one has to live with one's eyes open all the time?

VALET: To *live*, did you say?

GARCIN: Don't let's quibble over words. With one's eyes open. Forever. Always broad daylight in my eyes—and in my head. [*Short silence.*] And suppose I took that contraption on the mantelpiece and dropped it on the lamp—wouldn't it go out?

VALET: You can't move it. It's too heavy.

GARCIN [*seizing the bronze ornament and trying to lift it*]: You're right. It's too heavy.

[*A short silence follows.*]

VALET: Very well, sir, if you don't need me any more, I'll be off.

GARCIN: What? You're going? [*The VALET goes up to the door.*] Wait. [VALET *looks round.*] That's a bell, isn't it? [VALET *nods.*] And if I ring, you're bound to come?

VALET: Well, yes, that's so—in a way. But you can never be sure about that bell. There's something wrong with the wiring, and it doesn't always work. [GARCIN *goes to the bell-push and presses the button. A bell purrs outside.*]

GARCIN: It's working all right.

VALET [*looking surprised*]: So it is. [*He, too, presses the button.*] But I shouldn't count on it too much if I were you. It's—capricious. Well, I really must go now. [GARCIN *makes a gesture to detain him.*] Yes, sir?

GARCIN: No, never mind. [*He goes to the mantelpiece and picks up a paper-knife.*] What's this?

VALET: Can't you see? An ordinary paper-knife.

GARCIN: Arc there books here?

VALET: No.

GARCIN: Then what's the use. of this? [VALET *shrugs his shoulders.*] Very well. You can go. [VALET *goes out.*] [GARCIN *is by himself. He goes to the bronze ornament and strokes it reflectively. He sits down; then gets up, goes to the bell-push, and presses the button. The bell remains silent. He tries two or three times, without success. Then he tries to open the door, also without success. He calls the VALET several times, but*

gets no result. He beats the door with his fists, still call-
ing. Suddenly he grows calm and sits down again. At
the same moment the door opens and INEZ *enters,*
followed by the VALET.]

VALET: Did you call, sir?

GARCIN [*on the point of answering "Yes"—but then his*
eyes fall on INEZ]: No.

VALET [*turning to* INEZ]: This is your room, madam.
[INEZ *says nothing.*] If there's any information you
require—? [INEZ *still keeps silent, and the* VALET *looks*
slightly huffed.] Most of our guests have quite a lot
to ask me. But I won't insist. Anyhow, as regards the
toothbrush, and the electric bell, and that thing on the
mantelshelf, this gentleman can tell you anything you
want to know as well as I could. We've had a little
chat, him and me. [VALET *goes out.*] [GARCIN *refrains*
from looking at INEZ, *who is inspecting the room.*
Abruptly she turns to GARCIN.]

INEZ: Where's Florence? [GARCIN *does not reply.*] Didn't
you hear? I asked you about Florence. Where is she?

GARCIN: I haven't an idea.

INEZ: Ah, that's the way it works, is it? Torture by sepa-
ration. Well, as far as I'm concerned, you won't get
anywhere. Florence was a tiresome little fool, and
I shan't miss her in the least.

GARCIN: I beg your pardon. Who do you suppose I am?

INEZ: You? Why, the torturer, of course.

GARCIN [*looks startled, then bursts out laughing*]: Well,
that's a good one! Too comic for words. I the torturer!
So you came in, had a look at me, and thought I was
—er—one of the staff. Of course, it's that silly fellow's
fault; he should have introduced us. A torturer indeed!
I'm Joseph Garcin, journalist and man of letters by
profession. And as we're both in the same boat, so to
speak, might I ask you, Mrs.—?

INEZ [*testily*]: Not "Mrs." I'm unmarried.

GARCIN: Right. That's a start, anyway. Well, now that
we've broken the ice, do you *really* think I look like
a torturer? And, by the way, how does one recognize

torturers when one sees them? Evidently you've ideas
on the subject.

INEZ: They look frightened.

GARCIN: Frightened! But how ridiculous! Of whom should
they be frightened? Of their victims?

INEZ: Laugh away, but I know what I'm talking about.
I've often watched my face in the glass.

GARCIN: In the glass? [*He looks around him.*] How beastly
of them! They've removed everything in the least re-
sembling a glass. [*Short silence.*] Anyhow, I can assure
you I'm not frightened. Not that I take my position
lightly; I realize its gravity only too well. But I'm not
afraid.

INEZ [*shrugging her shoulders*]: That's your affair. [*Silence.*] Must you be here all the time, or do you take
a stroll outside, now and then?

GARCIN: The door's locked.

INEZ: Oh! . . . That's too bad.

GARCIN: I can quite understand that it bores you having
me here. And I, too—well, quite frankly, I'd rather
be alone. I want to think things out, you know; to set
my life in order, and one does that better by oneself.
But I'm sure we'll manage to pull along together somehow. I'm no talker, I don't move much; in fact I'm
a peaceful sort of fellow. Only, if I may venture on
a suggestion, we should make a point of being ex-
tremely courteous to each other. That will ease the
situation for us both.

INEZ: I'm not polite.

GARCIN: Then I must be polite for two.

[*A longish silence.* GARCIN *is sitting on a sofa, while*
INEZ *paces up and down the room.*]

INEZ [*fixing her eyes on him*]: Your mouth!

GARCIN [*as if waking from a dream*]: I beg your
pardon.

INEZ: Can't you keep your mouth still? You keep twisting it about all the time. It's grotesque.

GARCIN: So sorry. I wasn't aware of it.

INEZ: That's just what I reproach you with. [GARCIN's

mouth twitches.] There you are! You talk about politeness, and you don't even try to control your face. Remember you're not alone; you've no right to inflict the sight of your fear on me.

GARCIN [*getting up and going towards her*]: How about you? Aren't you afraid?

INEZ: What would be the use? There was some point in being afraid *before;* while one still had hope.

GARCIN [*in a low voice*]: There's no more hope—but it's still "before." We haven't yet begun to suffer.

INEZ: That's so. [*A short silence.*] Well? What's going to happen?

GARCIN: I don't know. I'm waiting.

[*Silence again.* GARCIN *sits down and* INEZ *resumes her pacing up and down the room.* GARCIN'S *mouth twitches; after a glance at* INEZ *he buries his face in his hands. Enter* ESTELLE *with the* VALET. ESTELLE *looks at* GARCIN, *whose face is still hidden by his hands.*]

ESTELLE [*to* GARCIN]: No! Don't look up. I know what you're hiding with your hands. I know you've no face left. [GARCIN *removes his hands.*] What! [*A short pause. Then, in a tone of surprise*] But I don't know you!

GARCIN: I'm not the torturer, madam.

ESTELLE: I never thought you were. I—I thought someone was trying to play a rather nasty trick on me. [*To the* VALET] Is anyone else coming?

VALET: No, madam. No one else is coming.

ESTELLE: Oh! Then we're to stay by ourselves, the three of us, this gentleman, this lady, and myself. [*She starts laughing.*]

GARCIN [*angrily*]: There's nothing to laugh about.

ESTELLE [*still laughing*]: It's those sofas. They're so hideous. And just look how they've been arranged. It makes me think of New Year's Day—when I used to visit that boring old aunt of mine, Aunt Mary. Her house is full of horrors like that. . . . I suppose each of us has a sofa of his own. Is that one mine? [*To the* VALET] But you can't expect me to sit on that

one. It would be too horrible for words. I'm in pale
blue and it's vivid green.

INEZ: Would you prefer mine?

ESTELLE: That claret-colored one, you mean? That's very
sweet of you, but really—no, I don't think it'd be so
much better. What's the good of worrying, anyhow?
We've got to take what comes to us, and I'll stick to
the green one. [Pauses.] The only one which might
do, at a pinch, is that gentleman's. [Another pause.]

INEZ: Did you hear, Mr. Garcin?

GARCIN [with a slight start]: Oh—the sofa, you mean.
So sorry. [He rises.] Please take it, madam.

ESTELLE: Thanks. [She takes off her coat and drops it
on the sofa. A short silence.] Well, as we're to live
together, I suppose we'd better introduce ourselves.
My name's Rigault. Estelle Rigault. [GARCIN bows and
is going to announce his name, but INEZ steps in front
of him.]

INEZ: And I'm Inez Serrano. Very pleased to meet you.

GARCIN [bowing again]: Joseph Garcin.

VALET: Do you require me any longer?

ESTELLE: No, you can go. I'll ring when I want you.
[Exit VALET, with polite bows to everyone.]

INEZ: You're very pretty. I wish we'd had some flowers
to welcome you with.

ESTELLE: Flowers? Yes, I loved flowers. Only they'd fade
so quickly here, wouldn't they? It's so stuffy. Oh, well,
the great thing is to keep as cheerful as we can, don't
you agree? Of course, you, too, are—

INEZ: Yes. Last week. What about you?

ESTELLE: I'm—quite recent. Yesterday. As a matter of
fact, the ceremony's not quite over. [Her tone is natural
enough, but she seems to be seeing what she describes.]
The wind's blowing my sister's veil all over the place.
She's trying her best to cry. Come, dear! Make another
effort. That's better. Two tears, two little tears are
twinkling under the black veil. Oh dear! What a sight
Olga looks this morning! She's holding my sister's arm,
helping her along. She's not crying, and I don't blame

her; tears always mess one's face up, don't they? Olga was my bosom friend, you know.

INEZ: Did you suffer much?

ESTELLE: No. I was only half conscious, mostly.

INEZ: What was it?

ESTELLE: Pneumonia. [*In the same tone as before*] It's over now, they're leaving the cemetery. Good-by. Good-by. Quite a crowd they are. My husband's stayed at home. Prostrated with grief, poor man. [*To* INEZ] How about you?

INEZ: The gas stove.

ESTELLE: And you, Mr. Garcin?

GARCIN: Twelve bullets through my chest. [ESTELLE *makes a horrified gesture.*] Sorry! I fear I'm not good company among the dead.

ESTELLE: Please, please don't use that word. It's so—so crude. In terribly bad taste, really. It doesn't mean much, anyhow. Somehow I feel we've never been so much alive as now. If we've absolutely got to mention this—this state of things, I suggest we call ourselves —wait!—absentees. Have you been—been absent for long?

GARCIN: About a month.

ESTELLE: Where do you come from?

GARCIN: From Rio.

ESTELLE: I'm from Paris. Have you anyone left down there?

GARCIN: Yes, my wife. [*In the same tone as* ESTELLE *has been using*] She's waiting at the entrance of the barracks. She comes there every day. But they won't let her in. Now she's trying to peep between the bars. She doesn't yet know I'm—absent, but she suspects it. Now she's going away. She's wearing her black dress. So much the better, she won't need to change. She isn't crying, but she never did cry, anyhow. It's a bright sunny day and she's like a black shadow creeping down the empty street. Those big tragic eyes of hers—with that martyred look they always had. Oh, how she got on my nerves!

[*A short silence.* GARCIN *sits on the central sofa and buries his head in his hands.*]

INEZ: Estelle!

ESTELLE: Please, Mr. Garcin!

GARCIN: What is it?

ESTELLE: You're sitting on my sofa.

GARCIN: I beg your pardon. [*He gets up.*]

ESTELLE: You looked so—so far away. Sorry I disturbed you.

GARCIN: I was setting my life in order. [INEZ *starts laughing.*] You may laugh, but you'd do better to follow my example.

INEZ: No need. My life's in perfect order. It tidied itself up nicely of its own accord. So I needn't bother about it now.

GARCIN: Really? You imagine it's so simple as that. [*He runs his hand over his forehead.*] Whew! How hot it is here! Do you mind if—? [*He begins taking off his coat.*]

ESTELLE: How dare you! [*More gently*] No, please don't. I loathe men in their shirt-sleeves.

GARCIN [*putting on his coat again*]: All right. [*A short pause.*] Of course, I used to spend my nights in the newspaper office, and it was a regular Black Hole, so we never kept our coats on. Stiflingly hot it could be. [*Short pause. In the same tone as previously*] Stifling, that it *is*. It's night now.

ESTELLE: That's so. Olga's undressing; it must be after midnight. How quickly the time passes, on earth!

INEZ: Yes, after midnight. They've sealed up my room. It's dark, pitch-dark, and empty.

GARCIN: They've slung their coats on the backs of the chairs and rolled up their shirt-sleeves above the elbow. The air stinks of men and cigar-smoke. [*A short silence.*] I used to like living among men in their shirt-sleeves.

ESTELLE [*aggressively*]: Well, in that case our tastes differ. That's all it proves. [*Turning to* INEZ] What about you? Do you like men in their shirt-sleeves?

INEZ: Oh, I don't care much for men any way.

ESTELLE [*looking at the other two with a puzzled air*]: Really I can't imagine why they put us three together. It doesn't make sense.

INEZ [*stifling a laugh*]: What's that you said?

ESTELLE: I'm looking at you two and thinking that we're going to live together. . . . It's so absurd. I expected to meet old friends, or relatives.

INEZ: Yes, a charming old friend—with a hole in the middle of his face.

ESTELLE: Yes, him too. He danced the tango so divinely. Like a professional. . . . But why, why should we of all people be put together?

GARCIN: A pure fluke, I should say. They lodge folks as they can, in the order of their coming. [*To* INEZ] Why are you laughing?

INEZ: Because you amuse me, with your "flukes." As if they left anything to chance! But I suppose you've got to reassure yourself somehow.

ESTELLE [*hesitantly*]: I wonder, now. Don't you think we may have met each other at some time in our lives?

INEZ: Never. I shouldn't have forgotten you.

ESTELLE: Or perhaps we have friends in common. I wonder if you know the Dubois-Seymours?

INEZ: Not likely.

ESTELLE: But *everyone* went to their parties.

INEZ: What's their job?

ESTELLE: Oh, they don't do anything. But they have a lovely house in the country, and hosts of people visit them.

INEZ: I didn't. I was a post-office clerk.

ESTELLE [*recoiling a little*]: Ah, yes. . . . Of course, in that case— [*A pause.*] And you, Mr. Garcin?

GARCIN: We've never met. I always lived in Rio.

ESTELLE: Then you must be right. It's mere chance that has brought us together.

INEZ: Mere chance? Then it's by chance this room is furnished as we see it. It's an accident that the sofa on the right is a livid green, and that one on the left's wine-red. Mere chance? Well, just try to shift the sofas and you'll see the difference quick enough. And that statue on the mantelpiece, do you think it's there by accident? And what about the heat here? How about that? [*A short silence.*] I tell you they've thought it all out. Down to the last detail. Nothing was left to chance. This room was all set for us.

ESTELLE: But really! Everything here's so hideous; all in angles, so uncomfortable. I always loathed angles.

INEZ [*shrugging her shoulders*]: And do you think I lived in a Second Empire drawing-room?

ESTELLE: So it was all fixed up beforehand?

INEZ: Yes. And they've put us together deliberately.

ESTELLE: Then it's not mere chance that *you* precisely are sitting opposite *me*? But what can be the idea behind it?

INEZ: Ask me another! I only know they're waiting.

ESTELLE: I never could bear the idea of anyone's expecting something from me. It always made me want to do just the opposite.

INEZ: Well, do it. Do it if you can. You don't even know what they expect.

ESTELLE [*stamping her foot*]: It's outrageous! So something's coming to me from you two? [*She eyes each in turn.*] Something nasty, I suppose. There are some faces that tell me everything at once. Yours don't convey anything.

GARCIN [*turning abruptly towards* INEZ]: Look here! Why are we together? You've given us quite enough hints, you may as well come out with it.

INEZ [*in a surprised tone*]: But I know nothing, absolutely nothing about it. I'm as much in the dark as you are.

GARCIN: We've *got* to know. [*Ponders for a while.*]

INEZ: If only each of us had the guts to tell—

GARCIN: Tell what?

INEZ: Estelle!

ESTELLE: Yes?

INEZ: What have you done? I mean, why have they sent you here?

ESTELLE [*quickly*]: That's just it. I haven't a notion, not the foggiest. In fact, I'm wondering if there hasn't been some ghastly mistake. [*To* INEZ] Don't smile. Just think of the number of people who—who become absentees every day. There must be thousands and thousands, and probably they're sorted out by—by understrappers, you know what I mean. Stupid employees who don't know their job. So they're bound to make mistakes sometimes. . . . Do stop smiling. [*To* GARCIN] Why don't you speak? If they made a mistake in my case, they may have done the same about you. [*To* INEZ] And you, too. Anyhow, isn't it better to think we've got here by mistake?

INEZ: Is that all you have to tell us?

ESTELLE: What else should I tell? I've nothing to hide. I lost my parents when I was a kid, and I had my young brother to bring up. We were terribly poor and when an old friend of my people asked me to marry him I said yes. He was very well off, and quite nice. My brother was a very delicate child and needed all sorts of attention, so really that was the right thing for me to do, don't you agree? My husband was old enough to be my father, but for six years we had a happy married life. Then two years ago I met the man I was fated to love. We knew it the moment we set eyes on each other. He asked me to run away with him, and I refused. Then I got pneumonia and it finished me. That's the whole story. No doubt, by certain standards, I did wrong to sacrifice my youth to a man nearly three times my age. [*To* GARCIN] Do *you* think that could be called a sin?

GARCIN: Certainly not. [*A short silence.*] And now, tell me, do you think it's a crime to stand by one's principles?

ESTELLE: Of course not. Surely no one could blame a man for that!

GARCIN: Wait a bit! I ran a pacifist newspaper. Then war broke out. What was I to do? Everyone was watching me, wondering: "Will he dare?" Well, I dared. I folded my arms and they shot me. Had I done anything wrong?

ESTELLE [*laying her hand on his arm*]: Wrong? On the contrary. You were—

INEZ [*breaks in ironically*]:—a hero! And how about your wife, Mr. Garcin?

GARCIN: That's simple. I'd rescued her from—from the gutter.

ESTELLE [*to* INEZ]: You see! You see!

INEZ: Yes, I see. [*A pause.*] Look here! What's the point of play-acting, trying to throw dust in each other's eyes? We're all tarred with the same brush.

ESTELLE [*indignantly*]: How dare you!

INEZ: Yes, we are criminals—murderers—all three of us. We're in hell, my pets; they never make mistakes, and people aren't damned for nothing.

ESTELLE: Stop! For heaven's sake—

INEZ: In hell! Damned souls—that's us, all three!

ESTELLE: Keep quiet! I forbid you to use such disgusting words.

INEZ: A damned soul—that's you, my little plaster saint. And ditto our friend there, the noble pacifist. We've had our hour of pleasure, haven't we? There have been people who burned their lives out for our sakes—and we chuckled over it. So now we have to pay the reckoning.

GARCIN [*raising his fist*]: Will you keep your mouth shut, damn it!

INEZ [*confronting him fearlessly, but with a look of vast surprise*]: Well, well! [*A pause.*] Ah, I understand now. I know why they've put us three together.

GARCIN: I advise you to—to think twice before you say any more.

INEZ: Wait! You'll see how simple it is. Childishly simple. Obviously there aren't any physical torments —you agree, don't you? And yet we're in hell. And no one else will come here. We'll stay in this room together, the three of us, for ever and ever. . . . In short, there's someone absent here, the official torturer.

GARCIN [*sotto voce*]: I'd noticed that.

INEZ: It's obvious what they're after—an economy of man-power—or devil-power, if you prefer. The same idea as in the cafeteria, where customers serve themselves.

ESTELLE: What ever do you mean?

INEZ: I mean that each of us will act as torturer of the two others.

[*There is a short silence while they digest this information.*]

GARCIN [*gently*]: No, I shall never be your torturer. I wish neither of you any harm, and I've no concern with you. None at all. So the solution's easy enough; each of us stays put in his or her corner and takes no notice of the others. You here, you here, and I there. Like soldiers at our posts. Also, we mustn't speak. Not one word. That won't be difficult; each of us has plenty of material for self-communings. I think I could stay ten thousand years with only my thoughts for company.

ESTELLE: Have *I* got to keep silent, too?

GARCIN: Yes. And that way we—we'll work out our salvation. Looking into ourselves, never raising our heads. Agreed?

INEZ: Agreed.

ESTELLE [*after some hesitation*]: I agree.

GARCIN: Then—good-by.

[*He goes to his sofa and buries his head in his hands. There is a long silence; then* INEZ *begins singing to herself.*]

INEZ [*singing*]:

> What a crowd in Whitefriars Lane!
> They've set trestles in a row,
> With a scaffold and the knife,
> And a pail of bran below.
> Come, good folks, to Whitefriars Lane,
> Come to see the merry show!

The headsman rose at crack of dawn,
He'd a long day's work in hand,
Chopping heads off generals,
Priests and peers and admirals,
All the highest in the land.
What a crowd in Whitefriars Lane!

See them standing in a line,
Ladies all dressed up so fine.
But their heads have got to go,
Heads and hats roll down below.
Come, good folks, to Whitefrairs Lane,
Come to see the merry show!

[*Meanwhile* ESTELLE *has been plying her powder-puff
and lipstick. She looks round for a mirror, fumbles in
her bag, then turns towards* GARCIN.]

ESTELLE: Excuse me, have you a glass? [GARCIN *does not
answer.*] Any sort of glass, a pocket-mirror will do.
[GARCIN *remains silent.*] Even if you won't speak to
me, you might lend me a glass.

[*His head still buried in his hands,* GARCIN *ignores her.*]

INEZ [*eagerly*]: Don't worry. I've a glass in my bag. [*She
opens her bag. Angrily*] It's gone! They must have taken
it from me at the entrance.

ESTELLE: How tiresome!

[*A short silence.* ESTELLE *shuts her eyes and sways, as
if about to faint.* INEZ *runs forward and holds her up.*]

INEZ: What's the matter?

ESTELLE [*opens her eyes and smiles*]: I feel so queer.
[*She pats herself.*] Don't you ever get taken that way?
When I can't see myself I begin to wonder if I really
and truly exist. I pat myself just to make sure, but it
doesn't help much.

INEZ: You're lucky. I'm always conscious of myself—in
my mind. Painfully conscious.

ESTELLE: Ah yes, in your mind. But everything that goes
on in one's head is so vague, isn't it? It makes one

want to sleep. [*She is silent for a while.*] I've six big mirrors in my bedroom. There they are. I can see them. But they don't see me. They're reflecting the carpet, the settee, the window—but how empty it is, a glass in which I'm absent! When I talked to people I always made sure there was one near by in which I could see myself. I watched myself talking. And somehow it kept me alert, seeing myself as the others saw me. . . . Oh dear! My lipstick! I'm sure I've put it on all crooked. No, I can't do without a looking-glass for ever and ever, I simply can't.

INEZ· Suppose I try to be your glass? Come and pay me a visit, dear. Here's a place for you on my sofa.

ESTELLE: But— [*Points to* GARCIN.]

INEZ: Oh, he doesn't count.

ESTELLE: But we're going to—to hurt each other. You said it yourself.

INEZ: Do I look as if I wanted to hurt you?

ESTELLE: One never can tell.

INEZ: Much more likely *you'll* hurt *me*. Still, what does it matter? If I've got to suffer, it may as well be at your hands, your pretty hands. Sit down. Come closer. Closer. Look into my eyes. What do you see?

ESTELLE: Oh, I'm there! But so tiny I can't see myself properly.

INEZ: But I can. Every inch of you. Now ask me questions. I'll be as candid as any looking-glass.

[ESTELLE *seems rather embarrassed and turns to* GARCIN, *as if appealing to him for help.*]

ESTELLE: Please, Mr. Garcin. Sure our chatter isn't boring you?

[GARCIN *makes no reply.*]

INEZ: Don't worry about him. As I said, he doesn't count. We're by ourselves. . . . Ask away.

ESTELLE: Are my lips all right?

INEZ: Show! No, they're a bit smudgy.

ESTELLE: I thought as much. Luckily [*throws a quick glance at* GARCIN] no one's seen me. I'll try again.

INEZ: That's better. No. Follow the line of your lips. Wait! I'll guide your hand. There. That's quite good.

ESTELLE: As good as when I came in?

INEZ: Far better. Crueler. Your mouth looks quite diabolical that way.

ESTELLE: Good gracious! And you say you like it! How maddening, not being able to see for myself! You're quite sure, Miss Serrano, that it's all right now?

INEZ: Won't you call me Inez?

ESTELLE: Are you sure it looks all right?

INEZ: You're lovely, Estelle.

ESTELLE: But how can I rely upon your taste? Is it the same as *my* taste? Oh, how sickening it all is, enough to drive one crazy!

INEZ: I *have* your taste, my dear, because I like you so much. Look at me. No, straight. Now smile. I'm not so ugly, either. Am I not nicer than your glass?

ESTELLE: Oh, I don't know. You scare me rather. My reflection in the glass never did that; of course, I knew it so well. Like something I had tamed. . . . I'm going to smile, and my smile will sink down into your pupils, and heaven knows what it will become.

INEZ: And why shouldn't you "tame" *me*? [*The women gaze at each other,* ESTELLE *with a sort of fearful fascination.*] Listen! I want you to call me Inez. We must be great friends.

ESTELLE: I don't make friends with women very easily.

INEZ: Not with postal clerks, you mean? Hullo, what's that—that nasty red spot at the bottom of your cheek? A pimple?

ESTELLE: A pimple? Oh, how simply foul! Where?

INEZ: There. . . . You know the way they catch larks—with a mirror? I'm your lark-mirror, my dear, and you can't escape me. . . . There isn't any pimple, not a trace of one. So what about it? Suppose the mirror started telling lies? Or suppose I covered my eyes—as he is doing—and refused to look at you, all that loveliness of yours would be wasted on the desert air. No, don't be afraid, I can't help looking at you, I shan't turn my eyes away. And I'll be nice to you, ever so nice. Only you must be nice to me, too.

[*A short silence.*]

ESTELLE: Are you really—attracted by me?

INEZ: Very much indeed.

[*Another short silence.*]

ESTELLE [*indicating* GARCIN *by a slight movement of her head*]: But I wish he'd notice me, too.

INEZ: Of course! Because he's a Man! [*To* GARCIN] You've won. [GARCIN *says nothing.*] But look at her, damn it! [*Still no reply from* GARCIN.] Don't pretend. You haven't missed a word of what we've said.

GARCIN: Quite so; not a word. I stuck my fingers in my ears, but your voices thudded in my brain. Silly chatter. Now will you leave me in peace, you two? I'm not interested in you.

INEZ: Not in me, perhaps—but how about this child? Aren't you interested in her? Oh, I saw through your game; you got on your high horse just to impress her.

GARCIN: I asked you to leave me in peace. There's someone talking about me in the newspaper office and I want to listen. And, if it'll make you any happier, let me tell you that I've no use for the "child," as you call her.

ESTELLE: Thanks.

GARCIN: Oh, I didn't mean it rudely.

ESTELLE: You cad!

[*They confront each other in silence for some moments.*]

GARCIN: So's that's that. [*Pause.*] You know I begged you not to speak.

ESTELLE: It's *her* fault; she started. I didn't ask anything of her and she came and offered me her—her glass.

INEZ: So you say. But all the time you were making up to him, trying every trick to catch his attention.

ESTELLE: Well, why shouldn't I?

GARCIN: You're crazy, both of you. Don't you see where this is leading us? For pity's sake, keep your mouths

shut. [*Pause.*] Now let's all sit down again quite
quietly; we'll look at the floor and each must try to
forget the others are there.

[*A longish silence.* GARCIN *sits down. The women return hesitantly to their places. Suddenly* INEZ *swings
round on him.*]

INEZ: To forget about the others? How utterly absurd!
I *feel* you there, in every pore. Your silence clamors
in my ears. You can nail up your mouth, cut your
tongue out—but you can't prevent your *being there.*
Can you stop your thoughts? I hear them ticking away
like a clock, tick-tock, tick-tock, and I'm certain you
hear mine. It's all very well skulking on your sofa,
but you're everywhere, and every sound comes to me
soiled, because you've intercepted it on its way. Why,
you've even stolen my face; you know it and I don't!
And what about her, about Estelle? You've stolen her
from me, too; if she and I were alone do you suppose
she'd treat me as she does? No, take your hands from
your face, I won't leave you in peace—that would suit
your book too well. You'd go on sitting there, in a sort
of trance, like a yogi, and even if I didn't see her I'd
feel it in my bones—that she was making every sound,
even the rustle of her dress, for your benefit, throwing
you smiles you didn't see. . . . Well, I won't stand for
that, I prefer to choose my hell; I prefer to look you
in the eyes and fight it out face to face.

GARCIN: Have it your own way. I suppose we were bound
to come to this; they knew what they were about, and
we're easy game. If they'd put me in a room with men
—men can keep their mouths shut. But it's no use
wanting the impossible. [*He goes to* ESTELLE *and lightly
fondles her neck.*] So I attract you, little girl? It seems
you were making eyes at me?

ESTELLE: Don't touch me.

GARCIN: Why not? We might, anyhow, be natural. . . .
Do you know, I used to be mad about women? And
some were fond of me. So we may as well stop posing,
we've nothing to lose. Why trouble about politeness,

and decorum, and the rest of it? We're between ourselves. And presently we shall be naked as—as new-born babes.

ESTELLE: Oh, let me be!

GARCIN: As new-born babes. Well, I'd warned you, anyhow. I asked so little of you, nothing but peace and a little silence. I'd put my fingers in my ears. Gomez was spouting away as usual, standing in the center of the room, with all the pressmen listening. In their shirtsleeves. I tried to hear, but it wasn't too easy. Things on earth move so quickly, you know. Couldn't you have held your tongues? Now it's over, he's stopped talking, and what he thinks of me has gone back into his head. Well, we've got to see it through somehow. . . . Naked as we were born. So much the better; I want to know whom I have to deal with.

INEZ: You know already. There's nothing more to learn.

GARCIN: You're wrong. So long as each of us hasn't made a clean breast of it—why they've damned him or her —we know nothing. Nothing that counts. You, young lady, you shall begin. Why? Tell us why. If you are frank, if we bring our specters into the open, it may save us from disaster. So—out with it! Why?

ESTELLE: I tell you I haven't a notion. They wouldn't tell me why.

GARCIN: That's so. They wouldn't tell me, either. But I've a pretty good idea. . . . Perhaps you're shy of speaking first? Right. I'll lead off. [*A short silence.*] I'm not a very estimable person.

INEZ: No need to tell us that. We know you were a deserter.

GARCIN: Let that be. It's only a side-issue. I'm here because I treated my wife abominably. That's all. For five years. Naturally, she's suffering still. There she is: the moment I mention her, I see her. It's Gomez who interests me, and it's she I see. Where's Gomez got to? For five years. There! They've given her back my things; she's sitting by the window, with my coat on her knees. The coat with the twelve bullet-holes. The blood's like rust; a brown ring round each hole. It's quite a museum-piece, that coat; scarred with history. And I used to wear it, fancy! . . . Now, can't you shed a tear, my love? Surely you'll squeeze one out—at last? No? You can't manage it? . . . Night after night I came home blind drunk, stinking of wine and women. She'd sat up for me, of course. But she never cried, never uttered a word of reproach. Only her eyes spoke. Big, tragic eyes. I don't regret anything. I must pay the price, but I shan't whine. . . . It's snowing in the street. Won't you cry, confound you? That woman was a born martyr, you know; a victim by vocation.

INEZ [*almost tenderly*]: Why did you hurt her like that?

GARCIN: It was so easy. A word was enough to make her flinch. Like a sensitive-plant. But never, never a reproach. I'm fond of teasing. I watched and waited. But no, not a tear, not a protest. I'd picked her up out of the gutter, you understand. . . . Now she's stroking the coat. Her eyes are shut and she's feeling with her fingers for the bullet-holes. What are you after? What do you expect? I tell you I regret nothing. The truth is, she admired me too much. Does that mean anything to you?

INEZ: No. Nobody admired *me*.

GARCIN: So much the better. So much the better for you. I suppose all this strikes you as very vague. Well, here's something you can get your teeth into. I brought a half-caste girl to stay in our house. My wife slept upstairs; she must have heard—everything. She was an early riser and, as I and the girl stayed in bed late, she served us our morning coffee.

INEZ: You brute!

GARCIN: Yes, a brute, if you like. But a well-beloved brute. [*A far-away look comes to his eyes.*] No, it's nothing. Only Gomez, and he's not talking about *me*. . . . What were you saying? Yes, a brute. Certainly. Else why should I be here? [*To* INEZ] Your turn.

INEZ: Well, I was what some people down there called "a damned bitch." Damned already. So it's no surprise, being here.

GARCIN: Is that all you have to say?

INEZ: No. There was that affair with Florence. A dead men's tale. With three corpses to it. He to start with; then she and I. So there's no one left, I've nothing to worry about; it was a clean sweep. Only that room. I see it now and then. Empty, with the doors locked. . . . No, they've just unlocked them. "To Let." It's to let; there's a notice on the door. That's—too ridiculous.

GARCIN: Three. Three deaths, you said?

INEZ: Three.

GARCIN: One man and two women?

INEZ: Yes.

GARCIN: Well, well. [*A pause.*] Did he kill himself?

INEZ: He? No, he hadn't the guts for that. Still, he'd every reason; we led him a dog's life. As a matter of fact, he was run over by a tram. A silly sort of end. . . . I was living with them; he was my cousin.

GARCIN: Was Florence fair?

INEZ: Fair? [*Glances at* ESTELLE.] You know, I don't regret a thing; still, I'm not so very keen on telling you the story.

GARCIN: That's all right. . . . So you got sick of him?

INEZ: Quite gradually. All sorts of little things got on my nerves. For instance, he made a noise when he was drinking—a sort of gurgle. Trifles like that. He was rather pathetic really. Vulnerable. Why are you smiling?

GARCIN: Because I, anyhow, am *not* vulnerable.

INEZ: Don't be too sure. . . . I crept inside her skin, she saw the world through my eyes. When she left him, I had her on my hands. We shared a bed-sitting-room at the other end of the town.

GARCIN: And then?

INEZ: Then that tram did its job. I used to remind her every day: "Yes, my pet, we killed him between us." [*A pause.*] I'm rather cruel, really.

GARCIN: So am I.

INEZ: No, you're not cruel. It's something else.

GARCIN: What?

INEZ: I'll tell you later. When I say I'm cruel, I mean I can't get on without making people suffer. Like a live coal. A live coal in others' hearts. When I'm alone I flicker out. For six months I flamed away in her heart, till there was nothing but a cinder. One night she got up and turned on the gas while I was asleep. Then she crept back into bed. So now you know.

GARCIN: Well! Well!

INEZ: Yes? What's in your mind?

GARCIN: Nothing. Only that it's not a pretty story.

INEZ: Obviously. But what matter?

GARCIN: As you say, what matter? [To ESTELLE] Your turn. What have you done?

ESTELLE: As I told you, I haven't a notion. I rack my brain, but it's no use.

GARCIN: Right. Then we'll give you a hand. That fellow with the smashed face, who was he?

ESTELLE: Who—who do you mean?

INEZ: You know quite well. The man you were so scared of seeing when you came in.

ESTELLE: Oh, him! A friend of mine.

GARCIN: Why were you afraid of him?

ESTELLE: That's my business, Mr. Garcin.

INEZ: Did he shoot himself on your account?

ESTELLE: Of course not. How absurd you are!

GARCIN: Then why should you have been so scared? He blew his brains out, didn't he? That's how his face got smashed.

ESTELLE: Don't! Please don't go on.

GARCIN: Because of you. Because of you.

INEZ: He shot himself because of you.

ESTELLE: Leave me alone! It's—it's not fair, bullying me like that. I want to go! I want to go!

[She runs to the door and shakes it.]

GARCIN: Go if you can. Personally, I ask for nothing better. Unfortunately, the door's locked.

[ESTELLE *presses the bell-push, but the bell does not ring.* INEZ *and* GARCIN *laugh.* ESTELLE *swings round on them, her back to the door.*]

ESTELLE [*in a muffled voice*]: You're hateful, both of you.

INEZ: Hateful? Yes, that's the word. Now get on with it. That fellow who killed himself on your account—you were his mistress, eh?

GARCIN: Of course she was. And he wanted to have her to himself alone. That's so, isn't it?

INEZ: He danced the tango like a professional, but he was poor as a church mouse—that's right, isn't it?

[*A short silence.*]

GARCIN: Was he poor or not? Give a straight answer.

ESTELLE: Yes, he was poor.

GARCIN: And then you had your reputation to keep up. One day he came and implored you to run away with him, and you laughed in his face.

INEZ: That's it. You laughed at him. And so he killed himself.

ESTELLE: Did you use to look at Florence in that way?

INEZ: Yes.

[*A short pause, then* ESTELLE *bursts out laughing.*]

ESTELLE: You've got it all wrong, you two. [*She stiffens her shoulders, still leaning against the door, and faces them. Her voice grows shrill, truculent.*] He wanted me to have a baby. So there!

GARCIN: And you didn't want one?

ESTELLE: I certainly didn't. But the baby came, worse luck. I went to Switzerland for five months. No one knew anything. It was a girl. Roger was with me when she was born. It pleased him no end, having a daughter. It didn't please *me!*

GARCIN: And then?

ESTELLE: There was a balcony overlooking the lake. I brought a big stone. He could see what I was up to and he kept on shouting: "Estelle, for God's sake, don't!" I hated him then. He saw it all. He was leaning over the balcony and he saw the rings spreading on the water—

GARCIN: Yes? And then?

ESTELLE: That's all. I came back to Paris—and he did as he wished.

GARCIN: You mean he blew his brains out?

ESTELLE: It was absurd of him, really, my husband never suspected anything. [*A pause.*] Oh, how I loathe you! [*She sobs tearlessly.*]

GARCIN: Nothing doing. Tears don't flow in this place.

ESTELLE: I'm a coward. A coward! [*Pause.*] If you knew how I hate you!

INEZ [*taking her in her arms*]: Poor child! [*To* GARCIN] So the hearing's over. But there's no need to look like a hanging judge.

GARCIN: A hanging judge? [*He glances around him.*] I'd give a lot to be able to see myself in a glass. [*Pause.*] How hot it is! [*Unthinkingly he takes off his coat.*] Oh, sorry! [*He starts putting it on again.*]

ESTELLE: Don't bother. You can stay in your shirt-sleeves. As things are—

GARCIN: Just so. [*He drops his coat on the sofa.*] You mustn't be angry with me, Estelle.

ESTELLE: I'm not angry with you.

INEZ: And what about me? Are you angry with me?

ESTELLE: Yes.

[*A short silence.*]

INEZ: Well, Mr. Garcin, now you have us in the nude all right. Do you understand things any better for that?

GARCIN: I wonder. Yes, perhaps a trifle better. [*Timidly*] And now suppose we start trying to help each other.

INEZ: I don't need help.

GARCIN: Inez, they've laid their snare damned cunningly —like a cobweb. If you make any movement, if you raise your hand to fan yourself, Estelle and I feel a little tug. Alone, none of us can save himself or herself; we're linked together inextricably. So you can take your choice. [*A pause.*] Hullo? What's happening?

INEZ: They've let it. The windows are wide open, a man is sitting on my bed. *My* bed, if you please! They've let it, let it! Step in, step in, make yourself at home, you brute! Ah, there's a woman, too. She's going up to him, putting her hands on his shoulders. . . . Damn it, why don't they turn the lights on? It's getting dark. Now he's going to kiss her. But that's my room, *my* room! Pitch-dark now. I can't see anything, but I hear them whispering, whispering. Is he going to make love to her on *my* bed? What's that she said? That it's noon and the sun is shining? I must be going blind. [*A pause.*] Blacked out. I can't see or hear a thing. So I'm done with the earth, it seems. No more alibis for me! [*She shudders.*] I feel so empty, desiccated—really dead at last. All of me's here, in this room. [*A pause.*] What were you saying? Something about helping me, wasn't it?

GARCIN: Yes.

INEZ: Helping me to do what?

GARCIN: To defeat their devilish tricks.

INEZ: And what do you expect me to do, in return?

GARCIN: To help *me*. It only needs a little effort, Inez; just a spark of human feeling.

INEZ: Human feeling. That's beyond my range. I'm rotten to the core.

GARCIN: And how about me? [*A pause.*] All the same, suppose we try?

INEZ: It's no use. I'm all dried up. I can't give and I can't receive. How could *I* help you? A dead twig, ready for the burning. [*She falls silent, gazing at* ESTELLE, *who has buried her head in her hands.*] Florence was fair, a natural blonde.

GARCIN: Do you realize that this young woman's fated to be your torturer?

INEZ: Perhaps I've guessed it.

GARCIN: It's through her they'll get you. I, of course, I'm different—aloof. I take no notice of her. Suppose you had a try—

INEZ: Yes?

GARCIN: It's a trap. They're watching you, to see if you'll fall into it.

INEZ: I know. And you're another trap. Do you think they

haven't foreknown every word you say? And of course
there's a whole nest of pitfalls that we can't see. Everything here's a booby-trap. But what do I care? I'm a
pitfall, too. For her, obviously. And perhaps I'll catch
her.

GARCIN: You won't catch anything. We're chasing after
each other, round and round in a vicious circle, like the
horses on a roundabout. That's part of their plan, of
course. . . . Drop it, Inez. Open your hands and let
go of everything. Or else you'll bring disaster on all
three of us.

INEZ: Do I look the sort of person who lets go? I know
what's coming to me. I'm going to burn, and it's to last
forever. Yes, I *know* everything. But do you think I'll let
go? I'll catch her, she'll see you through my eyes, as
Florence saw that other man. What's the good of trying
to enlist my sympathy? I assure you I know everything,
and I can't feel sorry even for myself. A trap! Don't I
know it, and that I'm in a trap myself, up to the neck,
and there's nothing to be done about it? And if it suits
their book, so much the better!

GARCIN [*gripping her shoulders*]: Well, I, anyhow, can feel
sorry for you, too. Look at me, we're naked, naked right
through, and I can see into your heart. That's one link
between us. Do you think I'd want to hurt you? I don't
regret anything, I'm dried up, too. But for you I can
still feel pity.

INEZ [*who has let him keep his hands on her shoulders
until now, shakes herself loose*]: Don't. I hate being
pawed about. And keep your pity for yourself. Don't
forget, Garcin, that there are traps for you, too, in this
room. All nicely set for you. You'd do better to watch
your own interests. [*A pause.*] But, if you will leave us
in peace, this child and me, I'll see I don't do you any
harm.

GARCIN [*gazes at her for a moment, then shrugs his
shoulders*]: Very well.

ESTELLE [*raising her head*]: Please, Garcin.

GARCIN: What do you want of me?

ESTELLE [*rises and goes up to him*]: You can help *me*, anyhow.

GARCIN: If you want help, apply to her.

[INEZ *has come up and is standing behind* ESTELLE, *but without touching her. During the dialogue that follows she speaks almost in her ear. But* ESTELLE *keeps her eyes on* GARCIN, *who observes her without speaking, and she addresses her answers to him, as if it were he who is questioning her.*]

ESTELLE: I implore you, Garcin—you gave me your promise, didn't you? Help me quick. I don't want to be left alone. Olga's taken him to a cabaret.

INEZ: Taken whom?

ESTELLE: Peter. . . . Oh, now they're dancing together.

INEZ: Who's Peter?

ESTELLE: Such a silly boy. He called me his glancing stream—just fancy! He was terribly in love with me. . . . She's persuaded him to come out with her tonight.

INEZ: Do you love him?

ESTELLE: They're sitting down now. She's puffing like a grampus. What a fool the girl is to insist on dancing! But I dare say she does it to reduce. . . . No, of course I don't love him; he's only eighteen, and I'm not a baby-snatcher.

INEZ: Then why bother about them? What difference can it make?

ESTELLE: He belonged to me.

INEZ: Nothing on earth belongs to you any more.

ESTELLE: I tell you he was mine. All mine.

INEZ: Yes, he *was* yours—once. But now— Try to make him hear, try to touch him. Olga can touch him, talk to him as much as she likes. That's so, isn't it? She can squeeze his hands, rub herself against him—

ESTELLE: Yes, look! She's pressing her great fat chest against him, puffing and blowing in his face. But, my poor little lamb, can't you see how ridiculous she is? Why don't you laugh at her? Oh, once I'd have only had to glance at them and she'd have slunk away. Is there really nothing, nothing left of me?

INEZ: Nothing whatever. Nothing of you's left on earth—not even a shadow. All you own is here. Would you like that paper-knife? Or that ornament on the mantelpiece? That blue sofa's yours. And I, my dear, am yours forever.

ESTELLE: You mine! That's good! Well, which of you two would dare to call me his glancing stream, his crystal girl? You know too much about me, you know I'm rotten through and through. . . . Peter dear, think of me, fix your thoughts on me, and save me. All the time you're thinking "my glancing stream, my crystal girl," I'm only half here, I'm only half wicked, and half of me is down there with you, clean and bright and crystal-clear as running water. . . . Oh, just look at her face, all scarlet, like a tomato. No, it's absurd, we've laughed at her together, you and I, often and often. . . . What's that tune?—I always loved it. Yes, the *St. Louis Blues*. . . . All right, dance away, dance away. Garcin, I wish you could see her, you'd die of laughing. Only—she'll never know I *see* her. Yes, I see you, Olga, with your hair all anyhow, and you do look a dope, my dear. Oh, now you're treading on his toes. It's a scream! Hurry up! Quicker! Quicker! He's dragging her along, bundling her round and round—it's too ghastly! He always said I was so light, he loved to dance with me. [*She is dancing as she speaks.*] I tell you, Olga, I can see you. No, she doesn't care, she's dancing through my gaze. What's that? What's that you said? "Our poor dear Estelle"? Oh, don't be such a humbug! You didn't even shed a tear at the funeral. . . . And she has the nerve to talk to him about her poor dear friend Estelle! How dare she discuss me with Peter? Now then, keep time. She never could dance and talk at once. Oh, what's that? No, no. Don't tell him. Please, please don't tell him. You can keep him, do what you like with him, but please don't tell him about—that! [*She*

has stopped dancing.] All right. You can have him now.
Isn't it *foul*, Garcin? She's told him everything, about
Roger, my trip to Switzerland, the baby. "Poor Estelle
wasn't exactly—" No, I wasn't exactly— True enough.
He's looking grave, shaking his head, but he doesn't
seem so very much surprised, not what one would
expect. Keep him, then—I won't haggle with you over
his long eyelashes, his pretty girlish face. They're yours
for the asking. His glancing stream, his crystal. Well,
the crystal's shattered into bits. "Poor Estelle!" Dance,
dance, dance. On with it. But do keep time. One, two.
One, two. How I'd love to go down to earth for just a
moment, and dance with him again. [*She dances again
for some moments.*] The music's growing fainter.
They've turned down the lights, as they do for a tango.
Why are they playing so softly? Louder, please. I can't
hear. It's so far away, so far away. I—I can't hear a
sound. [*She stops dancing.*] All over. It's the end. The
earth has left me. [*To* GARCIN] Don't turn from me—
please. Take me in your arms. [*Behind* ESTELLE'S *back,*
INEZ *signs to* GARCIN *to move away.*]

INEZ [*commandingly*]: Now then, Garcin!

[GARCIN *moves back a step, and, glancing at* ESTELLE,
points to INEZ.]

GARCIN: It's to her you should say that.

ESTELLE [*clinging to him*]: Don't turn away. You're a
man, aren't you, and surely I'm not such a fright as all
that! Everyone says I've lovely hair and, after all, a man
killed himself on my account. You have to look at something, and there's nothing here to see except the sofas
and that awful ornament and the table. Surely I'm
better to look at than a lot of stupid furniture. Listen!
I've dropped out of their hearts like a little sparrow
fallen from its nest. So gather me up, dear, fold me to
your heart—and you'll see how nice I can be.

GARCIN [*freeing himself from her, after a short struggle*]:
I tell you it's to that lady you should speak.

ESTELLE: To her? But she doesn't count, she's a woman.

INEZ: Oh, I don't count? Is that what you think? But,

my poor little fallen nestling, you've been sheltering in my heart for ages, though you didn't realize it. Don't be afraid; I'll keep looking at you for ever and ever, without a flutter of my eyelids, and you'll live in my gaze like a mote in a sunbeam.

ESTELLE: A sunbeam indeed! Don't talk such rubbish! You've tried that trick already, and you should know it doesn't work.

INEZ: Estelle! My glancing stream! My crystal!

ESTELLE: *Your* crystal? It's grotesque. Do you think you can fool me with that sort of talk? Everyone knows by now what I did to my baby. The crystal's shattered, but I don't care. I'm just a hollow dummy, all that's left of me is the outside—but it's not for you.

INEZ: Come to me, Estelle. You shall be whatever you like: a glancing stream, a muddy stream. And deep down in my eyes you'll see yourself just as you want to be.

ESTELLE: Oh, leave me in peace. You haven't any eyes. Oh, damn it, isn't there anything I can do to get rid of you? I've an idea. [*She spits in* INEZ's *face.*] There!

INEZ: Garcin, you shall pay for this.

[*A pause.* GARCIN *shrugs his shoulders and goes to* ESTELLE.]

GARCIN: So it's a man you need?

ESTELLE: Not *any* man. You.

GARCIN: No humbug now. Any man would do your business. As I happen to be here, you want me. Right! [*He grips her shoulders.*] Mind, I'm not your sort at all, really; I'm not a young nincompoop and I don't dance the tango.

ESTELLE: I'll take you as you are. And perhaps I shall change you.

GARCIN: I doubt it. I shan't pay much attention; I've other things to think about.

ESTELLE: What things?

GARCIN: They wouldn't interest you.

ESTELLE: I'll sit on your sofa and wait for you to take some notice of me. I promise not to bother you at all.

INEZ [*with a shrill laugh*]: That's right, fawn on him, like the silly bitch you are. Grovel and cringe! And he hasn't even good looks to commend him!

ESTELLE [*to* GARCIN]: Don't listen to her. She has no eyes, no ears. She's—nothing.

GARCIN: I'll give you what I can. It doesn't amount to much. I shan't love you; I know you too well.

ESTELLE: Do you want me, anyhow?

GARCIN: Yes.

ESTELLE: I ask no more.

GARCIN: In that case— [*He bends over her.*]

INEZ: Estelle! Garcin! You must be going crazy. You're not alone. I'm here too.

GARCIN: Of course—but what does it matter?

INEZ: Under my eyes? You couldn't—couldn't do it.

ESTELLE: Why not? I often undressed with my maid looking on.

INEZ [*gripping* GARCIN'*s arm*]: Let her alone. Don't paw her with your dirty man's hands.

GARCIN [*thrusting her away roughly*]: Take care. I'm no gentleman, and I'd have no compunction about striking a woman.

INEZ: But you promised me; you promised. I'm only asking you to keep your word.

GARCIN: Why should I, considering you were the first to break our agreement?

[INEZ *turns her back on him and retreats to the far end of the room.*]

INEZ: Very well, have it your own way. I'm the weaker party, one against two. But don't forget I'm here, and watching. I shan't take my eyes off you, Garcin; when you're kissing her, you'll feel them boring into you. Yes, have it your own way, make love and get it over. We're in hell; my turn will come.

[*During the following scene she watches them without speaking.*]

GARCIN [*coming back to* ESTELLE *and grasping her shoulders*]: Now then. Your lips. Give me your lips.

[*A pause. He bends to kiss her, then abruptly straightens up.*]

ESTELLE [*indignantly*]: Really! [*A pause.*] Didn't I tell you not to pay any attention to her?

GARCIN: You've got it wrong. [*Short silence.*] It's Gomez; he's back in the press-room. They've shut the windows; it must be winter down there. Six months since I—.Well, I warned you I'd be absent-minded sometimes, didn't I? They're shivering, they've kept their coats on. Funny they should feel the cold like that, when I'm feeling so hot. Ah, this time he's talking about me.

ESTELLE: Is it going to last long? [*Short silence.*] You might at least tell me what he's saying.

GARCIN: Nothing. Nothing worth repeating. He's a swine, that's all. [*He listens attentively.*] A god-damned bloody swine. [*He turns to* ESTELLE.] Let's come back to—to ourselves. Are you going to love me?

ESTELLE [*smiling*]: I wonder now!

GARCIN: Will you trust me?

ESTELLE: What a quaint thing to ask! Considering you'll be under my eyes. all the time, and I don't think I've much to fear from Inez, so far as you're concerned.

GARCIN: Obviously. [*A pause. He takes his hands off* ESTELLE's *shoulders.*] I was thinking of another kind of trust. [*Listens.*] Talk away, talk away, you swine. I'm not there to defend myself. [*To* ESTELLE] Estelle, you *must* give me your trust.

ESTELLE: Oh, what a nuisance you are! I'm giving you my mouth, my arms, my whole body—and everything could be so simple. . . . My trust! I haven't any to give, I'm afraid, and you're making me terribly embarrassed. You must have something pretty ghastly on your conscience to make such a fuss about my trusting you.

GARCIN: They shot me.

ESTELLE: I know. Because you refused to fight. Well, why shouldn't you?

GARCIN: I—I didn't exactly refuse. [*In a far-away voice*] I must say he talks well, he makes out a good case against me, but he never says what I should have done instead. Should I have gone to the general and said: "General, I decline to fight"? A mug's game; they'd have promptly locked me up. But I wanted to show my colors, my true colors, do you understand? I wasn't going to be silenced. [To ESTELLE] So I—I took the train. . . . They caught me at the frontier.

ESTELLE: Where were you trying to go?

GARCIN: To Mexico. I meant to launch a pacifist newspaper down there. [A short silence.] Well, why don't you speak?

ESTELLE: What could I say? You acted quite rightly, as you didn't want to fight. [GARCIN makes a fretful gesture.] But, darling, how on earth can I guess what you want me to answer?

INEZ: Can't you guess? Well, I can. He wants you to tell him that he bolted like a lion. For "bolt" he did, and that's what's biting him.

GARCIN: "Bolted," "went away"—we won't quarrel over words.

ESTELLE: But you *had* to run away. If you'd stayed they'd have sent you to jail, wouldn't they?

GARCIN: Of course. [A *pause*.] Well, Estelle, am I a coward?

ESTELLE: How can I say? Don't be so unreasonable, darling. I can't put myself in your skin. You must decide that for yourself.

GARCIN [*wearily*]: I can't decide.

ESTELLE: Anyhow, you must remember. You must have had reasons for acting as you did.

GARCIN: I had.

ESTELLE: Well?

GARCIN: But were they the real reasons?

ESTELLE: You've a twisted mind, that's your trouble. Plaguing yourself over such trifles!

GARCIN: I'd thought it all out, and I wanted to make a stand. But was that my real motive?

INEZ: Exactly. That's the question. Was that your real motive? No doubt you argued it out with yourself, you weighed the pros and cons, you found good reasons for what you did. But fear and hatred and all the dirty little instincts one keeps dark—they're motives too. So carry on, Mr. Garcin, and try to be honest with yourself—for once.

GARCIN: Do I need you to tell me that? Day and night I paced my cell, from the window to the door, from the door to the window. I pried into my heart, I sleuthed myself like a detective. By the end of it I felt as if I'd given my whole life to introspection. But always I harked back to the one thing certain—that I had acted as I did, I'd taken that train to the frontier. But why? Why? Finally I thought: My death will settle it. If I face death courageously, I'll prove I am no coward.

INEZ: And how did you face death?

GARCIN: Miserably. Rottenly. [INEZ *laughs.*] Oh, it was only a physical lapse—that might happen to anyone; I'm not ashamed of it. Only everything's been left in suspense, forever. [*To* ESTELLE] Come here, Estelle. Look at me. I want to feel someone looking at me while they're talking about me on earth.-. . . I like green eyes.

INEZ: Green eyes! Just hark to him! And you, Estelle, do you like cowards?

ESTELLE: If you knew how little I care! Coward or hero, it's all one—provided he kisses well.

GARCIN: There they are, slumped in their chairs, sucking at their cigars. Bored they look. Half-asleep. They're thinking: "Garcin's a coward." But only vaguely, dreamily. One's got to think of something. "That chap Garcin was a coward." That's what they've decided, those dear friends of mine. In six months' time they'll be saying: "Cowardly as that skunk Garcin." You're lucky, you two; no one on earth is giving you another thought. But I—I'm long in dying.

INEZ: What about your wife, Garcin?

GARCIN: Oh, didn't I tell you? She's dead.

INEZ: Dead?

GARCIN: Yes, she died just now. About two months ago.

INEZ: Of grief?

GARCIN: What else should she die of? So all is for the best, you see; the war's over, my wife's dead, and I've carved out my place in history.

[*He gives a choking sob and passes his hand over his face.* ESTELLE *catches his arm.*]

ESTELLE: My poor darling! Look at me. Please look. Touch me. Touch me. [*She takes his hand and puts it on her neck.*] There! Keep your hand there. [GARCIN *makes a fretful movement.*] No, don't move. Why trouble what those men are thinking? They'll die off one by one. Forget them. There's only me, now.

GARCIN: But *they* won't forget *me*, not they! They'll die, but others will come after them to carry on the legend. I've left my fate in their hands.

ESTELLE: You think too much, that's your trouble.

GARCIN: What else is there to do now? I was a man of action once. . . . Oh, if only I could be with them again, for just one day—I'd fling their lie in their teeth. But I'm locked out; they're passing judgment on my life without troubling about me, and they're right, because I'm dead. Dead and done with. [*Laughs.*] A back number.

[*A short pause.*]

ESTELLE [*gently*]: Garcin.

GARCIN: Still there? Now listen! I want you to do me a service. No, don't shrink away. I know it must seem strange to you, having someone asking you for help; you're not used to that. But if you'll make the effort, if you'll only *will* it hard enough, I dare say we can really love each other. Look at it this way. A thousand of them are proclaiming I'm a coward; but what do numbers matter? If there's someone, just one person, to say quite positively I did not run away, that I'm not the sort who runs away, that I'm brave and decent and the rest of it—well, that one person's faith would save me. Will you have that faith in me? Then I shall love you and cherish you for ever. Estelle—will you?

ESTELLE [*laughing*]: Oh, you dear silly man, do you think I could love a coward?

GARCIN: But just now you said—

ESTELLE: I was only teasing you. I like men, my dear, who're real men, with tough skin and strong hands. You haven't a coward's chin, or a coward's mouth, or a coward's voice, or a coward's hair. And it's for your mouth, your hair, your voice, I love you.

GARCIN: Do you mean this? *Really* mean it?

ESTELLE: Shall I swear it?

GARCIN: Then I snap my fingers at them all, those below and those in here. Estelle, we shall climb out of hell. [INEZ *gives a shrill laugh. He breaks off and stares at her.*] What's that?

INEZ [*still laughing*]: But she doesn't mean a word of what she says. How can you be such a simpleton? "Estelle, am I a coward?" As if she cared a damn either way.

ESTELLE: Inez, how dare you? [To GARCIN] Don't listen to her. If you want me to have faith in you, you must begin by trusting me.

INEZ: That's right! That's right! Trust away! She wants a man—that far you can trust her—she wants a man's arm round her waist, a man's smell, a man's eyes glowing with desire. And that's all she wants. She'd assure you you were God Almighty if she thought it would give you pleasure.

GARCIN: Estelle, is this true? Answer me. Is it true?

ESTELLE: What do you expect me to say? Don't you realize how maddening it is to have to answer questions one can't make head or tail of? [*She stamps her foot.*] You do make things difficult. . . . Anyhow, I'd love you just the same, even if you were a coward. Isn't that enough?

[*A short pause.*]

GARCIN [*to the two women*]: You disgust me, both of you. [*He goes towards the door.*]

ESTELLE: What are you up to?

GARCIN: I'm going.

INEZ [*quickly*]: You won't get far. The door is locked.

GARCIN: I'll *make* them open it. [*He presses the bell-push. The bell does not ring.*]

ESTELLE: Please! Please!

INEZ [*to* ESTELLE]: Don't worry, my pet. The bell doesn't work.

GARCIN: I tell you they shall open. [*Drums on the door.*] I can't endure it any longer, I'm through with you both. [ESTELLE *runs to him; he pushes her away.*] Go away. You're even fouler than she. I won't let myself get bogged in your eyes. You're soft and slimy. Ugh! [*Bangs on the door again.*] Like an octopus. Like a quagmire.

ESTELLE: I beg you, oh, I beg you not to leave me. I'll promise not to speak again, I won't trouble you in any way—but don't go. I daren't be left alone with Inez, now she's shown her claws.

GARCIN: Look after yourself. I never asked you to come here.

ESTELLE: Oh, how mean you are! Yes, it's quite true you're a coward.

INEZ [*going up to* ESTELLE]: Well, my little sparrow fallen from the nest, I hope you're satisfied now. You spat in my face—playing up to him, of course—and we had a tiff on his account. But he's going, and a good riddance it will be. We two women will have the place to ourselves.

ESTELLE: You won't gain anything. If that door opens, I'm going, too.

INEZ: Where?

ESTELLE: I don't care where. As far from you as I can. [GARCIN *has been drumming on the door while they talk.*]

GARCIN: Open the door! Open, blast you! I'll endure anything, your red-hot tongs and molten lead, your racks and prongs and garrotes—all your fiendish gadgets, everything that burns and flays and tears—I'll put up with any torture you impose. Anything, anything would be better than this agony of mind, this creeping pain that gnaws and fumbles and caresses one and never hurts quite enough. [*He grips the door-knob and rattles it.*] Now will you open? [*The door flies open with a jerk, and he just avoids falling.*] Ah! [*A long silence.*]

INEZ: Well, Garcin? You're free to go.

GARCIN [*meditatively*]: Now I wonder why that door opened.

INEZ: What are you waiting for? Hurry up and go.

GARCIN: I shall not go.

INEZ: And you, Estelle? [ESTELLE *does not move.* INEZ *bursts out laughing.*] So what? Which shall it be? Which of the three of us will leave? The barrier's down, why are we waiting? . . . But what a situation! It's a scream! We're—inseparables!

[ESTELLE *springs at her from behind.*]

ESTELLE: Inseparables? Garcin, come and lend a hand. Quickly. We'll push her out and slam the door on her. That'll teach her a lesson.

INEZ [*struggling with* ESTELLE]: Estelle! I beg you, let me stay. I won't go, I won't go! Not into the passage.

GARCIN: Let go of her.

ESTELLE: You're crazy. She hates you.

GARCIN: It's because of her I'm staying here.

[ESTELLE *releases* INEZ *and stares dumbfoundedly at* GARCIN.]

INEZ: Because of me? [*Pause.*] All right, shut the door. It's ten times hotter here since it opened. [GARCIN *goes to the door and shuts it.*] Because of me, you said?

GARCIN: Yes. *You*, anyhow, know what it means to be a coward.

INEZ: Yes, I know.

GARCIN: And you know what wickedness is, and shame, and fear. There were days when you peered into yourself, into the secret places of your heart, and what you saw there made you faint with horror. And then, next day, you didn't know what to make of it, you couldn't interpret the horror you had glimpsed the day before. Yes, you know what evil *costs*. And when you say I'm a coward, you know from experience what that means. Is that so?

INEZ: Yes.

GARCIN: So it's you whom I have to convince; you are of my kind. Did you suppose I meant to go? No, I couldn't leave you here, gloating over my defeat, with all those thoughts about me running in your head.

INEZ: Do you really wish to convince me?

GARCIN: That's the one and only thing I wish for now. I can't hear them any longer, you know. Probably that means they're through with me. For good and all. The curtain's down, nothing of me is left on earth—not even the name of coward. So, Inez, we're alone. Only you two remain to give a thought to me. She—she doesn't count. It's you who matter; you who hate me. If you'll have faith in me I'm saved.

INEZ: It won't be easy. Have a look at me. I'm a hard-headed woman.

GARCIN: I'll give you all the time that's needed.

INEZ: Yes, we've lots of time in hand. *All* time.

GARCIN [*putting his hands on her shoulders*]: Listen! Each man has an aim in life, a leading motive; that's so, isn't it? Well, I didn't give a damn for wealth, or for love. I aimed at being a real man. A tough, as they say. I staked everything on the same horse. . . . Can one possibly be a coward when one's deliberately courted danger at every turn? And can one judge a life by a single action?

INEZ: Why not? For thirty years you dreamt you were a hero; and condoned a thousand petty lapses—because a hero, of course, can do no wrong. An easy method, obviously. Then a day came when you were up against it, the red light of real danger—and you took the train to Mexico.

GARCIN: I "dreamt," you say. It was no dream. When I chose the hardest path, I made my choice deliberately. A man is what he wills himself to be.

INEZ: Prove it. Prove it was no dream. It's what one does, and nothing else, that shows the stuff one's made of.

GARCIN: I died too soon. I wasn't allowed time to—to do my deeds.

INEZ: One always dies too soon—or too late. And yet one's whole life is complete at that moment, with a line drawn neatly under it, ready for the summing up. You are—your life, and nothing else.

GARCIN: What a poisonous woman you are! With an answer for everything.

INEZ: Now then! Don't lose heart. It shouldn't be so hard, convincing me. Pull yourself together, man, rake up some arguments. [GARCIN *shrugs his shoulders.*] Ah, wasn't I right when I said you were vulnerable? Now you're going to pay the price, and what a price! You're a coward, Garcin, because I wish it. I wish it—do you hear?—I wish it. And yet, just look at me, see how weak I am, a mere breath on the air, a gaze observing you, a formless thought that thinks you. [*He walks towards her, opening his hands.*] Ah, they're open now, those big hands, those coarse, man's hands! But what do you hope to do? You can't throttle thoughts with hands. So you've no choice, you must convince me, and you're at my mercy.

ESTELLE: Garcin!

GARCIN: What?

ESTELLE: Revenge yourself.

GARCIN: How?

ESTELLE: Kiss me, darling—then you'll hear her squeal.

GARCIN: That's true, Inez. I'm at your mercy, but you're at mine as well.

[*He bends over* ESTELLE. INEZ *gives a little cry.*]

INEZ: Oh, you coward, you weakling, running to women to console you!

ESTELLE: That's right, Inez. Squeal away.

INEZ: What a lovely pair you make! If you could see his big paw splayed out on your back, rucking up your skin and creasing the silk. Be careful, though! He's perspiring, his hand will leave a blue stain on your dress.

ESTELLE: Squeal away, Inez, squeal away! . . . Hug me tight, darling; tighter still—that'll finish her off, and a good thing too!

INEZ: Yes, Garcin, she's right. Carry on with it, press her to you till you feel your bodies melting into each other; a lump of warm, throbbing flesh. . . . Love's a grand solace, isn't it, my friend? Deep and dark as sleep. But I'll see you don't sleep.

[GARCIN *makes a slight movement.*]

ESTELLE: Don't listen to her. Press your lips to my mouth. Oh, I'm yours, yours, yours.

INEZ: Well, what are you waiting for? Do as you're told. What a lovely scene: coward Garcin holding baby-killer Estelle in his manly arms! Make your stakes, everyone. Will coward Garcin kiss the lady, or won't he dare? What's the betting? I'm watching you, everybody's watching, I'm a crowd all by myself. Do you hear the crowd? Do you hear them muttering, Garcin? Mumbling and muttering. "Coward! Coward! Coward! Coward!"—that's what they're saying. . . . It's no use trying to escape, I'll never let you go. What do you hope to get from her silly lips? Forgetfulness? But I shan't forget you, not I! "It's I you must convince." So come to me. I'm waiting. Come along, now. . . . Look how obedient he is, like a well-trained dog who comes when his mistress calls. You can't hold him, and you never will.

GARCIN: Will night never come?

INEZ: Never.

GARCIN: You will always see me?

INEZ: Always.

[GARCIN *moves away from* ESTELLE *and takes some steps across the room. He goes to the bronze ornament.*]

GARCIN: This bronze. [*Strokes it thoughtfully.*] Yes, now's the moment; I'm looking at this thing on the mantelpiece, and I understand that I'm in hell. I tell you, everything's been thought out beforehand. They knew I'd stand at the fireplace stroking this thing of bronze, with all those eyes intent on me. Devouring me. [*He swings round abruptly.*] What? Only two of you? I thought there were more; many more. [*Laughs.*] So this is hell. I'd never have believed it. You remember all we were told about the torture-chambers, the fire and brimstone, the "burning marl." Old wives' tales! There's no need for red-hot pokers. Hell is—other people!

ESTELLE: My darling! Please—

GARCIN [*thrusting her away*]: No, let me be. She is between us. I cannot love you when she's watching.

ESTELLE: Right! In that case, I'll stop her watching. [*She picks up the paper-knife from the table, rushes at* INEZ, *and stabs her several times.*]

INEZ [*struggling and laughing*]: But, you crazy creature, what do you think you're doing? You know quite well I'm dead.

ESTELLE: Dead?

[*She drops the knife. A pause.* INEZ *picks up the knife and jabs herself with it regretfully.*]

INEZ: Dead! Dead! Dead! Knives, poison, ropes—all useless. It has happened *already*, do you understand? Once and for all. So here we are, forever. [*Laughs.*]

ESTELLE [*with a peal of laughter*]: Forever. My God, how funny! Forever.

GARCIN [*looks at the two women, and joins in the laughter*]: For ever, and ever, and ever.

[*They slump onto their respective sofas. A long silence. Their laughter dies away and they gaze at each other.*]

GARCIN: Well, well, let's get on with it. . . .

CURTAIN

THE FLIES
(*Les Mouches*)

A PLAY IN THREE ACTS

CHARACTERS IN THE PLAY

ZEUS

ORESTES

ELECTRA

ÆGISTHEUS

CLYTEMNESTRA

THE TUTOR

FIRST FURY

SECOND FURY

THE HIGH PRIEST

A YOUNG WOMAN

AN OLD WOMAN

AN IDIOT BOY

FIRST SOLDIER

SECOND SOLDIER

MEN AND WOMEN, TOWNSFOLK OF ARGOS

FURIES, SERVANTS, PALACE GUARDS

Les Mouches (*The Flies*) was first played at the Théâtre de la Cité, Paris, under the direction of Charles Dullin

ACT I

A *public square in Argos, dominated by a statue of* ZEUS, *god of flies and death. The image has white eyes and blood-smeared cheeks.*

A *procession of* OLD WOMEN *in black, carrying urns, advances; they make libations to the statue. An* IDIOT BOY *is squatting in the background.* ORESTES *enters, accompanied by* THE TUTOR.

ORESTES: Listen, my good women.

[*The* OLD WOMEN *swing round, emitting little squeals.*]

THE TUTOR: Would you kindly tell us— [*The* OLD WOMEN *spit on the ground and move back a pace.*] Steady, good ladies, steady. I only want a piece of simple information. We are travelers and we have lost our way. [*Dropping their urns, the* WOMEN *take to their heels.*] Stupid old hags! You'd think I had intentions on their virtue! [*Ironically*] Ah, young master, truly this has been a pleasant journey. And how well inspired you were to come to this city of Argos, when there are hundreds of towns in Greece and Italy where the drink is good, the inns are hospitable, and the streets full of friendly, smiling people! But these uncouth hillmen—one would suppose they'd never seen a foreigner before. A hundred times and more I've had to ask our way, and never once did I get a straight answer. And then the grilling heat! This Argos is a nightmare city. Squeals of terror everywhere, people who panic the moment they set eyes on you, and scurry to cover, like black beetles, down the glaring streets. Pfoo! I can't think how you bear it—this emptiness, the shimmering air, that fierce sun overhead. What's deadlier than the sun?

ORESTES: I was born here.

THE TUTOR: So the story goes. But, if I were you, I

wouldn't brag about it.

ORESTES: I was born here—and yet I have to ask my way, like any stranger. Knock at that door.

THE TUTOR: What do you expect? That someone will open it? Only look at those houses and tell me how they strike you. You will observe there's not a window anywhere. They open on closed courtyards, I suppose, and turn their backsides to the street. [ORESTES *makes a fretful gesture.*] Very good, sir. I'll knock—but nothing will come of it.

[*He knocks. Nothing happens. He knocks again, and the door opens a cautious inch.*]

A VOICE: What do you want?

THE TUTOR: Just a word of information. Can you tell me where—? [*The door is slammed in his face.*] Oh, the devil take you! Well, my lord Orestes, is that enough, or must I try elsewhere? If you wish, I'll knock at every door.

ORESTES: No, that's enough.

THE TUTOR: Well, I never! There's someone here. [*He goes up to the* IDIOT BOY.] Excuse me, sir . . .

THE IDIOT: Hoo! Hoo! Hoo!

THE TUTOR [*bowing again*]: My noble lord . . .

THE IDIOT: Hoo!

THE TUTOR: Will Your Highness deign to show us where Ægistheus lives?

THE IDIOT: Hoo!

THE TUTOR: Ægistheus, King of Argos.

THE IDIOT: Hoo! Hoo! Hoo!

[ZEUS *passes by, back stage.*]

THE TUTOR: We're out of luck. The only one who doesn't run away is a half-wit. [ZEUS *retraces his steps.*] Ah, that's odd! He's followed us here.

ORESTES: Who?

THE TUTOR: That bearded fellow.

ORESTES: You're dreaming.

THE TUTOR: I tell you, I saw him go by.

ORESTES: You must be mistaken.

THE TUTOR: Impossible. Never in my life have I seen

such a beard—or, rather, only one: the bronze beard on the chin of Zeus Ahenobarbos at Palermo. Look, there he is again. What can he want of us?

ORESTES: He is only a traveler like ourselves.

THE TUTOR: Only that? We met him on the road to Delphi. And when we took the boat at Itea, there he was, fanning that great beard in the bows. At Nauplia we couldn't move a step without having him at our heels, and now—here he is again! Do you think that chance explains it? [*He brushes the flies off his face.*] These flies in Argos are much more sociable than its townsfolk. Just look at them! [*Points to the* IDIOT BOY.] There must be a round dozen pumping away at each of his eyes, and yet he's smiling quite contentedly; probably he likes having his eyes sucked. That's not surprising; look at that yellow muck oozing out of them. [*He flaps his hand at the flies.*] Move on, my little friends. Hah! They're on you now. Allow me! [*He drives them away.*] Well, this should please you —you who are always complaining of being a stranger in your native land. These charming insects, anyhow, are making you welcome; one would think they know who you are. [*He whisks them away.*] Now leave us in peace, you buzzers. We know you like us, but we've had enough of you. . . . Where can they come from? They're as big as bumble-bees and noisy as a swarm of locusts.

[*Meanwhile* ZEUS *has approached them.*]

ZEUS: They are only bluebottles, a trifle larger than usual. Fifteen years ago a mighty stench of carrion drew them to this city, and since then they've been getting fatter and fatter. Give them another fifteen years, and they'll be as big as toads.

[*A short silence.*]

THE TUTOR: Pray, whom have I the honor of addressing?

ZEUS: Demetrios is my name, and I hail from Athens.

ORESTES: Did I not see you on the boat, a fortnight ago?

ZEUS: Yes, and I saw you, too.

[*Hideous shrieks come from the palace.*]

THE TUTOR: Listen to that! I don't know if you will agree with me, young master, but I think we'd do better to leave this place.

ORESTES: Keep quiet!

ZEUS: You have nothing to fear. It's what they call Dead Men's Day today. Those cries announce the beginning of the ceremony.

ORESTES: You seem well posted on the local customs.

ZEUS: Yes, I often visit Argos. As it so happened, I was here on the great day of Agamemnon's homecoming, when the Greek fleet, flushed with victory, anchored in the Nauplia roads. From the top of the rampart one saw the bay dappled with their white sails. [*He drives the flies away.*] There were no flies then. Argos was only a small country town, basking in the sun, yawning the years away. Like everyone else I went up to the sentry-path to see the royal procession, and I watched it for many an hour wending across the plain. At sundown on the second day Queen Clytemnestra came to the ramparts, and with her was Ægistheus, the present King. The people of Argos saw their faces dyed red by the sunset, and they saw them leaning over the battlements, gazing for a long while seawards. And the people thought: "There's evil brewing." But they kept silence. Ægistheus, you should know, was the Queen's lover. A hard, brutal man, and even in those days he had the cast of melancholy. . . . But you're looking pale, young sir.

ORESTES: It's the long journey I have made, and this accursed heat. But pray go on; you interest me.

ZEUS: Agamemnon was a worthy man, you know, but he made one great mistake. He put a ban on public executions. That was a pity. A good hanging now and then—that entertains folk in the provinces and robs death of its glamour. . . . So the people here held their tongues; they looked forward to seeing, for once, a violent death. They still kept silent when they saw their King entering by the city gates. And when Clytemnestra stretched forth her graceful arms, fragrant and white as lilies, they still said nothing. Yet at that moment a word, a single word, might have sufficed. But no one said it; each was gloating in imagination over the picture of a huge corpse with a shattered face.

ORESTES: And you, too, said nothing?

ZEUS: Does that rouse your indignation? Well, my young friend, I like you all the better for it; it proves your heart's in the right place. No, I admit I, too, held my peace. I'm a stranger here, and it was no concern of mine. And next day when it started, when the folks of Argos heard their King screaming his life out in the palace, they still kept silence, but they rolled their eyes in a sort of ecstasy, and the whole town was like a woman in heat.

ORESTES: So now the murderer is on the throne. For fifteen years he has enjoyed the fruits of crime. And I thought the gods were just!

ZEUS: Steady, my friend. Don't blame the gods too hastily. Must they always punish? Wouldn't it be better to use such breaches of the law to point a moral?

ORESTES: And is this what they did?

ZEUS: They sent the flies.

THE TUTOR: The flies? How do the flies come in?

ZEUS: They are a symbol. But if you want to know what the gods did, look around you. See that old creature over there, creeping away like a beetle on her little black feet, and hugging the walls. Well, she's a good specimen of the squat black vermin that teem in every cranny of this town. Now watch me catch our specimen, it's well worth inspection. Here it is. A loathsome object, you'll agree. . . . Hah! You're blinking now. Still, you're an Argive and you should be used to the white-hot rapiers of the sun. . . . Watch her wriggling, like a hooked fish! . . . Now, old lady, let's hear your tale of woe. I see you're in black from head to foot. In mourning for a whole regiment of sons, is that it? Tell us, and I'll release you—perhaps. For whom are you in mourning?

OLD WOMAN: Sir, I am not in mourning. Everyone wears black at Argos.

ZEUS: Everyone wears black? Ah, I see. You're in mourning for your murdered King.

OLD WOMAN: Whisht! For God's sake, don't talk of that.

ZEUS: Yes, you're quite old enough to have heard those huge cries that echoed and re-echoed for a whole morning in the city streets. What did you do about it?

OLD WOMAN: My good man was in the fields, at work. What could I do, a woman alone? I bolted my door.

ZEUS: Yes, but you left your window not quite closed, so as to hear the better, and, while you peeped behind the curtains and held your breath, you felt a little tingling itch between your loins, and didn't you enjoy it!

OLD WOMAN: Oh, please stop, sir!

ZEUS: And when you went to bed that night, you had a grand time with your man. A real gala night.

OLD WOMAN: A what? . . . No, my lord, that was a dreadful, dreadful night.

ZEUS: A red gala, I tell you, and you've never been able to blot out its memory.

OLD WOMAN: Mercy on us! Are you—are you one of the Dead?

ZEUS: I dead? You're crazy, woman. . . . Anyhow, don't trouble your head who I am; you'd do better to think of yourself, and try to earn forgiveness by repenting of your sins.

OLD WOMAN: Oh, sir, I do repent, most heartily I repent. If you only knew how I repent, and my daughter too, and my son-in-law offers up a heifer every year, and my little grandson has been brought up in a spirit of repentance. He's a pretty lad, with flaxen hair, and he always behaves as good as gold. Though he's only seven, he never plays or laughs, for thinking of his original sin.

ZEUS: Good, you old bitch, that's as it should be—and be sure you die in a nice bitchy odor of repentance.

It's your one hope of salvation. [*The* OLD WOMAN *runs away*.] Unless I'm much mistaken, my masters, we have there the real thing, the good old piety of yore, rooted in terror.

ORESTES: What man are you?

ZEUS: Who cares what I am? We were talking of the gods. Well now, should they have struck Ægistheus down?

ORESTES: They should. . . . They should. . . . Oh, how would I know what they should have done? What do I care, anyhow? I'm a stranger here. . . . Does Ægistheus feel contrition?

ZEUS: Ægistheus? I'd be much surprised. But what matter? A whole city's repenting on his account. And it's measured by the bushel, is repentance. [*Eerie screams in the palace*.] Listen! Lest they forget the screams of the late King in his last agony, they keep this festival of death each year when the day of the King's murder comes round. A herdsman from the hills—he's chosen for his lung-power—is set to bellow in the Great Hall of the palace. [ORESTES *makes a gesture of disgust*.] Bah! That's nothing. I wonder what you'll say presently, when they let the Dead loose. Fifteen years ago, to a day, Agamemnon was murdered. And what a change has come over the light-hearted folk of Argos since that day; how near and dear to me they are at present!

ORESTES: Dear to *you*?

ZEUS: Pay no heed, young man. That was a slip of the tongue. Near and dear to the gods, I meant.

ORESTES: You surprise me. Then those blood-smeared walls, these swarms of flies, this reek of shambles and the stifling heat, these empty streets and yonder god with his gashed face, and all those creeping, half-human creatures beating their breasts in darkened rooms, and those shrieks, those hideous, blood-curdling shrieks—can it be that Zeus and his Olympians delight in these?

ZEUS: Young man, do not sit in judgment on the gods. They have their secrets—and their sorrows.

[*A short silence.*]

ORESTES: Am I right in thinking Agamemnon had a daughter? A daughter named Electra?

ZEUS: Yes. She lives there, in the palace—that building yonder.

ORESTES: So that's the palace? . . . And what does Electra think of—all this?

ZEUS: Oh, she's a mere child. There was a son, too, named Orestes. But he's dead, it seems.

ORESTES: Dead? Well, really . . .

THE TUTOR: Of course he's dead, young master. I thought you knew it. Don't you remember what they told us at Nauplia—about Ægistheus' having him murdered, soon after Agamemnon's death?

ZEUS: Still, some say he's alive. The story goes that the men ordered to kill the child had pity on him and left him in the forest. Some rich Athenians found him there and took him home. For my part, I'd rather he were dead.

ORESTES: Pray, why?

ZEUS: Suppose that one day he appeared in this city, and—

ORESTES: Continue, please.

ZEUS: As you wish. . . . Well, I'd say this to him. "My lad—" I'd say, "My lad," as he's your age or thereabouts —if he's alive, of course. By the way, young lord, may I know your name?

ORESTES: Philebus is my name, and I hail from Corinth. I am traveling to improve my mind, and this old slave accompanying me used to be my tutor.

ZEUS: Thank you. Well, I'd say something like this. "My lad, get you gone! What business have you here? Do you wish to enforce your rights? Yes, you're brave and strong and spirited. I can see you as a captain in an army of good fighters. You have better things to do than reigning over a dead-and-alive city, a carrion city plagued by flies. These people are great sinners but, as you see, they're working out their atonement. Let them be, young fellow, let them be; respect their sorrowful

endeavor, and begone on tiptoe. You cannot share in
their repentance, since you did not share their crime.
Your brazen innocence makes a gulf between you and
them. So if you have any care for them, be off! Be
off, or you will work their doom. If you hinder them
on their way, if even for a moment you turn their
thoughts from their remorse, all their sins will harden
on them—like cold fat. They have guilty consciences,
they're afraid—and fear and guilty consciences have a
good savor in the nostrils of the gods. Yes, the gods
take pleasure in such poor souls. Would you oust
them from the favor of the gods? What, moreover,
could you give them in exchange? Good digestions, the
gray monotony of provincial life, and the boredom—
ah, the soul-destroying boredom—of long days of mild
content. Go your way, my lad, go your way. The
repose of cities and men's souls hangs on a thread;
tamper with it and you bring disaster. [*Looking him in
the eyes*] A disaster which will recoil on you."

ORESTES: Yes? So that is what you'd say? Well, if I were
   that young man, I'd answer— [*They eye each other
   truculently.* THE TUTOR *coughs.*] No, I don't know how
 . I'd answer you. Perhaps you're right, and anyhow it's
   no concern of mine.

ZEUS: Good. I only hope Orestes would show as much
   sense. . . . Well, peace be with you, my friend; I must
   go about my business.

ORESTES: Peace be with you.

ZEUS: By the way, if those flies bother you, here's a way
   of getting rid of them. You see that swarm buzzing
   round your head? Right. Now watch! I flick my wrist
   —so—and wave my arm once, and then I say: Abraxas,
   galla, galla, tsay, tsay. See! They're falling down and
   starting to crawl on the ground like caterpillars.

ORESTES: By Jove!

ZEUS: Oh, that's nothing. Just a parlor trick. I'm a fly-
   charmer in my leisure hours. Good day to you. We
   shall meet again.

   [*Exit* ZEUS.]

THE TUTOR: Take care. That man knows who you are.

ORESTES: "Man," you say. But *is* he a man?

THE TUTOR: What else should he be? You grieve me, my young master. Have all my lessons, all my precepts, the smiling skepticism I taught you, been wasted on your ears? "Is he a man?" you ask. There's nothing else but men—what more would you have? And that bearded fellow is a man, sure enough; probably one of Ægistheus' spies.

ORESTES: A truce to your philosophy! It's done me too much harm already.

THE TUTOR: Harm? Do you call it doing harm to people when one emancipates their minds? Ah, how you've changed! Once I read you like an open book. . . . But at least you might tell me your plans. Why bring me to this city, and what's your purpose here?

ORESTES: Did I say I had a purpose? But that's enough. Be silent now. [*He takes some steps towards the palace.*] That is *my* palace. My father's birthplace. And it's there a whore and her paramour foully butchered him. I, too, was born there. I was nearly three when that usurper's bravoes carried me away. Most likely we went out by that door. One of them held me in his arms, I had my eyes wide open, and no doubt I was crying. And yet I have no memories, none whatever. I am looking at a huge, gloomy building, solemn and pretentious in the worst provincial taste. I am looking at it, but I *see* it for the first time.

THE TUTOR: No memories, master? What ingratitude, considering that I gave ten years of my life to stocking you with them! And what of all the journeys we have made together, all the towns we visited? And the course in archæology I composed specially for you? No memories, indeed! Palaces, shrines, and temples—with so many of them is your memory peopled that you could write a guide-book of all Greece.

ORESTES: Palaces—that's so. Palaces, statues, pillars—stones, stones, stones! Why, with all those stones in my head, am I not heavier? While you are about it, why not remind me of the three hundred and eighty-seven steps of the temple at Ephesus? I climbed them, one by one, and I remember each. The seventeenth, if my memory serves me, was badly broken. And yet—! Why, an old, mangy dog, warming himself at the hearth, and struggling to his feet with a little whimper to welcome his master home—why, that dog has more memories than I! At least he recognizes his master. *His* master. But what can I call mine?

THE TUTOR: And what of your culture, Lord Orestes? What of that? All that wise lore I culled for you with loving care, like a bouquet, matching the fruits of my knowledge with the finest flowers of my experience? Did I not, from the very first, set you a-reading all the books there are, so as to make clear to you the infinite diversity of men's opinions? And did I not remind you, time and again, how variable are human creeds and customs? So, along with youth, good looks, and wealth, you have the wisdom of far riper years; your mind is free from prejudice and superstition; you have no family ties, no religion, and no calling; you are free to turn your hand to anything. But you know better than to commit yourself—and there lies your strength. So, in a word, you stand head and shoulders above the ruck and, what's more, you could hold a chair of philosophy or architecture in a great university. And yet you cavil at your lot!

ORESTES: No, I do not cavil. What should I cavil at? You've left me free as the strands torn by the wind from spiders' webs that one sees floating ten feet above the ground. I'm light as gossamer and walk on air. I know I'm favored, I appreciate my lot at its full value. · [*A pause.*] Some men are born bespoken; a certain path has been assigned them, and at its end there is something they *must* do, a deed allotted. So on and on they trudge, wounding their bare feet on the flints. I suppose that strikes *you* as vulgar—the joy of going somewhere definite. And there are others, men of few words, who bear deep down in their

hearts a load of dark imaginings; men whose whole
life was changed because one day in childhood, at
the age of five or seven— Right; I grant you these
are no great men. When I was seven, I know I had
no home, no roots. I let sounds and scents, the patter
of rain on housetops, the golden play of sunbeams,
slip past my body and fall round me—and I knew
these were for others, I could never make them *my*
memories. For memories are luxuries reserved for people
who own houses, cattle, fields and servants. Whereas
I—! I'm free as air, thank God. My mind's my own,
gloriously aloof. [*He goes nearer to the palace.*] I might
have lived there. I'd not have read any of your books;
perhaps I'd not have learned to read. It's rare for a
Greek prince to know how to read. But I'd have come
in and gone out by that door ten thousand times. As
a child I'd have played with its leaves, and when I
pushed at them with all my little might, they'd have
creaked without yielding, and I'd have taken the measure of my weakness. Later on, I'd have pushed them
open furtively by night and gone out after girls. And
some years later, when I came of age, the slaves would
have flung the doors wide open and I'd have crossed
the threshold on horseback. My old wooden door! I'd
have been able to find your keyhole with my eyes
shut. And that notch there—I might have made it
showing off, the first day they let me hold a spear.
[*He steps back.*] Let's see. That's the Dorian style,
isn't it? And what do you make of that gold inlay?
I saw the like at Dodona; a pretty piece of craftsman-
ship. And now I'm going to say something that will rejoice you. This is not *my* palace, nor *my* door. And
there's nothing to detain us here.

THE TUTOR: Ah, that's talking sense. For what would you
have gained by living in Argos? By now your spirit
would be broken, you'd be wallowing in repentance.

ORESTES: Still, it would be *my* repentance. And this furnace heat singeing my hair would be *mine*. Mine, too,
the buzz of all these flies. At this moment I'd be lying

naked in some dark room at the back of the palace,
and watching a ribbon of red light lengthen across the
floor. I'd be waiting for sundown; waiting for the cool
dusk of an Argos evening to rise like perfume from
the parched earth; an Argos evening like many a thousand others, familiar yet ever new, another evening
that should be *mine*. . . . Well, well, my worthy peda-
gogue, let's be off. We've no business to be luxuriating
in others' heat.

THE TUTOR: Ah, my young lord, how you've eased my
mind! During these last few months—to be exact, ever
since I revealed to you the secret of your birth—I
could see you changing day by day, and it gave me
many a sleepless night. I was afraid—

ORESTES: Of what?

THE TUTOR: No, it will anger you.

ORESTES: Speak.

THE TUTOR: Be it so. Well, though from one's earliest
years one has been trained to skeptic irony, one can't
help having foolish fancies now and then. And I
wondered if you weren't hatching some wild scheme
to oust Ægistheus and take his place.

ORESTES [*thoughtfully*]: To oust Ægistheus. Ah— [*A
pause.*] No, my good slave, you need not fear; the
time for that is past. True, nothing could please me
better than to grip that sanctimonious ruffian by the
beard and drag him from my father's throne. But what
purpose would it serve? These folk are no concern of
mine. I have not seen one of their children come into
the world, nor been present at their daughters' wed-
dings; I don't share their remorse, I don't even know
a single one of them by name. That bearded fellow
was right; a king should share his subjects' memories. So
we'll let them be, and begone on tiptoe. . . . But,
mind you, if there were something I could do, something to give me the freedom of the city; if, even by
a crime, I could acquire their memories, their hopes
and fears, and fill with these the void within me, yes,
even if I had to kill my own mother—

THE TUTOR: Hush! For heaven's sake, hush!

ORESTES: Yes, these are idle dreams. Let's be off. Now go and see if we can get some horses here, and we'll move on to Sparta, where I have good friends.

[ELECTRA *comes forward, carrying a large ash-can. She goes up to the statue of* ZEUS, *without seeing them.*]

ELECTRA: Yes, you old swine, scowl away at me with your goggle eyes and your fat face all smeared with raspberry juice—scowl away, but you won't scare me, not you! They've been to worship you, haven't they? —those pious matrons in black dresses. They've been padding around you in their big creaky shoes. And you were pleased, old bugaboo, it warmed your silly wooden heart. You like them old, of course; the nearer they're to corpses, the more you love them. They've poured their choicest wines out at your feet, because it's your festival today, and the stale smell from their petticoats tickled your nostrils. [*She rubs herself against him.*] Now smell me for a change, smell the perfume of a fresh, clean body. But, of course, I'm young, I'm alive—and you loathe youth and life. I, too, am bringing you offerings, while all the others are at prayers. Here they are: ashes from the hearth, peelings, scraps of offal crawling with maggots, a chunk of bread too filthy even for our pigs. But your darling flies will love it, won't they, Zeus? A good feast-day to you, old idol, and let's hope it is your last. I'm not strong enough to pull you down. All I can do is to spit at you. But some day he will come, the man I'm waiting for, carrying a long, keen sword. He'll look you up and down and chuckle, with his hands on his hips, like this, and his head thrown back. Then he'll draw his sword and chop you in two, from top to bottom— like this! So the two halves of Zeus will fall apart, one to the left, one to the right, and everyone will see he's made of common wood. Just a lump of cheap white deal, the terrible God of Death! And all that frightfulness, the blood on his face, his dark-green eyes, and all the rest—they'll see it was only a coat of paint.

You, anyhow, you know you're white inside, white as
a child's body, and you know, too, that a sword can
rip you limb from limb, and you won't even bleed.
Just a log of deal—anyhow it will serve to light our
fires next winter. [*She notices* ORESTES.] Oh!

ORESTES: Don't be alarmed.

ELECTRA: I'm not alarmed. Not a bit. Who are you?

ORESTES: A stranger.

ELECTRA: Then you are welcome. All that's foreign to
this town is dear to me. Your name?

ORESTES: Philebus. I've come from Corinth.

ELECTRA: Ah? From Corinth. My name's Electra.

ORESTES: Electra— [*To* THE TUTOR] Leave us.
[*Exit* THE TUTOR.]

ELECTRA: Why are you looking at me like that?

ORESTES: You're very beautiful. Not at all like the people
in these parts.

ELECTRA: I beautiful? Can you really mean it? As beautiful as the Corinthian girls?

ORESTES: Yes.

ELECTRA. Well, here they never tell me that I'm beautiful. Perhaps they don't want me to know it. Anyhow,
what use would beauty be to me? I'm only a servant.

ORESTES: What! You a servant?

ELECTRA: The least of the servants in the palace. I wash
the King's and the Queen's underlinen. And how dirty
it is, all covered with spots and stains! Yes, I have to
wash everything they wear next their skin, the shifts
they wrap their rotting bodies in, the nightdresses
Clytemnestra has on when the King shares her bed.
I shut my eyes and scrub with all my might. I have
to wash up, too. You don't believe me? See my hands,
all chapped and rough. Why are you looking at them
in that funny way? Do they, by any chance, look like
the hands of a princess?

ORESTES: Poor little hands. No, they don't look like a
princess's hands. . . . But tell me more. What else do
they make you do?

ELECTRA: Every morning I've to empty the ash-can. I

drag it out of the palace, and then—well, you saw
what I do with the refuse. That big fellow in wood
is Zeus, God of Death and Flies. The other day, when
the High Priest came here to make his usual bows and
scrapings, he found himself treading on cabbage-stumps
and rotten turnips and mussel-shells. He looked startled,
I can tell you! I say! You won't tell on me, will you?

ORESTES: No.

ELECTRA: Really I don't care if you do. They can't make
things much worse for me than they are already. I'm
used to being beaten. Perhaps they'd shut me up in one
of the rooms in the tower. That wouldn't be so bad;
at least I wouldn't have to see their faces. Just imagine
what I get by way of thanks at bedtime, when my day's
work is done. I go up to a tall, stout lady with dyed
hair, with thick lips and very white hands, a queen's
hands, that smell of honey. Then she puts her hands
on my shoulders and dabs my forehead with her lips
and says: "Good night, Electra. Good night." Every
evening. Every evening I have to feel that woman
slobbering on my face. Ugh! Like a piece of raw
meat on my forehead. But I hold myself up, I've never
fallen yet. She's my mother, you know. If I was up
in the tower, she wouldn't kiss me any more.

ORESTES: Have you never thought of running away?

ELECTRA: I haven't the courage; I daren't face the country roads at night all by myself.

ORESTES: Is there no one, no girl friend of yours, who'd
go with you?

ELECTRA: No, I am quite alone. Ask any of the people
here, and they'll tell you I'm a pest, a public nuisance.
I've no friends.

ORESTES: Not even an old nurse, who saw you into the
world and has kept a little affection for you?

ELECTRA: Not even an old nurse. Mother will tell you; I
freeze even the kindest hearts—that's how I am.

ORESTES: Do you propose to spend your life here?

ELECTRA [*excitedly*]: My life? Oh no, no! Of course not!
Listen. I'm waiting for—for something.

ORESTES: Something, or someone?

ELECTRA: That's my secret. Now it's your turn to speak. You're good-looking, too. Will you be here long?

ORESTES: Well, I'd thought of leaving today. But, as it is—

ELECTRA: Yes?

ORESTES: As it is, I'm not so sure.

ELECTRA: Is Corinth a pretty place?

ORESTES: Very pretty.

ELECTRA: Do you like it? Are you proud of Corinth?

ORESTES: Yes.

ELECTRA: How strange that sounds! I can't imagine myself being proud of my home town. Tell me what it feels like.

ORESTES: Well— No, I don't know. I can't explain.

ELECTRA: You can't? I wonder why. [*A short silence.*] What's Corinth like? Are there shady streets and squares? Places where one can stroll in the cool of the evening?

ORESTES: Yes.

ELECTRA: And everyone comes out of doors? People go for walks together?

ORESTES: Almost everyone is out and about at sundown.

ELECTRA: Boys and girls together?

ORESTES: Oh yes, one often sees them going for walks together.

ELECTRA: And they always find something to say to each other? They like each other's company, and one hears them laughing in the streets quite late at night?

ORESTES: Yes.

ELECTRA: I suppose you think I'm very childish. But it's so hard for me to picture a life like that—going for walks, laughing and singing in the streets. Everybody here is sick with fear. Everyone except me. And I—

ORESTES: Yes? And you?

ELECTRA: Oh, I—I'm sick with—hatred. And what do they do all day, the girls at Corinth?

ORESTES: Well, they spend quite a while making themselves pretty; then they sing or play on lutes. Then they call on their friends, and at night they go to dances.

ELECTRA: But don't they have any worries?

ORESTES: Only quite little ones.

ELECTRA: Yes? Now listen well, please. Don't the people at Corinth feel remorse?

ORESTES: Sometimes. Not very often.

ELECTRA: So they do what they like and, afterwards, don't give another thought to it?

ORESTES: That's their way.

ELECTRA: How strange! [*A short silence.*] Please tell me something else; I want to know it because of—of someone I'm expecting. Suppose one of the young fellows you've been telling about, who walk and laugh with girls in the evenings—suppose one of these young men came home after a long journey and found his father murdered, and his mother living with the murderer, and his sister treated like a slave—what would he do, that young man from Corinth? Would he just take it for granted and slink out of his father's house and look for consolation with his girl friends? Or would he draw his sword and hurl himself at the assassin, and slash his brains out? . . . Why are you silent?

ORESTES: I was wondering—

ELECTRA: What? You can't say what he'd do?

CLYTEMNESTRA [*off stage, calling*]: Electra!

ELECTRA: Hush!

ORESTES: What is it?

ELECTRA: That was my mother, Queen Clytemnestra. [CLYTEMNESTRA *enters.*] What's this, Philebus? Are you afraid of her?

ORESTES [*to himself*]: So that's the face I tried to picture, night after night, until I came to see it, really *see* it, drawn and haggard under the rosy mask of paint. But I hadn't counted on those dead eyes.

CLYTEMNESTRA: Electra, hear the King's order. You are to make ready for the ceremony. You must wear your black dress and your jewels. . . . Well, what does this behavior mean? Why are you pressing your elbows to

your hips and staring at the ground? Oh, I know your
tricks, my girl, but they don't deceive me any longer.
Just now I was watching at the window and I saw a
very different Electra, a girl with flashing eyes, bold
gestures. . . . Why don't you answer?

ELECTRA: Do you really think a scullery-maid would add
to the splendor of your festival?

CLYTEMNESTRA: No play-acting. You are a princess, Electra, and the townsfolk expect to see you, as in former
years.

ELECTRA: A princess—yes, the princess of a day. Once a
year, when this day comes round, you remember who
I am; because, of course, the people want an edifying
glimpse of our family life. A strange princess, indeed,
who herds pigs and washes up. Tell me, will Ægistheus
put his arm round my neck as he did last time? Will
he smile tenderly on me, while he mumbles horrible
threats in my ear?

CLYTEMNESTRA: If you would have him otherwise, it rests
with you.

ELECTRA: Yes—if I let myself be tainted by your remorse;
if I beg the gods' forgiveness for a crime I never committed. Yes—if I kiss your royal husband's hand and
call him father. Ugh! The mere thought makes me sick.
There's dry blood under his nails.

CLYTEMNESTRA: Do as you will. I have long ceased giving
you orders in my name. It is the King's command I
bring you.

ELECTRA: And why should I obey him? Ægistheus is your
husband, Mother, your dearly beloved husband—not
mine.

CLYTEMNESTRA: That is all I have to say, Electra. Only
too well I see you are determined to bring ruin on
yourself, and on us all. Yet who am I to counsel you,
I who ruined my whole life in a single morning? You
hate me, my child, but what disturbs me more is your
likeness to me, as I was once. I used to have those
clean-cut features, that fever in the blood, those smoldering eyes—and nothing good came of them.

ELECTRA: No! Don't say I'm like you! Tell me, Philebus —you can see us side by side—am I really like her?

ORESTES: How can I tell? Her face is like a pleasant garden that hail and storms have ravaged. And upon yours I see a threat of storm; one day passion will sear it to the bone.

ELECTRA: A threat of storm? Good! So far I welcome the likeness. May your words come true!

CLYTEMNESTRA: And you, young man, who stare so boldly at us, who are you and why have you come here? Let me look at you more closely.

ELECTRA [*quickly*]: He's a Corinthian, of the name of Philebus. A traveler.

CLYTEMNESTRA: Philebus? Ah!

ELECTRA: You seemed to fear another name.

CLYTEMNESTRA: To fear? If the doom I brought on my life has taught me anything, it is that I have nothing left to fear. . . . Welcome to Argos, stranger. Yes, come nearer. How young you seem! What's your age?

ORESTES: Eighteen.

CLYTEMNESTRA: Are your parents alive?

ORESTES: My father's dead.

CLYTEMNESTRA: And your mother? Is she about my age? Ah, you don't answer. I suppose she looks much younger; she still laughs and sings when you are with her. Do you love her? Answer me, please. Why did you leave her?

ORESTES: I am on my way to Sparta, to enlist in the army.

CLYTEMNESTRA: Most travelers give our city a wide berth. Some go twenty leagues out of their way to avoid it. Were you not warned? The people of the Plain have put us in quarantine; they see our repentance as a sort of pestilence and are afraid of being infected.

ORESTES: I know.

CLYTEMNESTRA: Did they tell you that we bear the burden of an inexpiable crime, committed fifteen years ago?

ORESTES: Yes, they told me that.

CLYTEMNESTRA: And that Queen Clytemnestra bears the

heaviest load of guilt—that men shudder at her name?

ORESTES: That, too, I heard.

CLYTEMNESTRA: And yet you've come here! Stranger, I am Queen Clytemnestra.

ELECTRA: Don't pity her, Philebus. The Queen is indulging in our national pastime, the game of public confession. Here everyone cries his sins on the housetops. On holidays you'll often see a worthy shopkeeper dragging himself along on his knees, covering his hair with dust, and screaming out that he's a murderer, a libertine, a liar, and all the rest of it. But the folk of Argos are getting a little tired of these amusements; everyone knows his neighbor's sins by heart. The Queen's, especially, have lost interest; they're official—our basic crimes, in fact. So you can imagine her delight when she finds someone like you, somebody raw and young, who doesn't even know her name, to hear her tale of guilt. A marvelous opportunity! It's as if she were confessing for the first time.

CLYTEMNESTRA: Be silent. Anyone has the right to spit in my face, to call me murderess and whore. But no one has the right to speak ill of my remorse.

ELECTRA: Note her words, Philebus. That's a rule of the game. People will beg you to condemn them, but you must be sure to judge them only on the sins they own to; their other evil deeds are no one's business, and they wouldn't thank you for detecting them.

CLYTEMNESTRA: Fifteen years ago men said I was the loveliest woman in Greece. Look at me now and judge my sufferings. Let me be frank, young stranger; it is not the death of that old lecher that I regret. When I saw his blood tingeing the water in the bath, I sang and danced for joy. And even now, after fifteen years, whenever I recall it, I have a thrill of pleasure. But—but I had a son; he would be your age now. When Ægistheus handed him over to his bravoes, I—

ELECTRA: You had a daughter too, my mother; if I'm not mistaken. And you've made of her a scullion. But that crime, it seems, sits lightly on your conscience.

CLYTEMNESTRA: You are young, Electra. It is easy for young people, who have not yet had a chance of sinning, to condemn. But wait, my girl; one day you, too, will be trailing after you an inexpiable crime. At every step you will think that you are leaving it behind, but it will remain as heavy as before. Whenever you look back you will see it there, just at arm's length, glowing darkly like a black crystal. And you will have forgotten what it really is, and murmur to yourself: "It wasn't I, it could not have been I, who did that." Yet, though you disown it time and time again, always it will be there, a dead weight holding you back. And then at last you will realize that you staked your life on a single throw of the dice, and nothing remains for you but to drag your crime after you until you die. For that is the law, just or unjust, of repentance. Ah, then we'll see a change come over your young pride.

ELECTRA: My young pride? So it's your lost youth you are regretting, still more than your crime. It's my youth you detest, even more than my innocence.

CLYTEMNESTRA: What I detest in you, Electra, is—myself. Not your youth—far from it!—but my own.

ELECTRA: And I—it's you, it's *you* I hate.

CLYTEMNESTRA: For shame, Electra! Here we are, scolding each other like two women of the same age in love with the same man! And yet I am your mother. . . . I do not know who you are, young man, nor what brings you here, but your presence bodes no good. Electra hates me—that, of course, I always knew. But for fifteen years we have kept the peace; only our eyes betrayed our feelings. And now you have come, you have spoken, and here we are showing our teeth and snapping at each other like two curs in the street. An ancient law of Argos compels us to give you hospitality, but, I make no secret of it, I had rather you were gone. As for you, my child, too faithful copy of myself, 'tis true I have no love for you. But I had rather cut off my right hand than do you harm. Only too well you know it, and you trade on my weakness. But I advise you not to rear your anxious little head against Ægistheus; he has a short way with vipers. Mark my words, do his bidding—or you will rue it.

ELECTRA: Tell the King that I shall not attend the rite. Do you know what they do, Philebus? Above the town there's a great cavern; none of our young men, not even the bravest, has ever found its end. People say that it leads down to hell, and the High Priest has had the entrance blocked with a great stone. Well—would you believe it?—each year when this anniversary comes round, the townspeople gather outside the cavern, soldiers roll away the stone, and our dead, so they say, come up from hell and roam the city. Places are laid for them at every table, chairs and beds made ready, and the people in the house huddle in corners to make room for them during the night-watches. For the dead are everywhere, the whole town's at their mercy. You can imagine how our townsfolk plead with them. "My poor dead darling, I didn't mean to wrong you. Please be kind." Tomorrow, at cock-crow, they'll return underground, the stone will be rolled back, and that will be the end of it until this day next year. Well, I refuse to take part in this mummery. Those dead folk are *their* dead, not mine.

CLYTEMNESTRA: If you will not obey his summons willingly, the King will have you brought to him by force.

ELECTRA: By force? . . . I see. Very well, then. My good, kind mother, will you please tell the King that I shall certainly obey. I shall attend the rite, and if the townsfolk wish to see me, they won't be disappointed. . . . Philebus, will you do something for me? Please don't go at once, but stay here for the ceremony. Perhaps some parts of it may entertain you. Now I'll go and make myself ready.

[*Exit* ELECTRA.]

CLYTEMNESTRA [*to* ORESTES]: Leave this place. I feel that you are going to bring disaster on us. You have no cause to wish us ill; we have done nothing to you.

So go, I beg you. By all you hold most sacred, for your mother's sake, I beg you, go.

[*Exit* CLYTEMNESTRA.]

ORESTES [*thoughtfully*]: For my mother's sake.

· [ZEUS *enters and comes up to him.*]

ZEUS: Your attendant tells me you wish to leave. He has been looking for horses all over Argos, but can find none. Well, I can procure for you two sturdy mares and riding-gear at a very low figure.

ORESTES: I've changed my mind. I am not leaving Argos.

ZEUS [*meditatively*]: Ah, so you're not leaving, after all. [*A short pause. Then, in a quicker tempo*] In that case I shall stay with you and be your host. I know an excellent inn in the lower town where we can lodge together. You won't regret my company, I can assure you. But first—Abraxas, galla, galla, tsay, tsay—let me rid you of those flies. A man of my age can often be very helpful to lads like you. I'm old enough to be your father; you must tell me all about yourself and your troubles. So come, young man, don't try to shake me off. Meetings like this are often of more use than one would think. Consider the case of Telemachus— you know whom I mean, King Ulysses' son. One fine day he met an old worthy of the name of Mentor, who joined forces with him. Now I wonder if you know who that old fellow Mentor really was. . . .

[*He escorts* ORESTES *off the stage, holding him in conversation, while the curtain falls.*]

ACT II

SCENE I

A mountain terrace, with a cavern on the right. Its entrance is blocked by a large black boulder. On the left is a flight of steps leading up to a temple. A crowd of men and women have gathered for the ceremony.

A WOMAN [*kneeling before her little son, as she straightens the kerchief round his neck*]: There! That's the third time I've had to straighten it for you. [*She dusts his clothes.*] That's better. Now try to behave properly, and mind you start crying when you're told.

THE CHILD: Is that where they come from?

THE WOMAN: Yes.

THE CHILD: I'm frightened.

THE WOMAN: And so you should be, darling. Terribly frightened. That's how one grows up into a decent, god-fearing man.

A MAN: They'll have good weather today.

ANOTHER MAN: Just as well. It seems they still like sunlight, shadows though they are. Last year, when it rained, they were fierce, weren't they?

FIRST MAN: Ay, that's the word. Fierce.

SECOND MAN: A shocking time we had!

THIRD MAN: Once they've gone back to their cave and left us to ourselves, I'll climb up here again and look at that there stone, and I'll say to myself: "Now we've a year's peace before us."

FOURTH MAN: Well, I'm not like you, I ain't consoled that easily. From tomorrow I'll start wondering how they'll be next year. Every year they're getting nastier and nastier, and—

SECOND MAN: Hold your tongue, you fool! Suppose one of them has crept out through a crevice and is prowling round us now, eavesdropping, like. There's some of the Dead come out ahead of time, so I've heard tell.

[*They eye each other nervously.*]

A YOUNG WOMAN: If only it would start! What are they up to, those palace folk? They're never in a hurry, and it's all this waiting gets one down, what with the blazing sun and only that big black stone to look at. Just think! They're all there, crowded up behind the stone, gloating over the cruel things they're going to do to us.

AN OLD WOMAN: That's enough, my girl. . . . We all know she's no better than she should be; that's why she's so scared of her ghost. Her husband died last spring, and for ten years she'd been fooling the poor man.

YOUNG WOMAN: I don't deny it. Sure enough, I fooled him to the top of his bent; but I always liked him and I led him a pleasant life, that he can't deny. He never knew a thing about the other men, and when he died, you should have seen the way he looked at me, so tenderly, like a grateful dog. Of course, he knows everything now, and it's bitter pain for him, poor fellow, and all his love has turned to hate. Presently I'll feel him coiling round me, like a wisp of smoke, and he'll cling to me more closely than any living man has ever clung. I'll bring him home with me, wound round my neck like a tippet. I've a tasty little meal all ready, with the cakes and honey that he always liked. But it's all no use, I know. He'll never forgive me, and tonight—oh, how I dread it!—he will share my bed.

A MAN: Ay, she's right. What's Ægistheus doing? We can't bear this suspense much longer. It ain't fair to keep us waiting like this.

ANOTHER MAN: Sorry for yourself, are you? But do you think Ægistheus is less afraid than we? Tell me, how'd you like to be in his shoes, and have Agamemnon gibbering at you for twenty-four hours?

YOUNG WOMAN: Oh, this horrible, horrible suspense! Do you know, I have a feeling that all of you are drifting miles and miles away, leaving me alone. The stone is not yet rolled aside, but each of us is shut up with his dead, and lonely as a raindrop.

[ZEUS *enters, followed by* ORESTES *and* THE TUTOR.]

ZEUS: This way, young man; you'll have a better view.

ORESTES: So here we have them, the citizens of Argos, King Agamemnon's loyal subjects!

THE TUTOR: What an ugly lot! Observe, young master, their sallow cheeks and sunken eyes. These folk are perishing of fear. What better example could we have of the effects of superstition? Just look at them! And if you need another proof of the soundness of my teaching, look on me and my rosy cheeks.

ZEUS: Much good they do you, your pink cheeks. For all your roses, my good man, you're no more than a sack of dung, like all those others, in the eyes of Zeus. Yes, though you may not guess it, you stink to heaven. These folk, at least, are wise in their generation; they know how bad they smell.

A MAN [*climbing on to the temple steps, harangues the crowd*]: Do they want to drive us mad? Let's raise our voices all together and summon Ægistheus. Make him understand we will not suffer any more delay.

THE CROWD: Ægistheus! King Ægistheus! Have pity on us!

A WOMAN: Pity, yes, pity, you cry. And will none have pity on me? He'll come with his slit throat, the man I loathed so bitterly, and clammy, unseen arms will maul me in the darkness, all through the night.

ORESTES: But this is madness! Why doesn't someone tell these wretched people—?

ZEUS: What's this, young man? Why this ado over a woman who's lost her nerve? Wait and see; there's worse to come.

A MAN [*falling on his knees*]: I stink! Oh, how I stink! I am a mass of rottenness. See how the flies are teeming round me, like carrion crows. . . . . That's right, my harpies; sting and gouge and scavenge me; bore through my flesh to my black heart. I have sinned a thousand times, I am a sink of ordure, and I reek to heaven.

ZEUS: O worthy man!

SOME MEN [*helping him to his feet*]: That's enough. You shall talk about it later, when *they* are out.

[*Gasping, rolling his eyes, the man stares at them.*]

THE CROWD: Ægistheus! Ægistheus! For mercy's sake, give the order to begin. We can bear no more.

[Ægistheus *comes on to the temple steps, followed by* CLYTEMNESTRA, THE HIGH PRIEST, *and* BODYGUARDS.]

ÆGISTHEUS: Dogs! How dare you bewail your lot? Have you forgotten your disgrace? Then, by Zeus, I shall refresh your memories. [*He turns to* CLYTEMNESTRA.] We must start without her, it seems. But let her beware! My punishment will be condign.

CLYTEMNESTRA: She promised to attend. No doubt she is making ready, lingering in front of her mirror.

ÆGISTHEUS [*to* THE SOLDIERS]: Go seek Electra in the palace and bring her here by force, if need be. [SOLDIERS *file out. He addresses* THE CROWD.] Take your usual places. The men on my right, women and children on my left. Good.

[*A short silence.* ÆGISTHEUS *is waiting.*]

HIGH PRIEST: Sire, these people are at breaking-point.

ÆGISTHEUS: I know. But I am waiting for—

[THE SOLDIERS *return.*]

A SOLDIER: Your Majesty, we have searched for the princess everywhere. But there is no one in the palace.

ÆGISTHEUS: So be it. We shall deal with her tomorrow. [*To* THE HIGH PRIEST] Begin.

HIGH PRIEST: Roll away the stone.

THE CROWD: Ah!

[THE SOLDIERS *roll away the stone.* THE HIGH PRIEST *goes to the entrance of the cavern.*]

HIGH PRIEST: You, the forgotten and forsaken, all you whose hopes were dupes, who creep along the ground darkling like smoke wraiths and have nothing left you but your great shame—you, the dead, arise; this is your day of days. Come up, pour forth like a thick cloud of fumes of brimstone driven by the wind; rise from the bowels of the earth, ye who have died a hundred deaths,

ye whom every heartbeat in our breasts strikes dead
again. In the name of anger unappeased and unap-
peasable, and the lust of vengeance, I summon you to
wreak your hatred on the living. Come forth and scatter
like a dark miasma in our streets, weave between the
mother and her child, the lover and his beloved; make
us regret that we, too, are not dead. Arise, spectres,
harpies, ghouls, and goblins of our nights. Soldiers, arise,
who died blaspheming; arise, downtrodden victims,
children of disgrace; arise, all ye who died of hunger,
whose last sigh was a curse. See, the living are here to
greet you, fodder for your wrath. Arise and have at them
like a great rushing wind, and gnaw them to the bone.
Arise! Arise! Arise!

[*A tomtom sounds, and* THE PRIEST *dances at the
entrance of the cavern, slowly at first, then quickening
his gyrations until he falls to the ground exhausted.*]

ÆGISTHEUS: They are coming forth.

THE CROWD: Heaven help us!

ORESTES: I can bear this no longer. I must go—

ZEUS: Look at me, young man. In the eyes. Good; you
understand. Now, keep quiet.

ORESTES: Who—who are you?

ZEUS: You shall know soon.

[ÆGISTHEUS *comes slowly down the temple steps.*]

ÆGISTHEUS: They are there. All of them. [*A short silence.*]
There he is, Aricië, the husband you used so ill. There
he is, beside you, kissing you tenderly, clasping you in
his dead arms. How he loves you! And ah, how he hates
you! . . . There she is, Nicias, your mother, who died
of your neglect. . . . And you there, Segestes, you
bloodsucker—they are all round you, the wretched men
who borrowed of you; those who starved to death, and
those who hanged themselves because of you. In your
debt they died, but today they are your creditors. And
you, fathers and mothers, loving parents, lower your
eyes humbly. They are there, your dead children,
stretching their frail arms towards you, and all the
happiness you denied them, all the tortures you inflicted,

weigh like lead on their sad, childish, unforgiving hearts.

THE CROWD: Have mercy!

ÆGISTHEUS: Mercy? You ask for mercy? Do you not know the dead have no mercy? Their grievances are time-proof, adamant; rancor without end. Do you hope, Nicias, to atone by deeds of kindness for the wrong you did your mother? But what act of kindness can ever reach her now? Her soul is like a sultry, windless noon, in which nothing stirs, nothing changes, nothing lives. Only a fierce unmoving sun beats down on bare rocks forever. The dead have ceased to be—think what that implies in all its ruthlessness—yes, they are no more, and in their eternal keeping your crimes have no reprieve.

THE CROWD: Mercy!

ÆGISTHEUS: Well you may cry mercy! Play your parts, you wretched mummers, for today you have a full house to watch you. Millions of staring, hopeless eyes are brooding darkly on your faces and your gestures. They can see us, read our hearts, and we are naked in the presence of the dead. Ah, that makes you squirm; it burns and sears you, that stern, calm gaze unchanging as the gaze of eyes remembered.

THE CROWD: Mercy!

THE MEN: Forgive us for living while you are dead.

THE WOMEN: Have mercy! Tokens of you are ever with us, we see your faces everywhere we turn. We wear mourning unceasingly, and weep for you from dawn till dusk, from dusk till dawn. But somehow, try as we may, your memory dwindles and slips through our fingers; daily it grows dimmer and we know ourselves the guiltier. Yes, you are leaving us, ebbing away like life-blood from a wound. And yet, know you well—if this can mollify your bitter hatred—that you, our dear departed, have laid waste our lives.

THE MEN: Forgive us for living while you are dead.

THE CHILDREN: Please forgive us. We didn't want to be born, we're ashamed of growing up. What wrong can we have done you? It's not our fault if we're alive. And only just alive; see how small we are, how pale and puny. We never laugh or sing, we glide about like ghosts. And we're so frightened of you, so terribly afraid. Have mercy on us.

THE MEN: Forgive us for living while you are dead.

ÆGISTHEUS: Hold your peace! If you voice your sorrow thus, what will be left for me, your King, to say? For my ordeal has begun; the earth is quaking, and the light failing, and the greatest of the dead is coming forth—he whom I slew with my own hand, King Agamemnon.

ORESTES [*drawing his sword*]: I forbid you to drag my father's name into this mummery.

ZEUS [*clutching his arms*]: Stop, young fellow! Stop that!

ÆGISTHEUS [*looking round*]: Who dares to—?
[ELECTRA, *wearing a white dress, comes on to the temple steps.* ÆGISTHEUS *sees her.*] Electra!

THE CROWD: Electra!

ÆGISTHEUS: What is the meaning of this, Electra? Why are you in white?

ELECTRA: It's my prettiest dress. The city holds high festival today, and I thought I'd look my best.

HIGH PRIEST: Would you insult our dead? This day is *their* day, and well you know it. You should be in mourning.

ELECTRA: Why? I'm not afraid of *my* dead, and yours mean nothing to me.

ÆGISTHEUS: That is so; your dead are not our dead. . . . Remember the breed she comes of, the breed of Atreus, who treacherously cut his nephews' throats. What are you, Electra, but the last survivor of an accursed race? Ay, that whorish dress becomes you. I suffered your presence in the palace out of pity, but now I know I erred; the old foul blood of the house of Atreus flows in your veins. And if I did not see to it, you would taint us all. But bide awhile, my girl, and you will learn how I can punish. Your eyes will be red with weeping for many a day.

THE CROWD: Sacrilege! Sacrilege! Away with her!

ÆGISTHEUS: Hear, miserable girl, the murmurs of these

good folk you have outraged. Were I not here to curb their anger, they would tear you in pieces.

THE CROWD: Away with her, the impious wretch!

ELECTRA: Is it impious to be gay? Why can't these good folk of yours be gay? What prevents them?

ÆGISTHEUS: She is laughing, the wanton—and her dead father is standing there, with blood on his face.

ELECTRA: How dare you talk of Agamemnon? How can you be so sure he doesn't visit me by night and tell me all his secrets? Ah, if you knew the love and longing that hoarse, dead voice breathes in my ears! Yes, I'm laughing—laughing for the first time in my life; for the first time I'm happy. And can you be so sure my new-won happiness doesn't rejoice my father's heart? More likely, if he's here and sees his daughter in her white dress—his daughter of whom you've made a wretched drudge—if he sees her holding her head high, keeping her pride intact, more likely the last thing he dreams of is to blame me. No, his eyes are sparkling in the havoc of his face, he's twisting his blood-stained lips in the shadow of a smile.

THE YOUNG WOMAN: Can it be true, what she says?

VOICES: No, no. She's talking nonsense. She's gone mad. Electra, go, for pity's sake, or your sins will be visited on us.

ELECTRA: But what is it you're so frightened of? I can see all round you and there's nothing but your own shadows. Now listen to what I've just been told, something you may not know. In Greece there are cities where men live happily. White, contented cities, basking like lizards in the sun. At this very moment, under this same sky, children are playing in the streets of Corinth. And their mothers aren't asking forgiveness for having brought them into the world. No, they're smiling tenderly at them, they're proud of their motherhood. Mothers of Argos, can't you understand? Does it mean nothing to you, the pride of a mother who looks at her son and thinks: "It's I who bore him, brought him up"?

ÆGISTHEUS: That's enough. Keep silent, or I'll thrust your words down your throat.

VOICES: Yes, yes. Make her stop. She's talked enough.

OTHER VOICES: No, let her speak. It's Agamemnon speaking through her.

ELECTRA: The sun is shining. Everywhere down in the plains men are looking up and saying: "It's a fine day," and they're happy. Are you so set on making yourselves wretched that you've forgotten the simple joy of the peasant who says as he walks across his fields: "It's a fine day"? No, there you stand hanging your heads, moping and mumbling, more dead than alive. You're too terrified to lift a finger, afraid of jolting your precious ghosts if you make any movement. That would be dreadful, wouldn't it, if your hand suddenly went through a patch of clammy mist, and it was your grandmother's ghost! Now look at me. I'm spreading out my arms freely, and I'm stretching like someone just roused from sleep. I have my place in the sunlight, my full place and to spare. And does the sky fall on my head? Now I'm dancing, see, I'm dancing, and all I feel is the wind's breath fanning my cheeks. Where are the dead? Do you think they're dancing with me, in step?

HIGH PRIEST: People of Argos, I tell you that this woman is a profaner of all we hold most holy. Woe to her and to all of you who listen to her words!

ELECTRA: Oh, my beloved dead—Iphigeneia, my elder sister, and Agamemnon, my father and my only King— hear my prayer. If I am an evil-doer, if I offend your sorrowing shades, make some sign that I may know. But if, my dear ones, you approve, let no leaf stir, no blade of grass be moved, and no sound break in on my sacred dance. For I am dancing for joy, for peace among men; I dance for happiness and life. My dead ones, I invoke your silence that these people around me may know your hearts are with me.

[*She dances.*]

VOICES IN THE CROWD: Look how she's dancing, light as a

flame. Look how her dress is rippling, like a banner in the wind. And the dead—the dead do nothing.

THE YOUNG WOMAN: And see her look of ecstasy—oh, no, no, that's not the face of a wicked woman. Well, Ægistheus, what have you to say? Why are you silent?

ÆGISTHEUS: I waste no words on her. Does one argue with malignant vermin? No, one stamps them out. My kindness to her in the past was a mistake, but a mistake that can be remedied. Have no fear, I shall make short work of her and end her accursed race.

VOICES IN THE CROWD: Answer us, King Ægistheus. Threats are no answer.

THE YOUNG WOMAN: She's dancing, smiling, oh, so happily, and the dead seem to protect her. Oh fortunate, too fortunate Electra! Look, I, too, am holding out my arms, baring my neck to the sunlight.

A VOICE IN THE CROWD: The dead hold their peace. Ægistheus, you have lied.

ORESTES: Dear Electra!

ZEUS: This is too much. I'll shut that foolish wench's tongue. [*Stretches out his right arm.*] Poseidon, carabou, carabou, roola. [*The big stone which blocked the entrance to the cavern rumbles across the stage and crashes against the temple steps.* ELECTRA *stops dancing.*]

THE CROWD: Ah! . . . Mercy on us!

[*A long silence.*]

HIGH PRIEST: Froward and fickle race, now you have seen how the dead avenge themselves. Mark how the flies are beating down on you, in thick, swirling clouds. You have hearkened to the tempter's voice, and a curse has fallen on the city.

THE CROWD: It is not our fault, we are innocent. That woman came and tempted us, with her lying tongue. To the river with her! Drown the witch.

AN OLD WOMAN [*pointing to the* YOUNG WOMAN]: That young huzzy there was lapping up her words like milk. Strip her naked and lash her till she squeals. [*The* WOMEN *seize the* YOUNG WOMAN, *while the* MEN *surge up the temple steps, towards* ELECTRA.]

ÆGISTHEUS [*straightening up*]: Silence, dogs! Back to your
places! Vengeance is mine, not yours. [*A short silence.*]
Well, you have seen what comes of disobeying me.
Henceforth you will know better than to misdoubt your
ruler. Disperse to your homes, the dead will keep you
company and be your guests until tomorrow's dawn.
Make place for them at your tables, at your hearths, and
in your beds. And see that your good behavior blots out
the memory of what has happened here. As for me—
grieved though I am by your mistrust, I forgive you.
But you, Electra—

ELECTRA: Yes? What of it? I failed to bring it off this
time. Next time I'll do better.

ÆGISTHEUS: There shall be no next time. The custom of
the city forbids my punishing you on the day the dead
are with us. This you knew, and you took advantage of
it. But you are no longer one of us; I cast you out forever. You shall go hence barefooted, with nothing in
your hands, wearing that shameless dress. And I hereby
order any man who sees you within our gates after the
sun has risen to strike you down and rid the city of its
bane.

[*He goes out, followed by* THE SOLDIERS. THE CROWD
file past ELECTRA, *shaking their fists at her.*]

ZEUS [*to* ORESTES]: Well, young master, were you duly
edified? For, unless I'm much mistaken, the tale has a
moral. The wicked have been punished and the good
rewarded. [*He points to* ELECTRA.] As for that woman—

ORESTES [*sharply*]: Mind what you say. That woman is my
sister. Now go; I want to talk to her.

ZEUS [*observes him for a moment, then shrugs his
shoulders*]: Very good.

[*Exit* ZEUS, *followed by* THE TUTOR.]

ORESTES: Electra!

ELECTRA [*Still standing on the temple steps, she raises her
eyes and gazes at him.*]: Ah, you're still there, Philebus?

ORESTES: You're in danger, Electra. You mustn't stay a
moment longer in this city.

ELECTRA: In danger? Yes, that's true. You saw how I

failed to bring it off. It was a bit your fault, you know
—but I'm not angry with you.

ORESTES: My fault? How?

ELECTRA: You deceived me. [*She comes down the steps
towards him.*] Let me look at your eyes. Yes, it was your
eyes that made a fool of me.

ORESTES: There's no time to lose. Listen, Electra! We'll
escape together. Someone's getting a horse for me and
you can ride pillion.

ELECTRA: No.

ORESTES: What? You won't come away with me?

ELECTRA: I refuse to run away.

ORESTES: I'll take you with me to Corinth.

ELECTRA [*laughing*]: Corinth? Exactly! I know you mean
well, but you're fooling me again. What could a girl like
me do in Corinth? I've got to keep a level head, you
know. Only yesterday my desires were so simple, so
modest. When I waited at table, with meek, downcast
eyes, I used to watch the two of them—the handsome
old woman with the dead face, and the fat, pale King
with the slack mouth and that absurd beard like a
regiment of spiders running round his chin. And then
I'd dream of what I'd see one day—a wisp of steam,
like one's breath on a cold morning, rising from their
split bellies. That was the only thing I lived for,
Philebus, I assure you. I don't know what you're after,
but this I know: that I mustn't believe you. Your eyes
are too bold for my liking. . . . Do you know what I
used to tell myself before I met you? That a wise person
can want nothing better from life than to pay back the
wrong that has been done him.

ORESTES: If you come with me, Electra, you'll see there
are many, many other things to ask of life—without
one's ceasing to be wise.

ELECTRA: No, I won't listen any more; you've done me
quite enough harm already. You came here with your
kind, girlish face and your eager eyes—and you made
me forget my hatred. I unlocked my hands and I let
my one and only treasure slip through them. You lured

me into thinking one could cure the people here by words. Well, you saw what happened. They nurse their disease; they've got to like their sores so much that they scratch them with their dirty nails to keep them festering. Words are no use for such as they. An evil thing is conquered only by another evil thing, and only violence can save them. So good-by, Philebus, and leave me to my bad dreams.·

ORESTES: They'll kill you.

ELECTRA: We have a sanctuary here, Apollo's shrine. Often criminals take shelter there, and so long as they are in the temple, no one can touch a hair of their heads. That's where I'll go.

ORESTES: But why refuse my help?

ELECTRA: It's not for you to help me. Someone else will come, to set me free. [*A short silence.*] My brother isn't dead; I know that. And I'm waiting for his coming.

ORESTES: Suppose he doesn't come?

ELECTRA: He *will* come; he's bound to come. He is of our stock, you see; he has crime and tragedy in his blood, as I have—the bad blood of the house of Atreus. I picture him as a big, strong man, a born fighter, with bloodshot eyes like our father's, always smoldering with rage. He, too, is doomed; tangled up in his destiny, like a horse whose belly is ripped open and his legs are caught up in his guts. And now at every step he tears his bowels out. Yes, one day he will come, this city draws him. Nothing can hinder his coming, for it is here he can do the greatest harm, and suffer the greatest harm. I often seem to see him coming, with lowered head, sullen with pain, muttering angry words. He scares me; every night I see him in my dreams, and I wake screaming with terror. But I'm waiting for him and I love him. I must stay here to direct his rage—for I, anyhow, keep a clear head—to point to the guilty and say: "Those are they, Orestes. Strike!"

ORESTES: And suppose he isn't like that at all?

ELECTRA: How can he be otherwise? Don't forget he's the son of Agamemnon and Clytemnestra.

ORESTES: But mightn't he be weary of all that tale of wickedness and bloodshed; if, for instance, he'd been brought up in a happy, peaceful city?

ELECTRA: Then I'd spit in his face, and I'd say: "Go away, you cur; go and keep company where you belong, with women. But you're reckoning without your doom, poor fool. You're a grandson of Atreus, and you can't escape the heritage of blood. You prefer shame to crime; so be it. But Fate will come and hunt you down in your bed; you'll have the shame to start with, and then you will commit the crime, however much you shirk it."

ORESTES: Electra, I am Orestes.

ELECTRA [*with a cry*]: Oh! . . . You liar!

ORESTES: By the shades of my father, Agamemnon, I swear I am Orestes. [*A short silence.*] Well? Why don't you carry out your threat and spit in my face?

ELECTRA: How could I? [*She gazes at him earnestly.*] So those shining eyes, that noble forehead, are—my brother's! Orestes. . . . Oh, I'd rather you had stayed Philebus, and my brother was dead. [*Shyly*] Was it true, what you said about your having lived at Corinth?

ORESTES: No. I was brought up by some well-to-do Athenians.

ELECTRA: How young you look! Have you ever been in battle? Has that sword you carry ever tasted blood?

ORESTES: Never.

ELECTRA: It's strange. I felt less lonely when I didn't know you. I was waiting for the Orestes of my dream; always thinking of his strength and of my weakness. And now you're there before me; Orestes, the real Orestes, was you all the time. I look at you and I see we're just a boy and a girl, two young orphans. But, you know, I love you. More than I'd have loved the other Orestes.

ORESTES: Then, if you love me, come away. We'll leave this place together.

ELECTRA: Leave Argos? No. It's here the doom of the Atrides must be played out, and I am of the house of

Atreus. I ask nothing of you. I've nothing more to ask
of Philebus. But here I stay.

[ZEUS *enters, back stage, and takes cover to listen to
them.*]

ORESTES: Electra, I'm Orestes, your brother. I, too, am
of the house of Atreus, and my place is at your side.

ELECTRA: No. You're not my brother; you're a stranger.
Orestes is dead, and so much the better for him. From
now on I'll do homage to his shade, along with my
father's and my sister's. You, Philebus, claim to be of
our house. So be it! But can you truly say that you are
one of *us?* Was *your* childhood darkened by the shadow
of a murder? No, more likely you were a quiet little boy
with happy, trustful eyes, the pride of your adoptive
father. Naturally you could trust people—they always
had a smile for you—just as you could trust the solid
friendly things around you: tables, beds, and stairs. And
because you were rich, and always nicely dressed, and
had lots of toys, you must have often thought the world
was quite a nice world to live in, like a big warm bath
in which one can splash and loll contentedly. My childhood was quite different. When I was six I was a
drudge, and I mistrusted everything and everyone. [A
short pause.] So go away, my noble-souled brother. I
have no use for noble souls; what I need is an accomplice.

ORESTES: How could I leave you alone; above all, now
that you've lost even your last hope? . . . What do
you propose to do here?

ELECTRA: That's my business. Good-by, Philebus.

ORESTES: So you're driving me away? [*He takes some
steps, then halts and faces her.*] Is it my fault if I'm
not the fierce young swashbuckler you expected? Him
you'd have taken by the hand at once and said:
"Strike!" Of me you asked nothing. But, good heavens,
why should I be outcast by my own sister—when I've
not even been put to the test?

ELECTRA: No, Philebus, I could never lay such a load upon

a heart like yours; a heart that has no hatred in it.

ORESTES: You are right. No hatred; but no love, either. You, Electra, I might have loved. And yet—I wonder. Love or hatred calls for self-surrender. He cuts a fine figure, the warm-blooded, prosperous man, solidly entrenched in his well-being, who one fine day surrenders all to love—or to hatred; himself, his house, his land, his memories. But who am I, and what have I to surrender? I'm a mere shadow of a man; of all the ghosts haunting this town today, none is ghostlier than I. The only loves I've known were phantom loves, rare and vacillating as will-o'-the-wisps. The solid passions of the living were never mine. Never! [A *short silence*.] But, oh, the shame of it! Here I am, back in the town where I was born, and my own sister disavows me. And now— where shall I go? What city must I haunt?

ELECTRA: Isn't there some pretty girl waiting for you— somewhere in the world?

ORESTES: Nobody is waiting for me anywhere. I wander from city to city, a stranger to all others and to myself, and the cities close again behind me like the waters of a pool. If I leave Argos, what trace of my coming will remain, except the cruel disappointment of your hope?

ELECTRA: You told me about happy towns—

ORESTES: What do I care for happiness? I want my share of memories, my native soil, my place among the men of Argos. [A *short silence*.] Electra, I shall not leave Argos.

ELECTRA: Please, please, Philebus, go away. If you have any love for me, go. It hurts me to think what may come to you here—nothing but evil, that I know—and your innocence would ruin all my plans.

ORESTES: I shall not go.

ELECTRA: How can you think I'd let you stay beside me— you with your stubborn uprightness—to pass silent judgment on my acts? Oh, why are you so obstinate? Nobody wants you here.

ORESTES: It's my one chance, and you, Electra—surely

you won't refuse it to me? Try to understand. I want
to be a man who belongs to some place, a man among
comrades. Only consider. Even the slave bent beneath
his load, dropping with fatigue and staring dully at the
ground a foot in front of him—why, even that poor
slave can say he's in *his* town, as a tree is in a forest,
or a leaf upon the tree. Argos is all around him, warm,
compact, and comforting. Yes, Electra, I'd gladly be
that slave and enjoy that feeling of drawing the city
round me like a blanket and curling myself up in it.
No, I shall not go.

ELECTRA: Even if you stayed a hundred years among us,
you'd still be a stranger here, and lonelier than if you
were tramping the highroads of Greece. The townspeople would be watching you all the time from the
corner of an eye, and they'd lower their voices when
you came near.

ORESTES: Is it really so hard to win a place among you?
My sword can serve the city, and I have gold to help
the needy.

ELECTRA: We are not short of captains, or of charitable
souls.

ORESTES: In that case— [*He takes some steps away from
her, with lowered eyes.* ZEUS *comes forward and gazes
at him, rubbing his hands.* ORESTES *raises his eyes
heavenwards.*] Ah, if only I knew which path to take!
O Zeus, our Lord and King of Heaven, not often have
I called on you for help, and you have shown me little
favor; yet this you know: that I have always tried to act
aright. But now I am weary and my mind is dark; I can
no longer distinguish right from wrong. I need a guide
to point my way. Tell me, Zeus, is it truly your will that
a king's son, hounded from his city, should meekly
school himself to banishment and slink away from his
ancestral home like a whipped cur? I cannot think it.
And yet—and yet you have forbidden the shedding of
blood. . . . What have I said? Who spoke of bloodshed? . . . O Zeus, I beseech you, if meek acceptance,

the bowed head and lowly heart are what you would
have of me, make plain your will by some sign; for no
longer can I see my path.

ZEUS [*aside*]: Ah, that's where I can help you, my young
friend. Abraxas, abraxas, tsou, tsou.

[*Light flashes out round the stone.*]

ELECTRA [*laughing*]: Splendid! It's raining miracles today!
See what comes of being a pious young man and asking
counsel of the gods. [*She is convulsed with laughter and
can hardly get the words out.*] Oh, noble youth,
Philebus, darling of the gods! "Show me a sign," you
asked. "Show me a sign." Well, now you've had your
sign—a blaze of light round that precious, sacred stone
of theirs. So off you go to Corinth! Off you go!

ORESTES [*staring at the stone*]: So that is the Right
Thing. To live at peace—always at perfect peace. I see.
Always to say "Excuse me," and "Thank you." That's
what's wanted, eh? [*He stares at the stone in silence
for some moments.*] The Right Thing. *Their* Right
Thing. [*Another silence.*] Electra!

ELECTRA: Hurry up and go. Don't disappoint your fatherly
old friend, who has bent down from Olympus to en-
lighten you. [*She stops abruptly, a look of wonder on
her face.*] But—but what's come over you?

ORESTES [*slowly, in a tone he has not used till now*]:
There is another way.

ELECTRA [*apprehensively*]: No, Philebus, don't be stubborn. You asked the gods for orders; now you have
them.

ORESTES: Orders? What do you mean? Ah yes, the light
round that big stone. But it's not for me, that light;
from now on I'll take no one's orders, neither man's
nor god's.

ELECTRA: You're speaking in riddles.

ORESTES: What a change has come on everything, and,
oh, how far away you seem! Until now I felt something
warm and living round me, like a friendly presence.
That something has just died. What emptiness! What
endless emptiness, as far as eye can reach! [*He takes*

some steps away from her.] Night is coming on. The
air is getting chilly, isn't it? But what was it—what was
it that died just now?

ELECTRA: Philebus—

ORESTES: I say there is another path—*my* path. Can't
you see it? It starts here and leads down to the city.
I must go down—do you understand?—I must go
down into the depths, among you. For you are living,
all of you, at the bottom of a pit. [*He goes up to*
ELECTRA.] You are *my* sister, Electra, and that city is
my city. My sister. [*He takes her arm.*]

ELECTRA: Don't touch me. You're hurting me, frightening
me—and I'm *not* yours.

ORESTES: I know. Not yet. I'm still too—too light. I must
take a burden on my shoulders, a load of guilt so heavy
as to drag me down, right down into the abyss of Argos.

ELECTRA: But what—what do you mean to do?

ORESTES: Wait. Give me time to say farewell to all the
lightness, the aery lightness that was mine. Let me
say good-by to my youth. There are evenings at Corinth
and at Athens, golden evenings full of songs and scents
and laughter; these I shall never know again. And
mornings, too,' radiant with promise. Good-by to them
all, good-by. . . . Come, Electra, look at our city.
There it lies, rose-red in the sun, buzzing with men and
flies, drowsing its doom away in the languor of a
summer afternoon. It fends me off with its high walls,
red roofs, locked doors. And yet it's mine for the taking;
I've felt that since this morning. You, too, Electra, are
mine for the taking—and I'll take you, too. I'll turn
into an ax and hew those walls asunder, I'll rip open
the bellies of those stolid houses and there will steam
up from the gashes a stench of rotting food and incense.
I'll be an iron wedge driven into the city, like a wedge
rammed into the heart of an oak tree.

ELECTRA: Oh, how you've changed! Your eyes have lost
their glow; they're dull and smoldering. I'm sorry for
that, Philebus; you were so gentle. But now you're
talking like the Orestes of my dreams.

ORESTES: Listen! All those people quaking with fear in their dark rooms, with their dear departed round them —supposing I take over all their crimes. Supposing I set out to win the name of "guilt-stealer," and heap on myself all their remorse; that of the woman unfaithful to her husband, of the tradesman who let his mother die, of the usurer who bled his victims white? Surely, once I am plagued with all those pangs of conscience, innumerable as the flies of Argos—surely then I shall have earned the freedom of your city. Shall I not be as much at home within your red walls as the red-aproned butcher in his shop, among the carcasses of flayed sheep and cattle?

ELECTRA: So you wish to atone for us?

ORESTES: To atone? No. I said I'd house your penitence, but I did *not* say what I'd do with all those cackling fowls; maybe I'll wring their necks.

ELECTRA: And how can you take over our sense of guilt?

ORESTES: Why, all of you ask nothing better than to be rid of it. Only the King and Queen force you to nurse it in your foolish hearts.

ELECTRA: The King and Queen— Oh, Philebus!

ORESTES: The gods bear witness that I had no wish to shed their blood.

[*A long silence.*]

ELECTRA: You're too young, too weak.

ORESTES: Are you going to draw back—*now*? Hide me somewhere in the palace, and lead me tonight to the royal bedchamber—and then you'll see if I am too weak!

ELECTRA: Orestes!

ORESTES: Ah! For the first time you've called me Orestes.

ELECTRA: Yes. I know you now. You are indeed Orestes. I didn't recognize you at first, I'd expected somebody quite different. But this throbbing in my blood, this sour taste on my lips—I've had them in my dreams, and I know what they mean. So at last you have come, Orestes, and your resolve is sure. And here I am beside you—just as in my dreams—on the brink of an act

beyond all remedy. And I'm frightened; that, too, was
in my dreams. How long I've waited for this moment,
dreading and hoping for it! From now on, all the
moments will link up, like the cogs in a machine, and
we shall never rest again until they both are lying on
their backs, with faces like crushed mulberries. In a
pool of blood. To think it's you who are going to shed
it, you with those gentle eyes! I'm sorry now, sorry that
never again I'll see that gentleness, never again see
Philebus. Orestes, you are my elder brother, and head
of our house; fold me in your arms, protect me. Much
suffering, many perils lie ahead of both of us.

[ORESTES *takes her in his arms.* ZEUS *leaves his hiding-
place and creeps out on tiptoe.*]

CURTAIN

SCENE II

*The throne-room in the palace. An awe-inspiring, blood-
smeared image of* ZEUS *occupies a prominent position.
The sun is setting.*

ELECTRA *enters: then beckons to* ORESTES *to follow her.*

ORESTES: Someone's coming.

[*He begins to draw his sword.*]

ELECTRA: It's the sentries on their rounds. Follow me. I
know where to hide.

[*Two* SOLDIERS *enter.*]

FIRST SOLDIER: I can't think what's come over the flies
this evening. They're all crazy-like.

SECOND SOLDIER: They smell the dead; that's why they're
in such a state. Why, I daren't open my mouth to
yawn for fear they all come teeming down my throat
and start a round dance in my gullet. [ELECTRA *peeps
from her hiding-place, then quickly withdraws her
head.*] Hear that? Something creaked yonder.

FIRST SOLDIER: Oh, it's only Agamemnon, sitting down on his throne.

SECOND SOLDIER: And the seat creaked when he planted his fat bottom on it? No, it couldn't be that; a dead man's light as air.

FIRST SOLDIER: That goes for common folk like you and me. But a king, he's different. Mind you, Agamemnon always did himself proud at table. Why, he weighed two hundred pounds or more if he weighed one. It would be surprising if there wasn't some pounds left of all that flesh.

SECOND SOLDIER: So—so you think he's here, do you?

FIRST SOLDIER: Where else should he be? If I was a dead king and I had twenty-four hours' leave each year, you may be sure I'd spend them squatting on my throne, just to remind me of the high old times I had when I was His Almighty Majesty. And I'd stay put; I wouldn't run round pestering folk in their houses.

SECOND SOLDIER: Ah, wouldn't you? You say that because you're alive. But if you were dead, you'd be just as nasty as the others. [FIRST SOLDIER *smacks his face.*] Hey! What are you up to?

FIRST SOLDIER: I'm doing you a good turn. Look, I've killed seven of 'em, all at a go.

SECOND SOLDIER: Seven what? Seven dead 'uns?

FIRST SOLDIER: O' course not. *Flies.* Look, my hand's all bloody. [*He wipes it on his pants.*] Ugh, the filthy brutes!

SECOND SOLDIER: Pity you can't swot the lot of them while you're about it. The dead men, now—they don't do nothing, they know how to behave. If the flies were all killed off, we'd have some peace.

FIRST SOLDIER: Peace, you say? No, if I thought there were ghost-flies here as well, that'd be the last straw.

SECOND SOLDIER: Why?

FIRST SOLDIER: Don't you see? They die by millions every day, the little buzzers. Well, if all the flies that have died since last summer were set loose in the town, there'd be three hundred and sixty-five dead flies for

every one that's here. The air'd be laced with flies,
we'd breathe flies, eat flies, sweat flies; they'd be
rolling down our throats in clusters and bunging up
our lungs. . . . I wonder, now—maybe that's why
there's such a funny smell in this room.

SECOND SOLDIER: No, no, it ain't that. They say our
dead men have foul breaths, you know. And this
room's not so big as it looks—a thousand square feet
or so, I should say. Two or three dead men would be
enough to foul the air.

FIRST SOLDIER: That's so. Fussing and fuming like they
do.

SECOND SOLDIER: I tell you there's something amiss here.
I heard a floor-board creak over there.

[*They go behind the throne to investigate.* ORESTES *and*
ELECTRA *slip out on the left and tiptoe past the steps
of the throne, returning to their hiding-place just as*
THE SOLDIERS *emerge on the left.*]

FIRST SOLDIER: You see, there ain't nobody. It's only
that old sod Agamemnon. Like as not, he's sitting on
them cushions, straight as a poker. I shouldn't be
surprised if he's watching you and me for want of
anything else to do.

SECOND SOLDIER: Ay, and we'd better have a good look
round, I ain't easy in my mind. These flies are something wicked, but it can't be helped.

FIRST SOLDIER: I wish I was back in the barracks. At least
the dead folk there are old chums come back to visit
us, just ordinary folk like us. But when I think that
His Late Lamented Majesty is there, like as not
counting the buttons missing on my tunic, well it
makes me dithery, like when the general's doing an
inspection.

[*Enter* ÆGISTHEUS *and* CLYTEMNESTRA, *followed by
servants carrying lamps.*]

ÆGISTHEUS: Go, all of you.

[*Exeunt* SOLDIERS *and* SERVANTS.]

CLYTEMNESTRA: What is troubling you tonight?

ÆGISTHEUS: You saw what happened? Had I not played

upon their fear, they'd have shaken off their remorse
in the twinkling of an eye.

CLYTEMNESTRA: Is that all? Then be reassured. You will
always find a way to freeze their courage when the
need arises.

ÆGISTHEUS: I know. Oh, I'm only too skillful in the art of
false pretense. [*A short silence.*] I am sorry I had to
rebuke Electra.

CLYTEMNESTRA: Why? Because she is my daughter? It
pleased you to so do, and all you do has my approval.

ÆGISTHEUS: Woman, it is not on your account that I
regret it.

CLYTEMNESTRA: Then—why? You used not to have much
love for Electra.

ÆGISTHEUS: I am tired. So tired. For fifteen years I have
been upholding the remorse of a whole city, and my
arms are aching with the strain. For fifteen years I
have been dressing a part, playing the scaremonger,
and the black of my robes has seeped through to my
soul.

CLYTEMNESTRA: But, sire, I, too—

ÆGISTHEUS: I know, woman, I know. You are going to
tell me of your remorse. I wish I shared it. It fills out
the void of your life. *I* have no remorse—and no man
in Argos is sadder than I.

CLYTEMNESTRA: My sweet lord—
[*She goes up to him affectionately.*]

ÆGISTHEUS: Keep off, you whore! Are you not ashamed
—under his eyes?

CLYTEMNESTRA: Under his eyes? Who can see us here?

ÆGISTHEUS: Why, the King. The dead came forth this
morning.

CLYTEMNESTRA: Sire, I beg you—the dead are underground and will not trouble us for many a long day.
Have you forgotten it was you yourself who invented
that fable to impress your people?

ÆGISTHEUS: That's so. Well, it only shows how tired I am,
how sick at heart. Now leave me to my thoughts.
[*Exit* CLYTEMNESTRA.] Have you in me, Lord Zeus,

the king you wished for Argos? I come and go among
my people, I speak in trumpet tones, I parade the
terror of my frown, and all who see me cringe in an
agony of repentance. But I—what am I but an empty
shell? Some creature has devoured me unawares,
gnawed out my inner self. And now, looking within,
I see I am more dead than Agamemnon. Did I say
I was sad? I lied. Neither sad nor gay is the desert—
a boundless waste of sand under a burning waste of
sky. Not sad, nor gay, but—sinister. Ah, I'd give my
kingdom to be able to shed a tear.

[ZEUS *enters.*]

ZEUS: That's right. Complain away! You're only a king,
like every other king.

ÆGISTHEUS: Who are you? What are you doing here?

ZEUS: So you don't recognize me?

ÆGISTHEUS: Be gone, stranger, or I shall have you thrown
out by my guards.

ZEUS: You don't recognize me? Still, you have seen me
often enough, in dreams. It's true I looked more awe-
inspiring. [*Flashes of lightning, a peal of thunder.* ZEUS
assumes an awe-inspiring air.] And now do you know
me?

ÆGISTHEUS: Zeus!

ZEUS: Good! [*Affable again, he goes up to the statue.*]
So that's meant to be me? It's thus the Argives picture
me at their prayers? Well, well, it isn't often that a
god can study his likeness, face to face. [*A short
silence.*] How hideous I am! They cannot like me
much.

ÆGISTHEUS: They fear you.

ZEUS: Excellent! I've no use for love. Do you, Ægistheus,
love me?

ÆGISTHEUS: What do you want of me? Have I not paid
heavily enough?

ZEUS: Never enough.

ÆGISTHEUS: But it's killing me, the task I have under-
taken.

ZEUS: Come now! Don't exaggerate! Your health is none

too bad; you're fat. Mind, I'm not reproaching you.
It's good, royal fat, yellow as tallow—just as it should
be. You're built to live another twenty years.

ÆGISTHEUS: Another twenty years!

ZEUS: Would you rather die?

ÆGISTHEUS: Yes.

ZEUS: So, if anyone came here now, with a drawn sword,
would you bare your breasts to him?

ÆGISTHEUS: I—I cannot say.

ZEUS: Now mark my words. If you let yourself be
slaughtered like a dumb ox, your doom will be exem-
plary. You shall be King in hell for all eternity. That's
what I came here to tell you.

ÆGISTHEUS: Is someone planning to kill me?

ZEUS: So it seems.

ÆGISTHEUS: Electra?

ZEUS: Not only Electra.

ÆGISTHEUS: Who?

ZEUS: Orestes.

ÆGISTHEUS: Oh! . . . Well, that's in the natural order of
things, no doubt. What can I do against it?

ZEUS [*mimicking his tone*]: What can I do? [*Imperiously*]
Bid your men arrest a young stranger going under the
name of Philebus. Have him and Electra thrown into
a dungeon—and if you leave them there to rot, I'll
think no worse of you. Well, what are you waiting for?
Call your men.

ÆGISTHEUS: No.

ZEUS: Be good enough to tell me why that no.

ÆGISTHEUS: I am tired.

ZEUS: Don't stare at the ground. Raise your big, bloodshot eyes and look at me. That's better. Yes, you're
majestically stupid, like a horse; a kingly fool. But yours
is not the stubbornness that vexes me; rather, it will
add a spice to your surrender. For I know you will
obey me in the end.

ÆGISTHEUS: I tell you I refuse to fall in with your plans.
I have done so far too often.

ZEUS: That's right. Show your mettle! Resist! Resist!

Ah, how I cherish souls like yours! Your eyes flash, you clench your fists, you fling refusal in the teeth of Zeus. None the less, my little rebel, my restive little horse, no sooner had I warned you than your heart said yes. Of course you'll obey. Do you think I leave Olympus without good reason? I wished to warn you of this crime because it is my will to avert it.

ÆGISTHEUS: To warn me! How strange!

ZEUS: Why "strange"? Surely it's natural enough. Your life's in danger and I want to save it.

ÆGISTHEUS: Who asked you to save it? What about Agamemnon? Did you warn *him*? And yet *he* wished to live.

ZEUS: O miserable man, what base ingratitude! You are dearer to me than Agamemnon, and when I prove this, you complain!

ÆGISTHEUS: Dearer than Agamemnon? I? No, it's Orestes whom you cherish. You allowed me to work my doom, you let me rush in, ax in hand, to King Agamemnon's bath—and no doubt you watched from high Olympus, licking your lips at the thought of another damned soul to gloat over. But today you are protecting young Orestes against himself; and I, whom you egged on to kill his father—you have chosen me to restrain the young man's hand. I was a poor creature, just qualified for murder; but for Orestes, it seems, you have higher destinies in view.

ZEUS: What strange jealousy is this! But have no fear; I love him no more than I love you. I love nobody.

ÆGISTHEUS: Then see what you have made of me, unjust god that you are. And tell me this. If today you hinder the crime Orestes has in mind, why did you permit mine of fifteen years ago?

ZEUS: All crimes do not displease me equally. And now, Ægistheus, I shall speak to you frankly, as one king to another. The first crime was mine; I committed it when I made man mortal. Once I had done that, what was left for you, poor human murderers, to do? To kill your victims? But they already had the seed of

death in them; all you could do was to hasten its
fruition by a year or two. Do you know what would
have befallen Agamemnon if you had not killed him?
Three months later he'd have died of apoplexy in a
pretty slave-girl's arms. But your crime served my ends.

ÆGISTHEUS: What ends? For fifteen years I have been
atoning for it—and you say it served your ends!

ZEUS: Exactly. It's because you are atoning for it that
it served my ends. I like crimes that *pay*. I like yours
because it was a clumsy, boorish murder, a crime that
did not know itself, a crime in the antique mode, more
like a cataclysm than an act of man. Not for one
moment did you defy me. You struck in a frenzy of
fear and rage. And then, when your frenzy had died
down, you looked back on the deed with loathing and
disowned it. Yet what a profit I have made on it!
For one dead man, twenty thousand living men wallowing in patience. Yes, it was a good bargain I struck
that day.

ÆGISTHEUS: I see what lies behind your words. Orestes
will have no remorse.

ZEUS: Not a trace of it. At this moment he is thinking
out his plan, coolly, methodically, cheerfully. What
good to me is a carefree murder, a shameless, sedate
crime, that lies light as thistledown on the murderer's
conscience? No, I won't allow it. Ah, how I loathe
the crimes of this new generation; thankless and sterile
as the wind! Yes, that nice-minded young man will kill
you as he'd kill a chicken; he'll go away with red
hands and a clean heart. In your place I should feel
humiliated. So—call your men!

ÆGISTHEUS: Again I tell you, I will *not*. The crime that
is being hatched displeases you enough for me to welcome it.

ZEUS: Ægistheus, you are a king, and it's to your sense of
kingship I appeal, for you enjoy wielding the scepter.

ÆGISTHEUS: Continue.

ZEUS: You may hate me, but we are akin; I made you

ın my image. A king is a god on earth, glorious and
terrifying as a god.

ÆGISTHEUS: You, terrifying?

ZEUS: Look at me. [*A long silence.*] I told you you were
made in my image. Each keeps order; you in Argos,
I in heaven and on earth—and you and I harbor the
same dark secret in our hearts.

ÆGISTHEUS: I have no secret.

ZEUS: You have. The same as mine. The bane of gods
and kings. The bitterness of knowing men are free.
Yes, Ægistheus, they are free. But your subjects do
not know it, and you do.

ÆGISTHEUS: Why, yes. If they knew it, they'd send my
palace up in flames. For fifteen years I've been playing
a part to mask their power from them.

ZEUS: So you see we are alike.

ÆGISTHEUS: Alike? A god likening himself to me—what
freak of irony is this? Since I camc to the throne, all
I said, all my acts, have been aimed at building up an
image of myself. I wish each of my subjects to keep
that image in the foreground of his mind, and to
feel, even when alone, that my eyes are on him,
severely judging his most private thoughts. But I have
been trapped in my own net. I have come to see
myself only as they see me. I peer into the dark pit
of their souls, and there, deep down, I see the image
that I have built up. I shudder, but I cannot take
my eyes off it. Almighty Zeus, who am I? Am I anything more than the dread that others have of me?

ZEUS: And I—who do you think I am? [*Points to the
statue.*] I, too, have my image, and do you suppose
it doesn't fill me with confusion? For a hundred
thousand years I havc been dancing a slow, dark ritual
dance before men's eyes. Their eyes are so intent on
me that they forget to look into themselves. If I
forgot myself for a single moment, if I let their eyes
turn away—

ÆGISTHEUS: Yes?

ZEUS: Enough. That is *my* business Ægistheus, I know that you are weary of it all; but why complain? You'll die one day—but I shall not. So long as there are men on earth, I am doomed to go on dancing before them.

ÆGISTHEUS: Alas! But who has doomed us?

ZEUS: No one but ourselves. For we have the same passion. You, Ægistheus, have, like me, a passion for order.

ÆGISTHEUS: For order? That is so. It was for the sake of order that I wooed Clytemnestra, for order that I killed my King; I wished that order should prevail, and that it should prevail through me. I have lived without love, without hope, even without lust. But I have kept order. Yes, I have kept good order in my kingdom. That has been my ruling passion; a godlike passion, but how terrible!

ZEUS: We could have no other, you and I; I am God, and you were born to be a king.

ÆGISTHEUS: Ay, more's the pity!

ZEUS: Ægistheus, my creature and my mortal brother, in the name of this good order that we serve, both you and I, I ask you—nay, I command you—to lay hands on Orestes and his sister.

ÆGISTHEUS: Are they so dangerous?

ZEUS: Orestes knows that he is free.

ÆGISTHEUS [*eagerly*]: He knows he's free? Then, to lay hands on him, to put him in irons, is not enough. A free man in a city acts like a plague-spot. He will infect my whole kingdom and bring my work to nothing. Almighty Zeus, why stay your hand? Why not fell him with a thunderbolt?

ZEUS [*slowly*]: Fell him with a thunderbolt? [*A pause. Then, in a muffled voice*] Ægistheus, the gods have another secret.

ÆGISTHEUS: Yes?

ZEUS: Once freedom lights its beacon in a man's heart, the gods are powerless against him. It's a matter between man and man, and it is for other men, and

for them only, to let him go his gait, or to throttle
him.

ÆGISTHEUS [*observing him closely*]: To throttle him? Be
it so. Well, I shall do your will, no doubt. But say no
more, and stay here no longer—I could not bear it.
[*As* ZEUS *departs,* ELECTRA *leaps forward and rushes
to the door.* ORESTES *comes forward.*]

ELECTRA: Strike him down! Don't give him time to call
for help. I'll bar the door.

ÆGISTHEUS: So you, young man, are Orestes?

ORESTES: Defend yourself.

ÆGISTHEUS: I shall not defend myself. It's too late for
me to call for help, and I am glad it is too late. No,
I shall not resist. I *wish* you to kill me.

ORESTES: Good. Little I care how it is done. . . . So I
am to be a murderer.

[ORESTES *strikes him with his sword.*]

ÆGISTHEUS [*tottering*]: Ah! You struck well, Orestes. [*He
clings to* ORESTES.] Let me look at you. Is it true you
feel no remorse?

ORESTES: Remorse? Why should I feel remorse? I am
only doing what is right.

ÆGISTHEUS: What is right is the will of God. You were
hidden here and you heard the words of Zeus.

ORESTES: What do I care for Zeus? Justice is a matter
between men, and I need no god to teach me it. It's
right to stamp you out, like the foul brute you are,
and to free the people of Argos from your evil in-
fluence. It is right to restore to them their sense of
human dignity.

ÆGISTHEUS [*groaning*]: Pain! What agony!

ELECTRA: Look! Look! He's swaying; his face has gone
quite gray. What an ugly sight's a dying man!

ORESTES: Keep silent! Let him carry with him to the
grave no other memory than the memory of our joy.

ÆGISTHEUS: My curse on you both!

ORESTES: Won't you have done with dying?

[*He strikes again.* ÆGISTHEUS *falls.*]

ÆGISTHEUS: Beware of the flies, Orestes, beware of the flies. All is not over.

[*Dies.*]

ORESTES [*giving the body a kick*]: For him, anyhow, all is over. Now lead me to the Queen's room.

ELECTRA: Orestes!

ORESTES: What?

ELECTRA: She—she can do us no more harm.

ORESTES: What of it? What has come over you? This is not how you spoke a little while ago.

ELECTRA: Orestes! You, too, have changed. I hardly recognize you.

ORESTES: Very well. I'll go alone.

[*Exit.*]

ELECTRA [*to herself*]: Will she scream? [*Silence. She is listening.*] He's walking down the passage. When he opens the fourth door— Oh, I wanted this to happen. And I—I want it now, I *must* want it. [*She looks at* ÆGISTHEUS.] That one—yes, he's dead. So *this* is what I wanted. I didn't realize how it would be. [*She comes closer to the body.*] A hundred times I've seen him, in my dreams, lying just where he is now, with a sword through his heart. His eyes were closed, he seemed asleep. How I hated him, what joy I got from hating him! But he doesn't seem asleep; his eyes are open, staring up at me. He is dead, and my hatred is dead, too. And I'm standing here, waiting, waiting. That woman is still alive, she's in her bedroom, and presently she'll be screaming. Screaming like an animal in pain. No, I can't bear those eyes any longer. [*Kneeling, she lays a mantle over the King's face.*] What was it, then, I wanted? What? [*A short silence.* CLYTEMNESTRA *screams.*] He's struck her. She was our mother—and he's struck her. [*She rises to her feet.*] It's done; my enemies are dead. For years and years I've reveled in the thought of this, and, now it's happened, my heart is like a lump of ice. Was I lying to myself all those years? No, that's not true, it can't be true. I'm not a coward. Only a moment ago I wanted it, and I haven't changed. I'm glad, glad, to see that swine lying at my feet. [*She jerks the mantle off the dead King's face.*] Those dead-fish eyes goggling up at nothing—why should they trouble me? That's how I wanted to see them, dead and staring, and I'm glad, glad— [CLYTEMNESTRA's *screams are weakening.*] Let her scream! Make her scream, Orestes. I want her to suffer. [*The screams cease.*] Oh joy, joy! I'm weeping for joy; my enemies are dead, my father is avenged.

[ORESTES *returns, his sword dripping blood.* ELECTRA *runs to him and flings herself into his arms.*]

ELECTRA: Orestes! . . . Oh! . . .

ORESTES: You're frightened. Why?

ELECTRA: I'm not frightened. I'm drunk. Drunk with joy. What did she say? Did she beg for mercy long?

ORESTES: Electra, I shall not repent of what I have done, but I think fit not to speak of it. There are some memories one does not share. It is enough for you to know she's dead.

ELECTRA: Did she die cursing us? That's all I want you to tell me. Did she curse us?

ORESTES: Yes. She died cursing us.

ELECTRA: Take me in your arms, beloved, and press me to your breast. How dark the night is! I never knew such darkness; those torches have no effect on it. . . . Do you love me?

ORESTES: It is not night; a new day is dawning. We are free, Electra. I feel as if I'd brought you into life and I, too, had just been born. Yes, I love you, and you belong to me. Only yesterday I was empty-handed, and today I have *you*. Ours is a double tie of blood; we two come of the same race and we two have shed blood.

ELECTRA: Let go your sword. Give me that hand, your strong right hand. [*She clasps and kisses it.*] Your fingers are short and square, made to grasp and hold. Dear hand! It's whiter than mine. But how heavy it became to strike down our father's murderers! Wait! [*She takes a torch and holds it near* ORESTES.] I must

light up your face; it's getting so dark that I can
hardly see you. And I *must* see you; when I stop seeing you, I'm afraid of you. I daren't take my eyes off
you. I must tell myself again and again that I love you.
But—how strange you look!

ORESTES: I am free, Electra. Freedom has crashed down
on me like a thunderbolt.

ELECTRA: Free? But I—I don't feel free. And you—can
you undo what has been done? Something has happened and we are no longer free to blot it out. Can
you prevent our being the murderers of our mother—
for all time?

ORESTES: Do you think I'd wish to prevent it? I have
done *my* deed, Electra, and that deed was good. I
shall bear it on my shoulders as a carrier at a ferry
carries the traveler to the farther bank. And when I
have brought it to the farther bank I shall take stock
of it. The heavier it is to carry, the better pleased I
shall be; for that burden is my freedom. Only yesterday I walked the earth haphazard; thousands of roads
I tramped that brought me nowhere, for they were
other men's roads. Yes, I tried them all; the haulers'
tracks along the riverside, the mule-paths in the mountains, and the broad, flagged highways of the charioteers.
But none of these was mine. Today I have one path
only, and heaven knows where it leads. But it is *my*
path. . . . What is it, Electra?

ELECTRA: I can't see you any more. Those torches give
no light. I hear your voice, but it hurts me, it cuts
like a knife. Will it always be as dark as this—always,
even in the daytime? . . . Oh, Orestes! There they are!

ORESTES: Who?

ELECTRA: There they are! Where have they come from?
They're hanging from the ceiling like clusters of black
grapes; the walls are alive with them; they're swirling
down across the torchlight and it's their shadows that
are hiding your face from me.

ORESTES: The flies—

ELECTRA: Listen! The sound of their wings is like a
roaring furnace. They're all round us, Orestes, watching, biding their time. Presently they'll swoop down
on us and I shall feel thousands of tiny clammy feet
crawling over me. Oh, look! They're growing bigger,
bigger; now they're as big as bees. We'll never escape
them, they'll follow us everywhere in a dense cloud.
Oh God, now I can see their eyes, millions of beady
eyes all staring at us!

ORESTES: What do the flies matter to us?

ELECTRA: They're the Furies, Orestes, the goddesses of
remorse.

VOICES [*from behind the door*]: Open! Open! . . . If you
don't, we'll smash the door in.

[*Heavy thuds. They are battering at the door.*]

ORESTES: Clytemnestra's cries must have brought them
here. Come! Lead me to Apollo's shrine. We will spend
the night there, sheltered from men and flies. And
tomorrow I shall speak to my people.

CURTAIN

ACT III

The temple of Apollo. Twilight. A statue of Apollo in the center of the stage. ELECTRA and ORESTES are sleeping at the foot of the statue, their arms clasped round its legs. The FURIES ring them round; they sleep standing, like cranes.
At the back is a huge bronze door.

FIRST FURY [*stretching herself*]: Aaaah! I slept the night out standing, stiff with rage, and my sleep was glorious with angry dreams. Ah, how lovely is the flower of anger, the red flower in my heart! [*She circles round* ORESTES *and* ELECTRA.] Still sleeping. How white and soft they are! I'll roll on their breasts and bellies, like a torrent over stones. And I shall polish hour by hour their tender flesh; rub it, scour it, wear it to the bone. [*She comes a few steps forward.*] Oh clear, bright dawn of hate! A superb awakening. They're sleeping, sweating, a smell of fever rises from them. But I am awake; cool and hard and gemlike. My soul is adamant —and I feel my sanctity.

ELECTRA [*sighing in her sleep*]: No! No!

FIRST FURY: She's sighing. Wait, my pretty one, wait till you feel our teeth. Soon you'll be screaming with the agony of our caresses. I'll woo you like a man, for you're my bride, and you shall feel my love crushing your life out. You, Electra, are more beautiful than I; but you'll see how my kisses age you. Within six months I'll have you raddled like an old hag; but I stay young forever. [*She bends over* ORESTES *and* ELECTRA.] Ah, this lovely human carrion, what a tasty meal we have in store! As I gaze down at them and breathe their breath, I choke with rage. Nothing is sweeter, nothing, than to feel a dawn of hatred spreading like quickfire in one's veins; teeth and talons ready for their task. Hatred is flooding through me, welling up in my breasts like milk. Awake, sisters, awake! The day has come.

SECOND FURY: I dreamt I was biting them.

FIRST FURY: Be patient. Today they are protected by a god, but soon hunger and thirst will drive them out of sanctuary. And then you shall bite them to your heart's content.

THIRD FURY: Aaah! How I want to claw them!

FIRST FURY: Your turn will come. In a little while your iron talons will be ribboning the flesh of those young criminals with angry red. Come closer, sisters, come and look at them.

A FURY: How young they are!

ANOTHER FURY: And how beautiful!

FIRST FURY: Yes, we are favored. Only too often criminals are old and ugly. Too seldom do we have the joy, the exquisite delight, of ruining what's beautiful.

THE FURIES: Heiah! Heiahah!

THIRD FURY: Orestes is almost a child. I shall mother him, oh so tenderly, with my hatred; I shall take his pale head on my knees and stroke his hair.

FIRST FURY: And then?

THIRD FURY: Then, when he least expects it, I shall dig these two fingers into his eyes.

[*All laugh.*]

FIRST FURY: See, they're stretching, sighing, on the brink of waking. And now, my sisters, flies my sisters, let's sing the sinners from their sleep.

THE FURIES [*together*]: Bzz. Bzz. Bzz. Bzz.

We shall settle on your rotten hearts like flies on butter;
Rotten hearts, juicy, luscious hearts.
Like bees we'll suck the pus and matter from your hearts,
And we'll turn it into honey, rich, green honey.
What love could ravish us as hatred does?

Bzz. Bzz. Bzz. Bzz.
We shall be the staring eyes of the houses,
The growls of the kenneled mastiff baring his fangs
    as you go by,
A drone of wings pulsing in high air,
Sounds of the forest,
Whistlings, whinings, creakings, hissings, howlings.
We shall be the darkness,
The clotted darkness of your souls.
Bzz. Bzz. Bzz. Bzz.
Heiah, heiah, heiahah!
Bzz. Bzz. Bzz. Bzz.
We are the flies, the suckers of pus,
We shall have open house with you,
We shall gather our food from your mouths,
And our light from the depths of your eyes.
All your life we will be with you,
Until we make you over to the worms.
[*They dance.*]

ELECTRA [*still half asleep*]: Was someone speaking? Who
    —who are you?

THE FURIES: Bzz. Bzz. Bzz.

ELECTRA: Ah, yes. There you are. Well? Have we really
    killed them?

ORESTES [*waking*]: Electra!

ELECTRA: You, who are you? Ah, yes. Orestes. Go away.

ORESTES: But—what's wrong, Electra?

ELECTRA: You frighten me. I had a dream. I saw our
    mother lying on her back. Blood was pouring from
    her, gushing under the doors. A dream. . . . Feel my
    hands. They're icy. No, don't. Don't touch me. Did
    she really bleed much?

ORESTES: Don't!

ELECTRA [*waking up completely*]: Let me look at you:
    You killed them. It was you, you who killed them.
    You are here beside me, you have just waked up,
    there's nothing written on your face, no brand. . . .
    And yet you killed them.

ORESTES: Why, yes. I killed them. [*A short silence.*]

You, too, make me afraid. Yesterday you were so
beautiful. And now you look as if some wild beast
had clawed your face.

ELECTRA: No beast. Your crime. It's tearing off my cheeks
and eyelids; I feel as if my eyes and teeth were naked.
. . . But what are those creatures?

ORESTES: Take no notice of them. They can do you no
harm.

FIRST FURY: No harm? Let her dare to come among us
and you'll see if we can do no harm!

ORESTES: Keep quiet. Back to your kennel, bitches! [*The
FURIES growl.*] Is it possible that the girl who only
yesterday was dancing in a white dress on the temple
steps—is it possible you were that girl?

ELECTRA: I've grown old. In a single night.

ORESTES: You have not lost your beauty, but— Where,
now, have I seen dead eyes like those? Electra—you
are like *her*. Like Clytemnestra. What use, then, was
it killing her? When I see my crime in those eyes, it
revolts me.

FIRST FURY: That is because *you* revolt *her*.

ORESTES: Is that true, Electra? Do I revolt you?

ELECTRA: Oh, let me be!

FIRST FURY: Well? Can you still have any doubt? How
should she not hate you? She lived in peace, dreaming
her dreams; and then you came, bringing murder and
impiety upon her. So now she has to share your guilt
and hug that pedestal, the only scrap of earth remaining
to her.

ORESTES: Do not listen.

FIRST FURY: Away! Away! Make him go, Electra; don't
let him touch you! He's a butcher. He reeks of fresh,
warm blood. He used the poor old woman very foully,
you know; he killed her piecemeal.

ELECTRA: Oh no! That's a lie, surely?

FIRST FURY: You can believe me; I was there all the time,
buzzing in the air around them.

ELECTRA: So he struck her several times?

FIRST FURY: Ten times at least. And each time the sword

squelched in the wound. She tried to shield her face
and belly with her hands, and he carved her hands to
ribbons.

ELECTRA: So it wasn't a quick death. Did she suffer much?

ORESTES: Put your fingers in your ears, do not look at
them, and, above all, ask no questions. If you question
them, you're lost.

FIRST FURY: Yes, she suffered—horribly.

ELECTRA [*covering her face with her hands*]: Oh!

ORESTES: She wants to part us, she is building up a wall
of solitude around you. But beware; once you are
alone, alone and helpless, they will fling themselves
upon you. Electra, we planned this crime together
and we should bear its brunt together.

ELECTRA: You dare to say I planned it with you?

ORESTES: Can you deny it?

ELECTRA: Of course I deny it. Wait! Well, perhaps—in
a way. . . . Oh, I don't know. I dreamt the crime, but
you carried it out, you murdered your own mother.

THE FURIES [*shrieking and laughing*]: Murderer! Murderer! Butcher!

ORESTES: Electra, behind that door is the outside world.
A world of dawn. Out there the sun is rising, lighting
up the roads. Soon we shall leave this place, we shall
walk those sunlit roads, and these hags of darkness
will lose their power. The sunbeams will cut through
them like swords.

ELECTRA: The sun—

FIRST FURY: You will never see the sun again, Electra.
We shall mass between you and the sun like a swarm
of locusts; you will carry darkness round your head
wherever you go.

ELECTRA: Oh, let me be! Stop torturing me!

ORESTES: It's your weakness gives them their strength.
Mark how they dare not speak to me. A nameless horror
has descended on you, keeping us apart. And yet why
should this be? What have you lived through that I
have not shared? Do you imagine that my mother's
cries will ever cease ringing in my ears? Or that my

eyes will ever cease to see her great sad eyes, lakes of
lambent darkness in the pallor of her face? And the
anguish that consumes you—do you think it will ever
cease ravaging my heart? But what matter? I am free.
Beyond anguish, beyond remorse. Free. And at one
with myself. No, you must not loathe yourself, Electra.
Give me your hand. I shall never forsake you.

ELECTRA: Let go of my hand! Those hell-hounds frighten
me, but you frighten me more.

FIRST FURY: You see! You see! . . . That's quite true,
little doll; you're less afraid of us than of that man.
Because you need us, Electra. You are our child, our
little girl. You need our nails to score your skin, our
teeth to bite your breast, and all our savage love to
save you from your hatred of yourself. Only the suffering of your body can take your mind off your suffering
soul. So come and let us hurt you. You have only those
two steps to come down, and we will take you in our
arms. And when our kisses sear your tender flesh, you'll
forget all in the cleansing fires of pain.

THE FURIES: Come down to us! Come down!

[*Slowly they dance round her, weaving their spell.*
ELECTRA *rises to her feet.*]

ORESTES [*gripping her arm*]: No, no, for pity's sake. Don't
go to them. Once they get you, all is lost.

ELECTRA [*freeing herself violently*]: Let go! Oh, how I
hate you! [*She goes down the steps, and the* FURIES
fling themselves on her.] Help!

[ZEUS *enters.*]

ZEUS: Kennel up!

FIRST FURY: The master!

[*The* FURIES *slink off reluctantly, leaving* ELECTRA *lying
on the ground.*]

ZEUS: Poor children. [*He goes up to* ELECTRA.] So to
this you've come, unhappy pair? My heart is torn between anger and compassion. Get up, Electra. So long
as I am here, my Furies will not hurt you. [*He helps
her to rise and gazes at her face.*] Ah, what a cruel
change! In a night, a single night, all the wild-rose

bloom has left your cheeks. In one night your body has gone to ruin, lungs, gall, and liver all burnt out. The pride of headstrong youth—see what it has brought you to, poor child.

ORESTES: Stop talking in that tone, fellow. It is unbecoming for the king of the gods.

ZEUS: And you, my lad, drop that haughty tone. It's unbecoming for a criminal atoning for his crime.

ORESTES: I am no criminal, and you have no power to make me atone for an act I don't regard as a crime.

ZEUS: So you may think, but wait awhile. I shall cure you of that error before long.

ORESTES: Torture me to your heart's content; I regret nothing.

ZEUS: Not even the doom you have brought upon your sister?

ORESTES: Not even that.

ZEUS: Do you hear, Electra? And this man professed to love you!

ORESTES: She is dearer to me than life. But her suffering comes from within, and only she can rid herself of it. For she is free.

ZEUS: And you? You, too, are free, no doubt?

ORESTES: Yes, and well you know it.

ZEUS: A pity you can't see yourself as you are now, you fool, for all your boasting! What a heroic figure you cut there, cowering between the legs of a protecting god, with a pack of hungry vixen keeping guard on you! If you *can* brag of freedom, why not praise the freedom of a prisoner languishing in fetters, or a slave nailed to the cross?

ORESTES: Certainly. Why not?

ZEUS: Take care. You play the braggart now because Apollo is protecting you. But Apollo is my most obedient servant. I have but to lift a finger and he will abandon you.

ORESTES: Then do so. Lift a finger, lift your whole hand while you are about it.

ZEUS: No, that is not my way. Haven't I told you that I

take no pleasure in punishment? I have come to save
you both.

ELECTRA: To save us? No, it is too cruel to make sport
of us. You are the lord of vengeance and of death,
but, god though you are, you have no right to delude
your victims with false hopes.

ZEUS: Within a quarter of an hour you can be outside
that door.

ELECTRA: Safe and sound?

ZEUS: You have my word for it.

ELECTRA: And what do you want from me in return?

ZEUS: Nothing, my child. Nothing.

ELECTRA: Nothing? Did I hear right? Then you are a
kind god, a lovable god.

ZEUS: Or next to nothing. A mere trifle. What you can
give most easily—a little penitence.

ORESTES: Take care, Electra. That trifle will weigh like
a millstone on your soul.

ZEUS [*to* ELECTRA]: Don't listen to him. Answer me,
instead. Why hesitate to disavow that crime? It was
committed by someone else; one could hardly say even
that you were his accomplice.

ORESTES: Electra! Are you going to go back on fifteen
years of hope and hatred?

ZEUS: What has she to go back on? Never did she really
wish that impious deed to be accomplished.

ELECTRA: If only that were true!

ZEUS: Come now! Surely you can trust my word. Do I
not read in men's hearts?

ELECTRA [*incredulously*]: And you read in mine that I
never really desired that crime? Though for fifteen years
I dreamt of murder and revenge?

ZEUS: Bah! I know you nursed bloodthirsty dreams—
but there was a sort of innocence about them. They
made you forget your servitude, they healed your
wounded pride. But you never really thought of making them come true. Well, am I mistaken?

ELECTRA: Ah, Zeus, dear Zeus, how I long to think you
are not mistaken!

ZEUS: You're a little girl, Electra. A mere child. Most little girls dream of becoming the richest or the loveliest woman on earth. But you were haunted by the cruel destiny of your race, you dreamt of becoming the saddest, most criminal of women. You never willed to do evil; you willed your own misfortune. At an age when most children are playing hopscotch or with their dolls, you, poor child, who had no friends or toys, you toyed with dreams of murder, because that's a game to play alone.

ELECTRA: Yes, yes! I'm beginning to understand.

ORESTES: Listen, Electra! It's *now* you are bringing guilt upon you. For who except yourself can know what you really wanted? Will you let another decide that for you? Why distort a past that can no longer stand up for itself? And why disown the firebrand that you were, that glorious young goddess, vivid with hatred, that I loved so much? Can't you see this cruel god is fooling you?

ZEUS: No, Electra, I'm not fooling you. And now hear what I offer. If you repudiate your crime, I'll see that you two occupy the throne of Argos.

ORESTES: Taking the places of our victims?

ZEUS: How else?

ORESTES: And I shall put on the royal robe, still warm from the dead King's wearing?

ZEUS: That or another. What can it matter?

ORESTES: Nothing of course—provided that it's black.

ZEUS: Are you not in mourning?

ORESTES: Yes, I was forgetting; in mourning for my mother. And my subjects—must I have them, too, wear black?

ZEUS: They wear it already.

ORESTES: True. We can give them time to wear out their old clothes. . . . Well, Electra, have you understood? If you shed some tears, you'll be given Clytemnestra's shifts and petticoats—those dirty, stinking ones you had to wash for fifteen years. And the part she played is yours for the asking. Now that you have come to

look so much like her, you will play the part superbly;
everyone will take you for your mother. But I—I fear
I am more squeamish—I refuse to wear the breeches
of the clown I killed.

ZEUS: You talk big, my boy. You butchered a defenseless
man and an old woman who begged for mercy. But,
to hear you speak, one would think you'd bravely
fought, one against a crowd, and were the savior of
your city.

ORESTES: Perhaps I was.

ZEUS: You a savior! Do you know what's afoot behind
that door? All the good folk of Argos are waiting there.
Waiting to greet you with stones and pikes and pitch-
forks. Oh, they are very grateful to their savior! . . .
You are lonely as a leper.

ORESTES: Yes.

ZEUS: So you take pride in being an outcast, do you?
But the solitude you're doomed to, most cowardly of
murderers, is the solitude of scorn and loathing.

ORESTES: The most cowardly of murderers is he who feels
remorse.

ZEUS: Orestes, I created you, and I created all things. Now
see! [*The walls of the temple draw apart, revealing the
firmament, spangled with wheeling stars.* ZEUS *is standing in the background. His voice becomes huge—am-
plified by loud-speakers—but his form is shadowy.*] See
those planets wheeling on their appointed ways, never
swerving, never clashing. It was I who ordained their
courses, according to the law of justice. Hear the music
of the spheres, that vast, mineral hymn of praise,
sounding and resounding to the limits of the firmament. [*Sounds of music.*] It is my work that living
things increase and multiply, each according to his kind.
I have ordained that man shall always beget man, and
dog give birth to dog. It is my work that the tides
with their innumerable tongues creep up to lap the
sand and draw back at the appointed hour. I make the
plants grow, and my breath fans round the earth the
yellow clouds of pollen. You are not in your own

home, intruder; you are a foreign body in the world, like a splinter in flesh, or a poacher in his lordship's forest. For the world is good; I made it according to my will, and I am Goodness. But you, Orestes, you have done evil, the very rocks and stones cry out against you. The Good is everywhere, it is the coolness of the wellspring, the pith of the reed, the grain of flint, the weight of stone. Yes, you will find it even in the heart of fire and light; even your own body plays you false, for it abides perforce by my law. Good is everywhere, in you and about you; sweeping through you like a scythe, crushing you like a mountain. Like an ocean it buoys you up and rocks you to and fro, and it enabled the success of your evil plan, for it was in the brightness of the torches, the temper of your blade, the strength of your right arm. And that of which you are so vain, the Evil that you think is your creation, what is it but a reflection in a mocking mirror, a phantom thing that would have no being but for Goodness. No, Orestes, return to your saner self; the universe refutes you, you are a mite in the scheme of things. Return to Nature, Nature's thankless son. Know your sin, abhor it, and tear it from you as one tears out a rotten, noisome tooth. Or else—beware lest the very seas shrink back at your approach, springs dry up when you pass by, stones and rocks roll from your path, and the earth crumbles under your feet.

ORESTES: Let it crumble! Let the rocks revile me, and flowers wilt at my coming. Your whole universe is not enough to prove me wrong. You are the king of gods, king of stones and stars, king of the waves of the sea. But you are not the king of man.

[*The walls draw together.* ZEUS *comes into view, tired and dejected, and he now speaks in his normal voice.*]

ZEUS: Impudent spawn! So I am not your king? Who, then, made you?

ORESTES: You. But you blundered; you should not have made me free.

ZEUS: I gave you freedom so that you might serve me.

ORESTES: Perhaps. But now it has turned against its giver. And neither you nor I can undo what has been done.

ZEUS: Ah, at last! So this is your excuse?

ORESTES: I am not excusing myself.

ZEUS: No? Let me tell you it sounds much like an excuse, this freedom whose slave you claim to be.

ORESTES: Neither slave nor master. I *am* my freedom. No sooner had you created me than I ceased to be yours.

ELECTRA: Oh, Orestes! By all you hold most holy, by our father's memory, I beg you do not add blasphemy to your crime!

ZEUS: Mark her words, young man. And hope no more to win her back by arguments like these. Such language is somewhat new to her ears—and somewhat shocking.

ORESTES: To my ears, too. And to my lungs, which breathe the words, and to my tongue, which shapes them. In fact, I can hardly understand myself. Only yesterday you were still a veil on my eyes, a clot of wax in my ears; yesterday, indeed, I had an excuse. *You* were my excuse for being alive, for you had put me in the world to fulfill your purpose, and the world was an old pandar prating to me about your goodness, day in, day out. And then you forsook me.

ZEUS: *I* forsook you? How?

ORESTES: Yesterday, when I was with Electra, I felt at one with Nature, this Nature of your making. It sang the praises of the Good—*your* Good—in siren tones, and lavished intimations. To lull me into gentleness, the fierce light mellowed and grew tender as a lover's eyes. And, to teach me the forgiveness of offenses, the sky grew bland as a pardoner's face. Obedient to your will, my youth rose up before me and pleaded with me like a girl who fears her lover will forsake her. That was the last time, the last, I saw my youth. Suddenly, out of the blue, freedom crashed down on me and swept me off my feet. Nature sprang back, my youth went with the wind, and I knew myself alone, utterly alone in the midst of this well-meaning little universe of yours. I was like a man who's lost his shadow. And there was nothing left in heaven, no right or wrong, nor anyone to give me orders.

ZEUS: What of it? Do you want me to admire a scabby sheep that has to be kept apart; or the leper mewed in a lazar-house? Remember, Orestes, you once were of my flock, you fed in my pastures among my sheep. Your vaunted freedom isolates you from the fold; it means exile.

ORESTES: Yes, exile.

ZEUS: But the disease can't be deeply rooted yet; it began only yesterday. Come back to the fold. Think of your loneliness; even your sister is forsaking you. Your eyes are big with anguish, your face is pale and drawn. The disease you're suffering from is inhuman, foreign to my nature, foreign to yourself. Come back. I am forgetfulness, I am peace.

ORESTES: Foreign to myself—I know it. Outside nature, against nature, without excuse, beyond remedy, except what remedy I find within myself. But I shall not return under your law; I am doomed to have no other law but mine. Nor shall I come back to nature, the nature you found good; in it are a thousand beaten paths all leading up to you—but I must blaze my trail. For I, Zeus, am a man, and every man must find out his own way. Nature abhors man, and you too, god of gods, abhor mankind.

ZEUS: That is true; men like you I hold in abhorrence.

ORESTES: Take care; those words were a confession of your weakness. As for me, I do not hate you. What have I to do with you, or you with me? We shall glide past each other, like ships in a river, without touching. You are God and I am free; each of us is alone, and our anguish is akin. How can you know I did not try to feel remorse in the long night that has gone by? And to sleep? But no longer can I feel remorse, and I can sleep no more.

[A *short silence.*]

ZEUS: What do you propose to do?

ORESTES: The folk of Argos are my folk. I must open their eyes.

ZEUS: Poor people! Your gift to them will be a sad one; of loneliness and shame. You will tear from their eyes the veils I had laid on them, and they will see their lives as they are, foul and futile, a barren boon.

ORESTES: Why, since it is their lot, should I deny them the despair I have in me?

ZEUS: What will they make of it?

ORESTES: What they choose. They're free; and human life begins on the far side of despair.

[*A short silence.*]

ZEUS: Well, Orestes, all this was foreknown. In the fullness of time a man was to come, to announce my decline. And you're that man, it seems. But seeing you yesterday—you with your girlish face—who'd have believed it?

ORESTES: Could I myself have believed it? . . . The words I speak are too big for my mouth, they tear it; the load of destiny I bear is too heavy for my youth and has shattered it.

ZEUS: I have little love for you, yet I am sorry for you.

ORESTES: And I, too, am sorry for *you*.

ZEUS: Good-by, Orestes. [*He takes some steps forward.*] As for you, Electra, bear this in mind. My reign is not yet over—far from it!—and I shall not give up the struggle. So choose if you are with me or against me. Farewell.

ORESTES: Farewell. [ZEUS *goes out.* ELECTRA *slowly rises to her feet.*] Where are you going?

ELECTRA: Leave me alone. I'm done with you.

ORESTES: I have known you only for a day, and must I lose you now forever?

ELECTRA: Would to God that I had never known you!

ORESTES: Electra! My sister, dear Electra! My only love, the one joy of my life, do not leave me. Stay with me.

ELECTRA: Thief! I had so little, so very little to call mine; only a few weak dreams, a morsel of peace

And now you've taken my all; you've robbed a pauper of her mite! You were my brother, the head of our house, and it was your duty to protect me. But no, you needs must drag me into carnage; I am red as a flayed ox, these loathsome flies are swarming after me, and my heart is buzzing like an angry hive.

ORESTES: Yes, my beloved, it's true, I have taken all from you, and I have nothing to offer in return; nothing but my crime. But think how vast a gift that is! Believe me, it weighs on my heart like lead. We were too light, Electra; now our feet sink into the soil, like chariot-wheels in turf. So come with me; we will tread heavily on our way, bowed beneath our precious load. You shall give me your hand, and we will go—

ELECTRA: Where?

ORESTES: I don't know. Towards ourselves. Beyond the rivers and mountains are an Orestes and an Electra waiting for us, and we must make our patient way towards them.

ELECTRA: I won't hear any more from you. All you have to offer me is misery and squalor. [*She rushes out into the center of the stage. The* FURIES *slowly close in on her.*] Help! Zeus, king of gods and men, my king, take me in your arms, carry me from this place, and shelter me. I will obey your law, I will be your creature and your slave, I will embrace your knees. Save me from the flies, from my brother, from myself! Do not leave me lonely and I will give up my whole life to atonement. I repent, Zeus. I bitterly repent.

[*She runs off the stage. The* FURIES *make as if to follow her, but the* FIRST FURY *holds them back.*]

FIRST FURY: Let her be, sisters. She is not for us. But that man is ours, and ours, I think, for many a day. His little soul is stubborn. He will suffer for two.

[*Buzzing, the* FURIES *approach* ORESTES.]

ORESTES: I am alone, alone.

FIRST FURY: No, no, my sweet little murderer, I'm staying with you, and you'll see what merry games I'll think up to entertain you.

ORESTES: Alone until I die. And after that——?

FIRST FURY: Take heart, sisters, he is weakening. See how his eyes dilate. Soon his nerves will be throbbing like harp-strings, in exquisite arpeggios of terror.

SECOND FURY: And hunger will drive him from his sanctuary before long. Before nightfall we shall know how his blood tastes.

ORESTES: Poor Electra!

[*The* TUTOR *enters.*]

THE TUTOR: Master! Young master! Where are you? It's so dark one can't see a thing. I'm bringing you some food. The townspeople have surrounded the temple; there's no hope of escape by daylight. We shall have to try our chance when night comes. Meanwhile, eat this food to keep your strength up. [*The* FURIES *bar his way.*] Hey! Who are these? More of those primitive myths! Ah, how I regret that pleasant land of Attica, where reason's always right.

ORESTES: Do not try to approach me, or they will tear you in pieces.

THE TUTOR: Gently now, my lovelies. See what I've brought you, some nice meat and fruit. Here you are! Let's hope it will calm you down.

ORESTES: So the people of Argos have gathered outside the temple, have they?

THE TUTOR: Indeed they have, and I can't say which are the fiercer, the thirstier for your blood: these charming young creatures here, or your worthy subjects.

ORESTES: Good. [*A short silence.*] Open that door.

THE TUTOR: Have you lost your wits? They're waiting behind it, and they're armed.

ORESTES: Do as I told you.

THE TUTOR: For once permit me, sir, to disobey your orders. I tell you, they will stone you. It's madness.

ORESTES: Old man, I am your master, and I order you to unbar that door.

[THE TUTOR *opens one leaf of the double doors a few inches.*]

THE TUTOR: Oh dear! Oh dear!

ORESTES: Open both leaves.

[THE TUTOR *half opens both leaves of the door and takes cover behind one of them. The* CROWD *surges forward, thrusting the doors wide open; then stops, bewildered, on the threshold. The stage is flooded with bright light. Shouts rise from the* CROWD: "Away with him!" "Kill him!" "Stone him!" "Tear him in pieces!"]*

ORESTES [*who has not heard them*]: The sun!

THE CROWD: Murderer! Butcher! Blasphemer! We'll tear you limb from limb. We'll pour molten lead into your veins.

A WOMAN: I'll pluck out your eyes.

A MAN: I'll eat your gizzard!

ORESTES [*drawing himself up to his full height*]: So here you are, my true and loyal subjects? I am Orestes, your King, son of Agamemnon, and this is my coronation day. [*Exclamations of amazement, mutterings among the* CROWD.] Ah, you are lowering your tone? [*Complete silence.*] I know; you fear me. Fifteen years ago to the day, another murderer showed himself to you, his arms red to the elbows, gloved in blood. But him you did not fear; you read in his eyes that he was of your kind, he had not the courage of his crimes. A crime that its doer disowns becomes ownerless—no man's crime; that's how you see it, isn't it? More like an accident than a crime?

So you welcomed the criminal as your King, and that crime without an owner started prowling round the city, whimpering like a dog that has lost its master. You see me, men of Argos, you understand that my crime is wholly mine; I claim it as my own, for all to know; it is my glory, my life's work, and you can neither punish me nor pity me. That is why I fill you with fear.

And yet, my people, I love you, and it was for your sake that I killed. For your sake. I had come to claim my kingdom, and you would have none of me because I was not of your kind. Now I am of your kind, my subjects; there is a bond of blood between us, and I have earned my kingship over you.

As for your sins and your remorse, your night-fears,

and the crime Ægistheus committed—all are mine, I take them all upon me. Fear your dead no longer; they are *my* dead. And, see, your faithful flies have left you and come to me. But have no fear, people of Argos. I shall not sit on my victim's throne or take the scepter in my blood-stained hands. A god offered it to me, and I said no. I wish to be a king without a kingdom, without subjects.

Farewell, my people. Try to reshape your lives. All here is new, all must begin anew. And for me, too, a new life is beginning. A strange life. . . .

Listen now to this tale. One summer there was a plague of rats in Scyros. It was like a foul disease; they soiled and nibbled everything, and the people of the city were at their wits' end. But one day a flute-player came to the city. He took his stand in the market-place. Like this. [ORESTES *rises to his feet.*] He began playing on his flute and all the rats came out and crowded round him. Then he started off, taking long strides— like this. [*He comes down from the pedestal.*] And he called to the people of Scyros: "Make way!" [*The* CROWD *makes way for him.*] And all the rats raised their heads and hesitated—as the flies are doing. Look! Look at the flies! Then all of sudden they followed in his train. And the flute-player, with his rats, vanished forever. Thus.

[*He strides out into the light. Shrieking, the* FURIES *fling themselves after him.*]

CURTAIN

DIRTY HANDS

(*Les Mains sales*)

A PLAY IN SEVEN ACTS

CHARACTERS IN THE PLAY

OLGA

HUGO

CHARLES

FRANTZ

LOUIS

IVAN

JESSICA

SLICK

GEORGE

HŒDERER

KARSKY

PRINCE PAUL

Les Mains sales (*Dirty Hands*) was presented for the first time at the Théâtre Antoine, Paris, on April 2, 1948.

ACT I

OLGA'S HOUSE

The ground floor of a small cottage along the highway. To the right, the front door of the house and a window with the blinds drawn. To the rear, a telephone on a chest of drawers. To the left rear, a door. Tables, chairs. Oddly assorted pieces, all of cheap make. It is evident that the tenant is totally indifferent to furnishings. To the left, next to the door, a fireplace; above the fireplace, a mirror. Cars can be heard from time to time going up the road. Motor horns.

OLGA, *alone, is sitting by the radio, turning the dial. Confused sounds and then a clear voice:*

SPEAKER: The German armies are in full retreat all along the front. The Soviet armies have taken Kischnar, some twenty-five miles from the Illyrian frontier. Wherever possible, the Illyrian troops are refusing to fight; many deserters have already gone over to the Allies. Illyrians, we know that you were forced to take up arms against the U.S.S.R.; we are fully aware of the profoundly democratic sentiments of the people of Illyria, and we . . .

[OLGA *turns off the radio. She remains motionless, staring straight ahead of her. A pause. A knock at the door. She starts to her feet. Another knock. She goes slowly to the door. More rapping.*]

OLGA: Who is it?

THE VOICE OF HUGO: Hugo.

OLGA: Who?

THE VOICE OF HUGO: Hugo Barine.

[OLGA *gives a start, then remains motionless by the door.*]

THE VOICE OF HUGO: Don't you recognize my voice? Come on, open up! Let me in.

[OLGA *goes quickly to the chest of drawers, takes an*

object from the drawer with her left hand, covers the hand with a towel, and goes to the door. She jumps back suddenly, ready for any emergency. A tall young man, about twenty-three years old, stands in the doorway.]

HUGO: It's me. [*They face each other silently for a moment.*] You're surprised?

OLGA: You've changed a lot.

HUGO: Yes. I've changed. [*A pause.*] You've had a good look? You recognize me? Absolutely sure? [*Pointing to the revolver hidden in the towel*] Then you can put that away.

OLGA [*still holding the revolver*]: I thought you got five years.

HUGO: Well, yes: I did get five years.

OLGA: Come in and shut the door. [*She takes a step backwards. The revolver is not trained directly on* HUGO, *but could cover him instantly if necessary.* HUGO *looks at the revolver with some amusement and slowly turns his back to* OLGA, *then shuts the door.*] Did you escape?

HUGO: Escape? I'm not that crazy. They had to push me out bodily. [*A pause.*] I was released for good behavior.

OLGA: Are you hungry?

HUGO: You'd like me to be, wouldn't you?

OLGA: Why should I?

HUGO: It is so comforting to give; it keeps the other person at a distance. And then, when a man is eating, he seems harmless. [*A pause.*] I'm sorry: I'm neither hungry nor thirsty.

OLGA: You might just have said no.

HUGO: Don't you remember what I'm like? I talked too much.

OLGA: I remember.

HUGO [*looking the place over*]: What a desert! And yet it's all here. My typewriter?

OLGA: Sold.

HUGO: Ah! [*A pause. He looks the room over once more.*] It's empty.

OLGA: What's empty?

HUGO [*with a sweep about the room*]: This place! The furniture seems set in a desert. Back there, when I put out my arms, I could touch both walls at once. Come closer. [*She maintains her distance.*] Of course; outside of prison people live at a respectful distance. What a waste of space! It's funny to be free; it makes me dizzy. I shall have to get used all over again to speaking to people without touching them.

OLGA: When were you released?

HUGO: Just now.

OLGA: You came straight here?

HUGO: Where would you want me to go?

OLGA: You didn't talk to anyone?

[HUGO *looks at her and begins to laugh.*]

HUGO: No, Olga. No. Relax. I spoke to nobody.

[OLGA *unfreezes a bit and looks at him.*]

OLGA: They didn't shave your head.

HUGO: No.

OLGA: But they took away your wave.

[*A pause.*]

HUGO: Aren't you glad to see me?

OLGA: I'm not sure. [*A car going up the road. Motor horns, the hum of an engine.* HUGO *shudders. The automobile fades.* OLGA *watches* HUGO *coldly.*] If it's true that they let you go, you don't have to be afraid.

HUGO [*ironically*]: You think not? [*He shrugs his shoulders. A pause.*] How's Louis?

OLGA: O.K.

HUGO: And Laurent?

OLGA: He—was unlucky.

HUGO: I thought as much. Somehow or other—I don't know why—I got into the habit of thinking of him as dead. There must have been changes.

OLGA: It has become much more difficult since the Germans are here.

HUGO [*with indifference*]: That's right. They are here.

OLGA: They've been here for three months. Five divisions.

Supposedly they were going on to Hungary. Then they stayed.

HUGO: Aha! [*With more interest*] There are new comrades?

OLGA: Many.

HUGO: Young ones?

OLGA: Quite a few young men. Recruiting is a little different now. There are vacancies to be filled. We are less—strict.

HUGO: Of course, of course; you have to adapt yourself. [*With a certain uneasiness*] But in all essentials the line is the same?

OLGA [*embarrassed*]: Well, yes! Roughly speaking, it's the same, naturally.

HUGO: In other words, you've kept on living. In prison it's hard to believe that others go on living. And you—is there somebody in your life?

OLGA: A few. [*In response to a gesture by* HUGO] But nobody at the moment.

HUGO: Did you—ever talk about me?

OLGA [*obviously lying*]: Sometimes.

HUGO: They came at night on their bikes, just as in my day; they'd sit around the table; Louis would be there stuffing his pipe and somebody would say: "You know, it was just on a night like this that the kid asked for his special permission."

OLGA: Something like that.

HUGO: And you would say: "The kid came through fine; he did the job cleanly and without compromising anyone."

OLGA: Yes, yes, yes.

HUGO: Sometimes the rain woke me; I'd say to myself: "They're going to have rain"; and then, before going back to sleep: "Maybe tonight they'll talk about me." That was my main advantage over the dead; I could still imagine that you were thinking of me. [OLGA *takes his arm with a sudden awkward and involuntary gesture. They look at each other.* OLGA *releases* HUGO'S *arm. He stiffens a bit.*] And then one day you said to yourself: "He has still three years to serve, and when he gets out [*changing his tone without taking his eyes off* OLGA], when he gets out they'll shoot him down like a dog for his trouble."

OLGA [*hastily stepping back*]: Are you crazy?

HUGO· Come on, Olga. Come on now. [*A pause.*] It was you they had send me the chocolates?

OLGA: What chocolates?

HUGO: Come, come, now!

OLGA [*imperiously*]: What chocolates?

HUGO: The brandied chocolates, in a pink box. For six months someone named Dresch sent me packages regularly. Since I knew nobody by that name, I assumed that the packages came from you, and it made me happy. Then the shipments stopped and I said to myself: "They are forgetting about me." And then, three months ago, a package arrived from the same address, with chocolates and cigarettes. I smoked the cigarettes and my cell-mate ate the chocolates. They had a bad effect on him, poor fellow, very bad. Then I thought: "They have not forgotten me."

OLGA: So?

HUGO: That's all.

OLGA: Hœderer had friends who don't exactly love you.

HUGO: They wouldn't have waited two years to let me know how they felt. No, Olga, I've had all the time in the world to think and there's only one way of explaining it: at first the party thought I could still be used in some way, and then it changed its mind.

OLGA [*without severity*]: You talk too much, Hugo. Always have. You have to talk to make sure you're alive.

HUGO: I won't argue about that; I do talk too much. I know it only too well, and you've never trusted me. No need to go any further. [*A pause.*] I'm not holding anything against you, you know. This whole affair began badly.

OLGA: Hugo, look at me. Do you really mean what you

said? [*She looks him full in the face.*] Yes, you meant
it. [*Violently*] Then why did you come here? Why?
Why?

HUGO: Because I knew that *you* couldn't shoot me. [*He
glances at the gun that she still holds and smiles.*] At
least I don't think so. [OLGA *ill-humoredly throws the
revolver, still wrapped in the towel, on the table.*] You
see.

OLGA: Look here, Hugo: I don't believe a word of what
you have told me and I have received no instructions
in regard to you. But if ever I should, you must know
that I will do as I am told. And if anyone from the
party asks me, I should say that you are here, even if
they were to shoot you down before my eyes. Have you
any money?

HUGO: No.

OLGA: I'll give you some, then you will go.

HUGO: Where? To wander around the alleys of the harbor
or on the docks? The water is cold, Olga. Here, whatever happens, it is light and warm. It's a more comfortable end.

OLGA: Hugo, I shall do as the party tells me. I swear to
you I shall do whatever they require of me.

HUGO: What did I tell you?

OLGA: Get out!

HUGO: No. [*Mimicking* OLGA] "I shall do as the party tells
me." You'll be surprised. With the best will in the
world what you can never do is exactly what the party
orders. "You will go to Hœderer and put three bullets
into his belly." A clear enough order, no? I went to
Hœderer and left him with three bullets in his belly.
But that was something else again. The orders? There
was no order, not any more. Orders leave you all alone,
after a certain point. The order stayed behind and I
went on alone and killed alone—and I no longer even
know why. I wish the party would order you to shoot
me. Just to see. Only to see what happens.

OLGA: You would see. [*A pause.*] What are you going to
do now?

HUGO: I don't know. I didn't make any plans. When they opened the prison gate, I thought that I would come here and I came.

OLGA: Where is Jessica?

HUGO: With her father. She wrote to me several times, in the beginning. I think she has dropped my name.

OLGA: Where could I put you up? Comrades come here every day. They come and go as they wish.

HUGO: Into your bedroom, too?

OLGA: No.

HUGO: I used to go in there. There was a red quilt on the bed; the wallpaper was covered with yellow and green diamonds; there were two photographs, and one was of me.

OLGA: What's this? An inventory?

HUGO: No: I remember. I often thought of it. But the other photo was a problem. I couldn't remember who it was.

[*A car on the road; he gives a start. They are both silent. The auto stops. The car door is slammed. A knock.*]

OLGA: Who's there?

THE VOICE OF CHARLES: Charles.

HUGO [*softly*]: Who is Charles?

OLGA [*softly*]: One of our men.

HUGO [*looking at her*]: Now what? [*A very brief pause. Charles knocks again.*]

OLGA [*to* HUGO]: Well? What are you waiting for? Go into my room. You can finish your reminiscing. [HUGO *goes out.* OLGA *goes to open the door.* CHARLES *and* FRANTZ *enter.*]

CHARLES: Where is he?

OLGA: Who?

CHARLES: The guy. He's been tailed ever since he— [*A brief pause.*] Isn't he here?

OLGA: Yes. He's here.

CHARLES: Where?

OLGA: There. [*She indicates her room.*]

CHARLES: Good.

[*He signals to* FRANTZ *to follow him, reaches into his coat pocket, and takes a step forward.* OLGA *bars the way.*]

OLGA: No.

CHARLES: It won't take long, Olga. If you like, you can take a walk. When you get back, there'll be nobody here and no traces. [*Indicating* FRANTZ] The kid is here to clean up afterwards.

OLGA: No.

CHARLES: Let me do my job, Olga.

OLGA: Louis sent you?

CHARLES: Yes.

OLGA: Where is he?

CHARLES: In the car.

OLGA: Go get him. [CHARLES *hesitates.*] Go on! I tell you go get him.

[CHARLES *makes a motion and* FRANTZ *goes out.* OLGA *and* CHARLES *face each other in silence.* OLGA, *without taking her eyes from his, gathers up the towel-covered revolver from the table.*]

LOUIS [*entering*]: What's got into you? Why don't you let them do their job?

OLGA: You are in too much of a hurry.

LOUIS: In too much of a hurry?

OLGA: Send them away.

LOUIS [*to the men*]: Wait for me outside. Come if I call. [*They go out.*] So. Now what have you to tell me? [*A pause.*]

OLGA [*gently*]: Louis, he worked for us.

LOUIS: Don't be a child, Olga. This fellow is dangerous. He must not talk.

OLGA: He won't talk.

LOUIS: Him? That damned chatterbox—

OLGA: He won't talk.

LOUIS: I wonder if you see him as he really is. You always were kind of sweet on him.

OLGA: And you were always prejudiced against him. [*A pause.*] Louis, I didn't send for you to discuss our personal prejudices. I am speaking to you in the interest of the party. We have lost many comrades since the Germans came. We can't afford to get rid of any young worker without even trying to find out if he's salvageable or not.

LOUIS: Salvageable? He is an undisciplined anarchistic individualist, an intellectual who thought only of striking an attractive pose, a bourgeois who worked when it pleased him and stopped at the slightest whim.

OLGA: He is also the guy who at twenty shot down Hœderer despite his bodyguards and managed to disguise a political assassination as a crime of passion.

LOUIS: But was it a political assassination? That part of the story was never cleared up.

OLGA: Exactly. We must get the true story here and now.

LOUIS: The story stinks. I don't want to have anything to do with it. And in any case I don't have the time to conduct a class examination.

OLGA: I have the time. [*A gesture by* LOUIS.] Louis, I'm afraid you are introducing too much personal feeling into this affair.

LOUIS: And I'm afraid you are much too involved yourself.

OLGA: Have you ever known me to put my feelings first? I'm not asking you to give him his life with no strings attached. I don't give a damn about his life. I just insist that before getting rid of him we ought to be sure that the party cannot take him back.

LOUIS: The party cannot take him back; not any more. Not now. You know that perfectly well.

OLGA: He worked under an assumed name and nobody knew him except Laurent, who is dead, and Dresden, who is at the front. You're afraid he'll talk? In the right spot he won't talk. You say he is an intellectual and an anarchist? Agreed, but he is also a desperate man. Properly supervised, he can serve as a strong-arm man for all sorts of jobs. He has proved that.

LOUIS: What do you suggest?

OLGA: What time is it?

LOUIS: Nine o'clock.

OLGA: Come back at midnight. I shall know by then why he killed Hœderer, and what he is today. If I am convinced that he can work with us, I will tell you so through the door; you will let him sleep in peace and give him an assignment tomorrow morning.

LOUIS: And if he isn't salvageable?

OLGA: I'll let you in.

LOUIS: A lot risked, little gained.

OLGA: Where is the risk? Are there men around the house?

LOUIS: Four.

OLGA: Let them stay there until midnight. [LOUIS *doesn't move*.] Louis, he worked for us. We must give him his chance.

LOUIS: All right. See you at midnight. [*He goes out.*] [OLGA *goes to the door and opens it.* HUGO *comes out from her room.*]

HUGO: It was your sister.

OLGA: Who?

HUGO: The picture on the wall is of your sister. [*A pause.*] My snapshot, you took it down. [OLGA *doesn't reply. He looks at her.*] You have a strange look. What did they want?

OLGA: They were looking for you.

HUGO: Ah! And you told them I was here?

OLGA: Yes.

HUGO: Very well. [*He is about to go out.*]

OLGA: The night is clear and there are comrades all around the house.

HUGO: Aha! [*He sits at the table.*] Give me something to eat. [OLGA *fetches a plate, bread, and ham. As she sets the food before him,* HUGO *chatters away.*] I had your room down pat. I was right about every detail. Everything is as it was in my memory. [*A pause.*] Only, when I was in jail, I said to myself: "This is just a memory. The real room is over there, on the other side of the wall." I went in, I looked at your room, and it seemed no more real than my recollection. The cell, too, was a dream. And the eyes of Hœderer, the day I shot him. Do you think there's a chance that I'll ever wake? Perhaps when your pals get to work on me with their playthings—

OLGA: As long as you are here they won't touch you.

HUGO: You managed that, did you? [*He pours a glass of wine.*] I'll have to leave eventually anyhow.

OLGA: Wait. You have one night. A lot can happen in one night.

HUGO: What do you expect to happen?

OLGA: Things can change.

HUGO: What?

OLGA: You. Me.

HUGO: You?

OLGA: That depends on you.

HUGO: So I have to change you? [*He laughs, looks at her, gets up, and goes toward her. On the alert, she slips quickly out of his reach.*]

OLGA: Not that way. That way I can be changed only if I really want to be.

[*A pause.* HUGO *shrugs his shoulders and sits down again. He begins to eat.*]

HUGO: And so?

OLGA: And so why don't you come in with us again?

HUGO [*breaking into laughter*]: You picked just the right moment to ask me that.

OLGA: But what if it were possible? What if this whole affair were due to a misunderstanding? Didn't you ever think about what you would do when you got out?

HUGO: No.

OLGA: What did you think of?

HUGO: About what I had done. I tried to understand why I did it.

OLGA: And did you come to understand? [HUGO *shrugs his shoulders.*] How did it happen? Is it true that Jessica was at the bottom of it?

HUGO: Yes.

OLGA: Then it was out of jealousy that—

HUGO: I don't know. I—don't think so.

OLGA: Tell me.

HUGO: What?

OLGA: Everything. From the beginning.

HUGO: Telling it, that's not hard; I know it by heart; I recited it to myself every day I was in prison. But what it means, that's something else again. It's an idiotic story, like all stories. If you look at it from a distance, everything holds together, more or less; but if you get up close to it, it busts apart. One action is over too quickly. It seems to happen almost spontaneously and you don't know whether you did it because you wanted to or because you couldn't hold it back. The fact is that I pulled the trigger—

OLGA: Begin at the beginning.

HUGO: You know the beginning as well as I do. Besides, does it really have a beginning? You could begin the story in March of '43 when Louis sent for me. Or a year earlier, when I joined the party. Or perhaps earlier still, with my birth. But never mind. Let's say that everything began in March 1943.

[*While he is speaking, the stage slowly darkens.*]

ACT II

*Same set. OLGA's place, two years earlier. It is night.
Through the back door, opening on the court, comes
the hum of voices, now rising, now falling. Evidently
several persons are engaged in heated discussion.*

*HUGO is typing. He seems much more youthful than in
the previous scene. IVAN is pacing back and forth.*

IVAN: Hey!

HUGO: What?

IVAN: Couldn't you stop typing?

HUGO: Why?

IVAN: It gets on my nerves.

HUGO: You don't seem the nervous type.

IVAN: I'm not! But right now it bothers me. Can't you
talk to me?

HUGO [*eagerly*]: I should like nothing better. What's your
name?

IVAN: In the underground I'm known as Ivan. What's
yours?

HUGO: Raskolnikov.

IVAN [*laughing*]: What a name!

HUGO: It's my name in the party.

IVAN: Where'd you dig that up?

HUGO: It's some guy in a novel.

IVAN: What does he do?

HUGO: He kills.

IVAN: Oh. And have you killed?

HUGO: No. [*A pause.*] Who sent you here?

IVAN: Louis.

HUGO: And what are you supposed to do?

IVAN: I'm supposed to wait here until ten o'clock.

HUGO: And then what?

[*A gesture by* IVAN *indicating that* HUGO *is not to pursue
this point.*]

[*Loud voices from the rear. Apparently there is some dispute.*]

IVAN: What are the boys cooking up, back there?

[*A gesture by* HUGO, *mimicking that of* IVAN *just before, indicating that* IVAN *is not to question him further.*]

HUGO: You see. That's what's such a mess; conversation can't go beyond a certain point. [*A pause.*]

IVAN: You been in the party long?

HUGO: Since 1942; that makes a year. I joined when the Regent declared war on the Soviet Union. How about you?

IVAN: I don't remember any more. I sometimes think I've always been in the party. [*A pause.*] You put out the paper, don't you?

HUGO: Myself and some others.

IVAN: I often get hold of it, but I seldom read it. It's not your fault of course, but your news is always a week behind the BBC or the Soviet radio.

HUGO: Where do you expect us to get the news? We listen to the radio just like you.

IVAN: I'm not complaining. You do your job; no offense. [*A pause.*] What time is it?

HUGO: Five minutes to ten.

IVAN: Whew! [*He yawns.*]

HUGO: What's wrong with you?

IVAN: Nothing.

HUGO: You're not feeling well.

IVAN: Sure. It's O.K.

HUGO: You're so fidgety.

IVAN: It's O.K., I tell you. I'm always like this just before.

HUGO: Before what?

IVAN: Never mind. [*A pause.*] When I'm on my bike I'll feel better. [*A pause.*] I'm too easy-going. If I didn't have to, I wouldn't hurt a fly. [*He yawns.*]

[OLGA *comes in through the front door. She sets a suitcase down by the door.*]

OLGA [*to* IVAN]: There it is. Can you tie it on your baggage-carrier?

IVAN: Let's have a look at it. Yes. Easily.

OLGA: It's ten o'clock. You can beat it now. You've been posted on the gateway and the house?

IVAN: Yes.

OLGA: Then good luck.

IVAN: None of that stuff. [*A pause.*] Are you going to kiss me?

OLGA: Sure. [*She kisses him on both cheeks.*]
[IVAN *picks up the suitcase and then, on the point of going out, turns round to face* HUGO.]

IVAN [*with comic emphasis*]: Good-by, Raskolnikov. [*He goes out.*]

HUGO [*smiling*]: Go to hell.

OLGA: You shouldn't have said that.

HUGO: Why not?

OLGA: One doesn't say things like that.

HUGO [*astonished*]: Olga, are *you* superstitious?

OLGA [*upset*]: Certainly not.
[HUGO *watches her attentively.*]

HUGO: What is he going to do?

OLGA: It's no business of yours.

HUGO: He's going to bomb the Korsk bridge?

OLGA: Why do you want me to tell you? If something goes wrong, the less you know, the better off you are.

HUGO: But *you* know, you know what he's going to do?

OLGA [*shrugging her shoulders*]: Oh, me!

HUGO: You, of course, you could keep your mouth shut. You're like Louis; you'd die before you'd talk. [*A brief silence.*] What makes you think I would talk? How will you ever be able to trust me if you don't put me to the test?

OLGA: The party isn't a night school. We're not testing your potentialities, but trying to make use of whatever capabilities you have now.

HUGO [*pointing to the typewriter*]: And my talents lie here?

OLGA: Do you know how to loosen railroad tracks?

HUGO: No.

OLGA: You see. [*A moment of silence.* HUGO *looks at himself in the mirror.*] Do you like your looks?

HUGO: I want to see if I look like my father. [*A pause.*]
  With a mustache the resemblance would be striking.
OLGA [*shrugging her shoulders*]: What of it?
HUGO: I don't like my father.
OLGA: We all know that.
HUGO: He said to me: "In my day I, too, belonged to a
  revolutionary group; I wrote for their paper. You'll get
  over it just as I did. . . ."
OLGA: Why are you telling me this?
HUGO: No reason. It's just that I think of it every time
  I look in the mirror. That's all.
OLGA [*pointing to the door behind which the meeting is
  being held*]: Is Louis in there?
HUGO: Yes.
OLGA: And Hœderer?
HUGO: I don't know him, but I suppose so. Just who is he?
OLGA: He was a deputy to the Landstag before it was
  dissolved. Now he's general secretary of the party.
  Hœderer is not his real name.
HUGO: What is his real name?
OLGA: I've already told you that you ask too many
  questions.
HUGO: What a racket! They must be squabbling.
OLGA: Hœderer called the committee here to have them
  vote on a proposition.
HUGO: What proposition?
OLGA: I don't know. I only know that Louis is against it.
HUGO [*smiling*]: If he's against it, then I am, too. I don't
  even have to know what the proposal is. [*A pause.*]
  Olga, you've got to help me.
OLGA: How?
HUGO: By convincing Louis that he should give me some-
  thing real to do. I'm tired of scribbling while our com-
  rades are dying.
OLGA: You run risks, too.
HUGO: Not the same thing. [*A pause.*] Olga, I have no
  wish to live.
OLGA: Really? Why not?
HUGO [*grimacing*]: Too difficult.

OLGA: Just the same, you got married.

HUGO: Bah!

OLGA: And you love your wife.

HUGO: Yes. Of course. [*A pause.*] A man who doesn't want
to live can do many things, if you know how to use
him. [*A pause. There is an uproar in the adjoining
room.*] It sounds bad in there.

OLGA [*disturbed*]: Very bad.

[LOUIS *emerges with two other men, who leave pre-
cipitately by the front door.*]

LOUIS: It's all over.

OLGA: Hœderer?

LOUIS: He went out the back way with Boris and Lucas.

OLGA: Well?

[LOUIS *shrugs his shoulders without replying. A pause.
Then:*]

LOUIS: The dirty bastards!

OLGA: It was put to a vote?

LOUIS: Yes. [*A pause.*] He is authorized to begin ne
gotiations. When he returns with a definite offer, he'l
carry it through.

OLGA: When is the next meeting?

LOUIS: In ten days. That gives us more than a week.
[OLGA *points to* HUGO.] What? Oh! Yes. So you're still
here, huh? [*He looks at him and repeats absent-
mindedly:*] You're still here. [HUGO *is about to leave.*]
Stay. I may have some work for you. [*To* OLGA] You
know him better than I do. What's he worth?

OLGA: He'll do.

LOUIS: You don't think he'd get cold feet in the middle?

OLGA: Oh no! Not that. On the contrary, he—

LOUIS: What?

OLGA: Nothing. He'll do.

LOUIS: Good. [*A pause.*] Has Ivan gone?

OLGA: A quarter of an hour ago.

LOUIS: We're sitting right up in the box seats; we should
be able to hear the explosion from here. [*A pause.
He turns toward* HUGO.] It seems you want to *act?*

HUGO: Yes.

LOUIS: Why?

HUGO: Just because.

LOUIS: Excellent. Only you can't do anything with your hands.

HUGO: That's true. I don't know how to do anything.

LOUIS: Well, then?

HUGO: In Russia at the end of the last century there were characters who would place themselves in the path of a grand duke with bombs in their pockets. The bombs would go off, the grand duke would get blown up, and the guys too. That's the sort of thing I can do.

LOUIS: They were anarchists. You think of them because you belong to the same type; you are an intellectual and an anarchist. You are fifty years behind the times. Terrorism, that's finished.

HUGO: Then I'm good for nothing.

LOUIS: In that field, yes.

HUGO: Let's drop the subject.

LOUIS: Wait. [*A pause.*] I may be able to find something for you to do.

HUGO: *Real* work?

LOUIS: Why not?

HUGO: You'll *really* trust me?

LOUIS: That depends on you.

HUGO: Louis, I shall do whatever you want, no matter what.

LOUIS: We shall see. Sit down. [*A pause.*] Here is the situation: on one side there is the fascist government of the Regent, which has lined itself up with the Axis; on the other side there is our party, which is fighting for democracy, for liberty, for a classless society. Between these two forces there is the Pentagon, which serves as a clandestine rallying-point for the bourgeois liberals and nationalists. Three groups with irreconcilable interests, three groups who hate each other. [*A pause.*] Hœderer had us meet tonight because he wants the Proletarian Party to join forces with the fascists and

the Pentagon and share power with them after the
war. What do you think of that?

HUGO [*smiling*]: You're pulling my leg.

LOUIS: Why?

HUGO: Because it's too idiotic.

LOUIS: And yet that's just what we've been discussing
here for three hours.

HUGO: It's [*confused*]—it's as if you told me that Olga
had denounced us all to the police and that the party
had voted to thank her for it.

LOUIS: What would you do if the majority of the party
came out in favor of conciliation?

HUGO: Are you serious?

LOUIS: Yes.

HUGO: I abandoned my family and my class the day I
understood what oppression was. Under no circumstances will I compromise with them.

LOUIS: But if it came down to that?

HUGO: Then I would get hold of a bomb and kill a cop
in Royal Square, or with a bit of luck one of the
military police. Then I would wait beside the body to
see what would happen. [*A pause.*] But this is all
a joke.

LOUIS: The Central Committee has accepted Hœderer's
proposal, four votes to three. Next week Hœderer is
to negotiate with the Regent's men.

HUGO: Has he sold out?

LOUIS: I don't know and I don't give a damn Objectively
he is a traitor; that's all that concerns me.

HUGO: But, Louis—I just don't understand; it's—it's
absurd. The Regent hates us, hunts us down, makes
war on the U.S.S.R. as the ally of Germany; he has
had our comrades shot; how could he—?

LOUIS: The Regent no longer believes in an Axis victory;
he wants to save his skin. If the Allies win, he wants
to be able to say he was playing a double game.

HUGO: But our pals—

LOUIS: The whole P.A.C., which I represent, is against

Hœderer. But the Proletarian Party, as you know, came into existence through the fusion of the P.A.C. and the Social Democrats. The Social Democrats have voted for Hœderer's proposal, and they are in the majority.

HUGO: But why did they——?

LOUIS: Because he scared them.

HUGO: Can't we break with them?

LOUIS: A split? Impossible. [*A pause.*] Are you with us, kid?

HUGO: Olga and you taught me all I know. I owe everything to you. To me, you are the party.

LOUIS [*to* OLGA]: Does he mean what he says?

OLGA: Yes.

LOUIS: Good. [*To* HUGO] You get the situation. As things stand, we can't walk out and we can't carry the matter to the committee. But the whole thing boils down to a maneuver of Hœderer's. If it weren't for Hœderer, we could put the others in our pocket. [*A pause.*] Last Tuesday Hœderer asked the party to furnish him with a male secretary. A student. Married.

HUGO: Why does he have to be married?

LOUIS: That I don't know. Are you married?

HUGO: Yes.

LOUIS: Fine! Do you accept?

[*They measure each other for a moment.*]

HUGO [*with energy*]: Yes.

LOUIS: Excellent. You can leave tomorrow with your wife. He lives about fifteen miles from here, in a country house turned over to him by a friend, with three strong-arm men, who are there in case of a sudden attack. Your job will be just to spy on him; we'll contact you once you are installed in the house. He must not see the envoys of the Regent, or in any case he mustn't see them twice. You understand?

HUGO: Yes.

LOUIS: On the night we set, you will open the door to three comrades who will finish the job; there'll be a car on the road and you can clear out with your wife in the meantime.

HUGO: Oh, Louis!

LOUIS: What's the matter?

HUGO: So that's it? Only that, huh? That's all you think I can handle?

LOUIS: You don't agree?

HUGO: No. Not at all; I won't be a decoy. People like me have pride, you know. An intellectual anarchist can't accept any old job.

OLGA: Hugo!

HUGO: This is what I propose; no need to contact me and no spying. I'll do the job myself.

LOUIS: You?

HUGO: Me.

LOUIS: It's tough work for a beginner.

HUGO: Your three killers may run into Hœderer's body-guard; what if they are knocked off? But if I become his secretary and win his confidence, I would be alone with him several hours a day.

LOUIS [*uncertain*]: I'm not—

OLGA: Louis!

LOUIS: What?

OLGA [*quietly*]: Trust him. It's a young kid after his big chance. He'll make good.

LOUIS: You'll answer for him?

OLGA: Without reservation.

LOUIS: Fine! Now listen!

[*A muffled explosion in the distance.*]

OLGA: He did it.

LOUIS: Lights out! Hugo, open the window!

[*They turn out the lights and open the window; far off there is the red glow of a fire.*]

OLGA: It's burning, it's burning. A regular fire! He did it!

[*They are all by the window.*]

HUGO: He did it. Before the end of the week you will be here, both of you, on a night such as this, and you will be waiting to hear from me; you'll be uneasy and you'll speak of me. I'll mean something to you then. You will ask yourselves: "What's he doing?"

And then there will be a ring on the phone or someone will knock on the door and you will smile just
the way you are smiling now and you will say: "He
did it."

CURTAIN

ACT III

A *summerhouse. A bed, cupboards, armchairs, chairs.
Women's clothes are strewn on all the chairs; there
are open suitcases on the bed.*

*JESSICA is putting the place in order. She goes to the
window and looks out. Returns. Goes to a packed
suitcase in a corner (it has the initials "H.B." on it),
drags it to the front of the stage, takes another look
out the window, fetches a suit of men's clothes from
a closet, searches the pockets, brings out a key, opens
the suitcase, rummages through it hastily, goes to look
out of the window, comes back to the suitcase, rummages in it again, finds what she has been looking for
while she has her back turned to the audience, and
looks once more out the window. She gives a start,
rapidly closes the suitcase, puts the key back in the
coat pocket, and hides under the mattress whatever it
is that she has found. HUGO enters.*

HUGO: It went on endlessly. Were you very bored?
JESSICA: Horribly.
HUGO: What did you do?
JESSICA: I slept.
HUGO: Well, time doesn't hang heavy when you sleep
JESSICA: I dreamed that I was bored, and that woke me
up and I unpacked the suitcases. How does the place
look now? [*She points to the jumble of clothes on
the bed and the chairs.*]
HUGO: I don't know. Is this arrangement temporary?
JESSICA [*firmly*]: No, final.
HUGO: Very good.
JESSICA: What do you think of him?
HUGO: Who?
JESSICA: Hœderer.
HUGO: Hœderer? Like anybody else.

JESSICA: How old is he?

HUGO: Middle-aged.

JESSICA: Middle between what and what?

HUGO: Twenty and sixty.

JESSICA: Tall or short?

HUGO: Medium.

JESSICA: Any unusual features?

HUGO: A big scar, a wig, and a glass eye.

JESSICA: What a monster!

HUGO: I made it up. He's perfectly ordinary.

JESSICA: You're just showing off. The truth is you couldn't describe him to me.

HUGO: Of course I could, if I wanted to.

JESSICA: No, not even if you wanted to.

HUGO: Yes, I could.

JESSICA: No. What color are his eyes?

HUGO: Gray.

JESSICA: My poor baby, you think all eyes are gray. There are blue eyes and black eyes and green eyes and hazel-colored eyes. There are even mauve-colored eyes. What color are mine? [*She covers her eyes with her hand.*] Don't look.

HUGO: They are two silk pavilions, two Andalusian gardens, two moonfish.

JESSICA: I asked you to tell me their color.

HUGO: Blue.

JESSICA: You looked.

HUGO: No, but you told me this morning.

JESSICA: Idiot. [*She comes closer to him.*] Now think carefully, Hugo: has he a mustache?

HUGO: No. [*A pause.*] I'm sure he hasn't.

JESSICA [*sadly*]: I wish I could believe you.

HUGO [*reflects a moment, then blurts out suddenly*]: He wore a polka-dot tie.

JESSICA: Polka-dot?

HUGO: Polka-dot.

JESSICA: Go 'way with you.

HUGO: You know the kind. [*He pretends he is looping a*

fancy ascot.]

JESSICA: You crawled before him, you gave in! All the while he was talking to you, you were looking at his tie. Hugo, he intimidated you!

HUGO: He did not!

JESSICA: He intimidated you!

HUGO: The fact is, he's not intimidating.

JESSICA: Then why did you look at his tie?

HUGO: In order not to intimidate him.

JESSICA: Uh-huh. But when I see him and you want to know what he looks like, you only have to ask me. What did he say to you?

HUGO: I told him that my father was vice-president of the Tosk Coke Manufacturers and that I broke with him to enter the party.

JESSICA: And what did he say to that?

HUGO: He said that was fine.

JESSICA: And then?

HUGO: I didn't conceal from him that I have my doctorate, but I made him understand that I am not an intellectual, that I am not ashamed to work as a clerk, and that my special point of honor is to require of myself the strictest discipline and obedience.

JESSICA: And what did he say to that?

HUGO: He said that was fine too.

JESSICA: And that took two hours?

HUGO: There were moments of silence.

JESSICA: You are one of those people who always repeat what you say to others and never what others say to you.

HUGO: That's because I think you are more interested in me than in the others.

JESSICA: Of course, my baby. But I have you. I don't have the others.

HUGO: Do you want Hœderer?

JESSICA: I want to have everybody.

HUGO: Hmmm. But he's vulgar.

JESSICA: How do you know if you didn't look at him?

HUGO: You have to be vulgar to wear a polka-dot tie.

JESSICA: The Greek empresses slept with barbarian generals.

HUGO: There were no empresses in Greece.

JESSICA: Then they were in Byzantium.

HUGO: In Byzantium there were barbarian generals and Greek empresses, but no one reports what they did together.

JESSICA: What else could they do? [*A brief silence.*] Did he ask you what I'm like?

HUGO: No.

JESSICA: You wouldn't have been able to tell him anything anyway: you don't know anything about me Didn't he ask about me at all?

HUGO: No, nothing.

JESSICA: He has no manners.

HUGO: You see. Anyway, there's no use your being interested in him now.

JESSICA: Why?

HUGO: You'll keep your mouth shut?

JESSICA: I'll hold it shut with both hands.

HUGO: He's going to die.

JESSICA: Is he sick?

HUGO: No, but he's going to be assassinated—like all men in politics.

JESSICA: Ah! [*A pause.*] And you, my little pet—are you in politics?

HUGO: Certainly.

JESSICA: And what is there for the widow of a political man to do?

HUGO: She can join her husband's party and complete his work.

JESSICA: Good Lord! I would rather kill myself beside your grave.

HUGO: Nowadays that only happens in Malabar.

JESSICA: Then here is what I would do: I would track down your assassins one by one, then I would make them burn with love for me, and when they began to think that they could console my haughty, despairing grief, I would stick a knife in their hearts.

HUGO: Which would you enjoy more? Killing them or seducing them?

JESSICA: You're stupid and vulgar.

HUGO: I thought you liked vulgar men. [JESSICA *doesn't reply*.] Are we playing our little game or not?

JESSICA: This isn't playing any more. Let me unpack the suitcases.

HUGO: Go ahead!

JESSICA: The only one left to unpack is yours. Give me the key.

HUGO: I gave it to you.

JESSICA [*pointing to the suitcase she opened at the beginning of the act*]: Not to that one.

HUGO: I'll unpack that myself.

JESSICA: That's not your job, my pet.

HUGO: Since when is it yours? Do you want to play at being a housewife?

JESSICA: You're certainly playing at being a revolutionary.

HUGO: Revolutionaries don't need wives who are homemakers: they cut off their heads.

JESSICA: They prefer she-wolves with black hair, like Olga.

HUGO: Are you jealous?

JESSICA: I should like to be. I never played that game. Shall we try?

HUGO: If you like.

JESSICA: Good. Then give me the key to the suitcase.

HUGO: Never!

JESSICA: What's in this suitcase?

HUGO: A shameful secret.

JESSICA: What secret?

HUGO: I am not my father's son.

JESSICA: How happy you would be to believe that, my poor baby! But it's not possible: you look too much like him.

HUGO: That's not true, Jessica! You think I resemble him?

JESSICA: Are we playing or not?

HUGO: Playing.

JESSICA: Then open the suitcase.

HUGO: I swore not to open it.

JESSICA: It's stuffed with letters from that she-wolf! Or snapshots, perhaps? Open it!

HUGO: No.

JESSICA: Open it! Open it!

HUGO: No, no, and no.

JESSICA: Are you playing?

HUGO: Yes.

JESSICA: Then, fins: I'm not playing any more. Open the suitcase.

HUGO: No more fins! I won't open it.

JESSICA: It's all the same to me, since I know what's inside.

HUGO: What's inside?

JESSICA: These. [*She reaches under the mattress, then, with one hand behind her back, flourishes the snapshots with the other.*] There!

HUGO: Jessica!

JESSICA [*triumphant*]: I found the key in your brown suit, and now I know who is your mistress, your princess, your empress. It's not me, and it's not the she-wolf. It's you, my pet, it's you yourself. Twelve snapshots of yourself in your suitcase.

HUGO: Give me those pictures.

JESSICA: Twelve snapshots of your wide-eyed youth. At three, at six, at eight, at ten, at twelve, at sixteen. You took them with you when your father threw you out, they go with you everywhere; how you must love yourself!

HUGO: Jessica, I'm not playing now.

JESSICA: At six you wore a starched collar, which must have scraped your tender neck, and then you had a velvet jacket with a fancy necktie. What a beautiful little man, what a well-behaved child! It's the well-behaved children, madame, that make the most formidable revolutionaries. They don't say a word, they don't hide under the table, they eat only one piece of chocolate at a time. But later on they make society pay dearly. Watch out for good boys.

[HUGO, *who had given the appearance of being resigned to her keeping the snapshots, lunges forward
suddenly and grabs her.*]

HUGO: Give them back to me, you witch! Give them
back to me.

JESSICA: Let go of me! [*He pushes her down on the bed.*]
Look out, you're going to get us killed.

HUGO: Give them back.

JESSICA: I tell you, the gun will go off! [HUGO *gets up;
she shows him the revolver she has held behind her
back.*] This was in the suitcase too.

HUGO: Give it to me. [*He takes it, goes to look in his
brown suit, takes out the key, goes to the suitcase,
opens it, collects the snapshots, and puts them and
the revolver into the suitcase. A pause.*]

JESSICA: What's that revolver doing here?

HUGO: I always have one with me.

JESSICA: That's not so. You never had one before we
came here. And you never had that suitcase either.
You bought them both at the same time. Why did
you get a revolver?

HUGO: Do you really want to know?

JESSICA: Yes, and be serious. You have no right to keep
things like this from me.

HUGO: You won't tell anybody?

JESSICA: I won't tell a soul.

HUGO: It's to kill Hœderer.

JESSICA: Don't tease me, Hugo. I tell you I'm not playing now.

HUGO [*he laughs*]: Am I playing? Or am I being serious?
There's a mystery for you. Jessica, you are going to be
the wife of an assassin!

JESSICA: But you could never do it, my poor little lamb;
would you like me to kill him for you? I'll go offer myself to him and then—

HUGO: Thanks, and anyhow you would fail! I shall act
for myself.

JESSICA: But why do you want to kill him? You don't
even know the man.

HUGO: So that my wife will take me seriously. Wouldn't you take me seriously then?

JESSICA: Me? I would admire you, hide you, feed you, and entertain you in your hide-away. And when the neighbors turned us in I would throw myself on you despite the police, and I would take you in my arms crying: "I love you.".

HUGO: Tell it to me now.

JESSICA: What?

HUGO: That you love me.

JESSICA: I love you.

HUGO: But mean it.

JESSICA: I love you.

HUGO: But you don't really mean it.

JESSICA: What's got into you? Are you playing?

HUGO: No, I'm not playing.

JESSICA: Then why did you ask me that? That's not like you.

HUGO: I don't know. I need to think that you love me. I have a right to that. Come on, say it. Say it as if you meant it.

JESSICA: I love you. I love you. No: I love you. Oh, go to the devil! Let's hear you say it.

HUGO: I love you.

JESSICA: You see, you don't say it any better than I.

HUGO: Jessica, you don't believe what I told you.

JESSICA: That you love me?

HUGO: That I'm going to kill Hœderer.

JESSICA: Of course I believe it.

HUGO: Try hard, Jessica. Be serious.

JESSICA: Why do I have to be serious?

HUGO: Because we can't always be playing.

JESSICA: I don't like to be serious, but I'll do the best I can: I'll play at being serious.

HUGO: Look me in the eyes. No. Don't laugh. Listen to me: it's true about Hœderer. That's why the party sent me here.

JESSICA: I believe you. But why didn't you tell me sooner?

HUGO: Perhaps you would have refused to come here with me.

JESSICA: Why should I refuse? It's a man's job and has nothing to do with me.

HUGO: This is going to be no joke, you know. He seems to be a hard guy.

JESSICA: Oh well, we'll chlorotorm him and tie him across a cannon's mouth.

HUGO: Jessica! I'm serious.

JESSICA: Me too.

HUGO: You are playing at being serious. You told me so yourself.

JESSICA: No. That's what you're doing.

HUGO: You've got to believe me, I beg you.

JESSICA: I'll believe you when you believe that I'm serious.

HUGO: All right, I believe you.

JESSICA: No. You're playing at believing me.

HUGO: This can go on forever! [*A rap on the door.*] Come in! [JESSICA *gets in front of the suitcase, her back to the audience, while* HUGO *goes to open the door.*]

[SLICK *and* GEORGE *enter, smiling. They carry submachine guns and wear holsters with revolvers. A moment of silence.*]

GEORGE: It's us.

HUGO: Well?

GEORGE: We came to give you a hand.

HUGO: A hand at what?

SLICK: To unpack.

JESSICA: Thanks very much, but I don't need any help.

GEORGE [*pointing at the women's clothes strewn over the furnishings*]: All that's got to be folded.

SLICK: If the four of us pitched in, we could get it done quicker.

JESSICA: You think so?

SLICK [*picks up a slip strewn over the back of a chair and holds it up at arm's length*]: This folds in the middle, right? And then you smooth down the sides?

JESSICA: Yes! That's right. But I rather think you would be better doing heavier work.

GEORGE: Don't play with that, Slick. It'll give you ideas. Excuse him, ma'am; we haven't seen a woman for six months.

SLICK: We don't even remember how they're stacked. [*They look at her.*]

JESSICA: It's coming back to you now?

GEORGE: A little.

JESSICA: Aren't there any women in the village?

SLICK: Sure, but we never get out.

GEORGE: The other secretary went over the wall every night; result: we find him one morning with his head in a pond. Then the old man decides that the new secretary ought to be a married man so as to have the necessary right at home.

JESSICA: That was very delicate of him.

SLICK: But he's against us getting ours.

JESSICA: Really? Why?

GEORGE: He says he wants us to stay tough.

HUGO: These are Hœderer's bodyguards.

JESSICA: You know it's funny—I guessed as much.

SLICK [*indicating his submachine gun*]: On account of this?

JESSICA: Because of that, too.

GEORGE: Mustn't take us for pros. Me, I'm a plumber. We're doing a little extra stuff 'cause the party asked us.

SLICK: You're not afraid of us?

JESSICA: On the contrary; but I should like [*indicating the machine guns and revolvers*] to see you put those playthings away. Put that in a corner.

GEORGE: We can't.

SLICK: Against orders.

JESSICA: Don't you put them away when you sleep?

GEORGE: No, ma'am.

JESSICA: No?

SLICK: No.

HUGO: They're sticklers for rules. When I went to see Hœderer they kept me covered with their machine guns.

GEORGE [*laughing*]: That's us all right.

SLICK [*laughing*]: If he'd 'uv made a wrong move you'd 'uv been a widow.

[*They all laugh.*]

JESSICA: Your boss must be awfully afraid of something.

SLICK: He's not afraid, he just don't want to be killed.

JESSICA: Why should anyone kill him?

SLICK: Search me. But people want to kill him. His pals came to warn him about two weeks ago.

JESSICA: That's interesting.

SLICK: Oh, you get used to it. It's not even exciting. You gotta keep on the lookout, that's all. [*During* SLICK's *reply* GEORGE *takes a turn about the room with an air of pretended nonchalance. He goes to the open closet and comes out with* HUGO's *suit.*]

GEORGE: Hey, Slick. Get a load of this; is this guy well fixed!

SLICK: It's part of the job. You look at a secretary, see; he's taking dictation, and if his looks don't please you, you forget what you're thinking about. [GEORGE *frisks the suit while pretending to brush it.*]

GEORGE: Watch out for the closet. The walls are filthy. [*He hangs the suit in the closet and returns to stand by* SLICK. JESSICA *and* HUGO *look at each other.*]

JESSICA: Why don't you sit down?

SLICK: No, thanks.

GEORGE: Never mind.

JESSICA: We can't offer you anything to drink.

SLICK: Doesn't matter. We can't drink on the job.

HUGO: Are you on the job now?

GEORGE: We are *always* on the job.

HUGO: Ah!

SLICK: Fact is, you gotta be a damned saint to stick at it.

HUGO: But I'm not on the job yet. I am at home, with my wife. Let's sit down, Jessica. [*They both sit down.*]

SLICK [*going to the window*]: Fine view.

GEORGE: It's nice here.

SLICK: And quiet.

GEORGE: Did you see the bed? It's big enough for three.

SLICK: For four; young married couples snuggle up close

GEORGE: All that space wasted while some people have to sleep on the floor.

SLICK: Shut up. I'm gonna dream about it tonight.

JESSICA: Don't you have a bed?

SLICK [*brightening up*]: George!

GEORGE [*laughing*]: Yeah.

SLICK: She's asking if we got a bed!

GEORGE [*pointing to* SLICK]: He sleeps on the rug in the office, and I sleep in the hall outside the old man's room.

JESSICA: And it's uncomfortable?

GEORGE: It would be tough on your husband; he seems like the delicate type. But we're used to that stuff. The worst of it is that we have no room ourselves. The garden isn't healthy, so we spend the day in the hall. [*He bends down and looks under the bed.*]

HUGO: What are you looking for?

GEORGE: Sometimes there are rats. [*He stands up straight.*]

HUGO: See any?

GEORGE: No.

HUGO: That's good. [*A pause.*]

JESSICA: Did you leave your boss all alone? Aren't you afraid that something might happen to him if you stay away too long?

SLICK: Leon's with him. [*Pointing to the telephone*] If there's any trouble he can always call us.

[*A pause.* HUGO *gets up, pale with exasperation.* JESSICA *stands up too.*]

HUGO: They're friendly, aren't they?

JESSICA: Delightful.

HUGO: And you see how they're built?

JESSICA: Like trucks! Well, you're going to have a trio of friends. My husband adores killers. He would have liked to be one himself.

SLICK: He's not built for it. He's built like a secretary.

HUGO: We'll get along marvelously. I shall be the brains,
Jessica the eyes, you the muscles. Feel his muscles,
Jessica! [*She feels them.*] Like iron. Feel them.

JESSICA: But maybe George doesn't want me, to.

GEORGE [*stiffens*]: I don't care.

HUGO: You see, he's delighted. Go on, feel his muscles,
Jessica, feel them. [JESSICA *feels them.*] Aren't they
like iron?

JESSICA: Like steel.

HUGO: We're so intimate now, aren't we?

SLICK: If you like it that way, kid.

JESSICA: It was so nice of you to come to see us.

SLICK: The pleasure was all ours. Ain't that right, George?

GEORGE: Does us good to see you so happy.

JESSICA: You'll have something to talk about in your hallway.

SLICK: That's right. 'Cause at night we can say to each
other: "They're so cozy now. He's holding his dear
wife in his arms."

GEORGE: That'll be a big help to us.

HUGO [*goes to the door and opens it*]: Come back whenever you like. The place is yours. [SLICK *calmly goes
to the door and shuts it.*]

SLICK: We're going. We'll go right away. There's just
one little formality.

HUGO: For instance?

SLICK: We gotta search the room.

HUGO: No.

GEORGE: No?

HUGO: You're not going to search anything!

SLICK: Don't knock yourself out. We got our orders.

HUGO: Orders from whom?

SLICK: Hœderer.

HUGO: Hœderer told you to search my room?

GEORGE: Look here, bud, don't be an ass. I told you
we've been warned; something's going to pop one
of these days. You don't suppose we're gonna let you
come in here without looking in your pockets. You
could be carrying grenades or any of that stuff, though

it looks to me like you couldn't hit the broad side of a barn.

HUGO: I want to know if Hœderer specifically instructed you to search my quarters.

SLICK [*to* GEORGE]: Specifically.

GEORGE: Specifically.

SLICK: No one gets in here without being frisked. That's the rule and that's all there is to it.

HUGO: And I say that you shall not search me. I'm to be the exception, and that's all there is to that.

GEORGE: Ain't you in the party?

HUGO: Yes.

GEORGE: Didn't they teach you anything? Don't you know what an assignment is?

HUGO: I know as well as you do.

SLICK: And when they give you an assignment, you know that you gotta carry it out?

HUGO: I know that.

SLICK: So?

HUGO: I respect orders, but I also respect myself. And I won't obey idiotic orders that were given expressly to make a fool of me.

SLICK: Did you hear that? Tell me, George, do you respect yourself?

GEORGE: I don't know. Do I look like I do? How about you, Slick?

SLICK: Are you crazy? You got no right to respect yourself if you're not at least a secretary.

HUGO: You stupid fools! I joined the party so that all men, secretaries or not, could have the right to respect themselves some day.

GEORGE: Make him cut it out, Slick, he's making me cry. No, kid, people join the party because they get fed up being hungry.

SLICK: So that guys like us will be able to eat some day.

GEORGE: Come on, Slick, cut the chatter. Open that one to begin with.

HUGO: You shan't touch it.

SLICK: Look, Junior, how do you plan to stop me?

HUGO: I can't fight against a steamroller, but if you just put one finger on that bag we'll leave this place tonight and Hœderer can find himself another secretary.

GEORGE: Oh, you scare me! A secretary like you—I can make one any day.

HUGO: Well, search then, if you're not afraid to. Go ahead and search!

[GEORGE *scratches his head.* JESSICA, *who has remained very calm during the whole scene, comes toward them.*]

JESSICA: Why don't you telephone Hœderer?

SLICK: Hœderer?

JESSICA: He'll settle this.

[GEORGE *and* SLICK *glance at each other inquiringly.*]

GEORGE: That's an idea. [*He goes to the phone and dials it.*] Hello. Leon? Go tell the old man that our pal here doesn't want us to search him. How's that? Oh! Thanks. [*Coming back to* SLICK] He's gonna see the old man.

SLICK: All right, but I want to tell you something, George. I like Hœderer and all that, but if he makes an exception for this rich little mamma's boy, when all the rest of us were stripped to the skin, even the postman, I'll quit.

GEORGE: Same here. They'd better go along or we'll be the ones who'll quit.

SLICK: So suppose I don't respect myself, I have my pride just like anybody else.

HUGO: Suit yourself. But if Hœderer gives the order to search, in five minutes I'll be outside this house.

GEORGE: Slick!

SLICK: Yes?

GEORGE: Don't you think the gentleman has an aristocratic pan?

HUGO: Jessica!

JESSICA: Yes?

HUGO: Don't you think these gentlemen look like real bruisers?

SLICK [*goes up to him and puts a hand on his shoulder*]:
Look, kid, if we really are bruisers, we're liable to
bruise you good!
·[*Enter* HŒDERER.]

HŒDERER: Why was I disturbed? [SLICK *takes a step backwards.*]

SLICK: He doesn't want to be searched.

HŒDERER: No?

HUGO: If you let them search me, I'll quit. That's final.

HŒDERER: Very well.

GEORGE: And if you stop us, we're the ones who are
gonna quit.

HŒDERER [*to his men*]: Sit down. [*They sit down reluctantly. He takes a slip and a pair of stockings from
the back of the armchair and is about to put them on
the bed.*]

JESSICA: Let me. [*She takes them in her hands, rolls
them into a ball, and then, without budging, throws
them onto the bed.*]

HŒDERER: What's your name?

JESSICA: Jessica.

HŒDERER [*looking her over*]: I expected you to be
homely.

JESSICA: Sorry to disappoint you.

HŒDERER [*still looking at her*]: Yes. It's regrettable.

JESSICA: Must I shave my head?

HŒDERER [*without taking his eyes from her*]: No. [*He
steps away from her.*] Was it over you they were about
to come to blows?

JESSICA: Not so far.

HŒDERER: Things must never come to that point. [*He
seats himself in the armchair.*] No need to search the
place.

SLICK: We—

HŒDERER: It's of no importance. We'll talk about it
later. [*To* SLICK] What's going on here? What do
you have against him? He's too well dressed? He
talks like a book?

SLICK: Question of looks.

HŒDERER: None of that here. We check our looks outside. [*He considers them.*] Look, fellows, you've started off badly. [*To* HUGO] You are insolent because you are the weakest. [*To* SLICK *and* GEORGE] You are just ill-humored. You began by disliking him. Tomorrow you'll play tricks on him, and next week when I have to dictate a letter to him you'll come and tell me that he was fished out of a pond.

HUGO: Not if I can help it.

HŒDERER: You can't help anything. Don't get excited, boy. Things don't have to come to that point, that's all. Four men who live together have to get along if there's not to be a massacre. So will you please do me the favor of trying to understand one another?

GEORGE [*with dignity*]: Feelings can't be ordered.

HŒDERER [*forcefully*]: They can and they must be among members of the same party when there's work to be done.

GEORGE: We're not in the same party.

HŒDERER [*to* HUGO]: Aren't you one of us?

HUGO: Of course.

HŒDERER: Well, then.

SLICK: We might belong to the same party, but we didn't get in for the same reasons.

HŒDERER: Everyone joins for the same reason.

SLICK: Let me tell you this: he joined to teach us how to respect each other.

HŒDERER: Come, come now.

GEORGE: That's what he said.

HUGO: And you—you joined just in order to be able to eat your fill. That's what you said.

HŒDERER: Is that right? Well, you are in agreement.

SLICK: How come?

HŒDERER: Slick! Didn't you tell me yourself that you were ashamed of being hungry? [*He turns toward* SLICK *and waits for a reply, but none is forthcoming.*] And how it infuriated you when you could think of nothing but your hunger? Didn't you say that a boy of twenty should have something better to do than be always thinking of his stomach?

SLICK: You didn't have to say that in front of him.

HŒDERER: Didn't you tell me that?

SLICK: What's that prove?

HŒDERER: It proves that you wanted your mouth full and a little something else besides. He calls that something else self-respect. Nothing objectionable in that. Everybody can use the words he likes.

SLICK: That's not self-respect. That makes me sick to call that self-respect. He uses words he finds in his head; he thinks with his head.

HUGO: What do you want me to think with?

SLICK: When your belly's growling, pal, it's not with your head that you think. It's true that I wanted to put a stop to that—good God, yes. Just for a moment, for a little moment, to think of something else— anything except myself. But that's not self-respect. You've never been hungry, and you've come in with us just to preach to us like the social workers who came to see my mother when she was drunk to tell her that she had no self-respect.

HUGO: That's not true.

GEORGE: Have you ever been hungry yourself? I'll bet you needed exercise before dinner to work up an appetite.

HUGO: For once you're right, my friend. I don't know what appetite is. If you could have seen the tonics they gave me as a kid; I always left half—what waste! Then they opened my mouth and told me: "One spoonful for Papa, one spoonful for Mamma, one spoonful for Aunt Anna." And they pushed the spoon down my throat. And I shot up too, believe me. But I never put on weight. Then they had me drink blood fresh from the slaughterhouse, because I was pale; after that I never touched meat. My father would say every night: "This child has no appetite." Every evening he would say: "Eat, Hugo, eat. You'll be sick." They had me take cod-liver oil; that's the height of luxury—medicine to make you hungry while others in the street would sell their souls for a beefsteak. I saw them pass under my window with their placards: "Give us bread." And then I would sit down at the table. "Eat, Hugo, eat." A spoonful for the night watchman who is on strike, a spoonful for the old woman who picks the parings out of the garbage can, a spoonful for the family of the carpenter who broke his leg. I left home. I joined the party, only to hear the same old song: "You've never been hungry, Hugo, what are you messing around here for? What can you know? You've never been hungry." Very well, then! I have never been hungry. Never! Never! Never! Now perhaps you can tell me what I can do to make you stop throwing it up to me. [*A pause.*]

HŒDERER: You heard him? Come on now, tell him. Tell him what he has to do. Slick, what do you want of him? Do you want him to cut off a hand? Or tear out one of his eyes? Or offer you his wife? What must he pay so that you will forgive him?

SLICK: I've got nothing to forgive him for.

HŒDERER: But you have. He joined the party without being driven to it by poverty.

GEORGE: We don't hold that against him. Only there's a big difference between us: him, he's just playing around. He joined up just because it was the thing to do. We did it because we couldn't do anything else.

HŒDERER: And do you think he could have done something else? The hunger of others is not so easy to bear, either.

GEORGE: There's plenty who manage to put up with it very nicely.

HŒDERER: That's because they have no imagination. The trouble with this kid here is that he has too much.

SLICK: O.K. No one's going to hurt him. We can't stand him, that's all. We have a right—

HŒDERER: What right? You have no right. None. "We can't stand him." You poor bastards, go look at your mugs in the mirror and then come back and talk about your delicate feelings if you dare. A man is judged by his work. And take care that I don't judge you by yours, because you're taking things mighty easy lately.

HUGO [*shouting*]: But don't defend me! Who asked you to defend me? You see perfectly well that there's nothing to be done about it; I'm used to it. When I saw them come in, before, I recognized their smile. Believe me, they weren't pretty; they came to pay me off for my father and for my grandfather and for all my family who had enough to eat. I tell you, I know them: they will never accept me; there are a hundred thousand of them with that smile. I struggled, I humiliated myself, I did all I could to make them forget, I told them that I loved them, that I envied them, that I admired them. Useless! There's nothing to be done about it. Nothing! I am a rich kid, an intellectual, a fellow who doesn't work with his hands. Well, let them think as they like. They're right, it's a matter of looks.

[SLICK *and* GEORGE *look at each other silently.*]

HŒDERER [*to his men*]: Well? [SLICK *and* GEORGE *shrug their shoulders uncertainly.*] I won't humor him any more than you: you know I don't humor anyone. He won't work with his hands, but I'll make him work, and hard. [*With irritation*] Well, let's get it over with.

SLICK [*making up his mind*]: O.K. [*To* HUGO] Look, buddy, it's not that I like you. It wouldn't help to try. There's something between us that just doesn't click. But I won't say that you're a bad guy, and it's true that we started off on the wrong foot. We'll try not to make life too hard. O.K.?

HUGO [*lamely*]: If you like.

SLICK: O.K., George?

GEORGE: Let it go at that. [*A pause.*]

KŒDERER [*calmly*]: Now about searching the place.

SLICK: Yes. The search. But now—

GEORGE: So all this was just talk.

SLICK: Just for the record.

HŒDERER [*changing his tone*]: Who asked your opinion? You'll search the place if I tell you to. [*To* HUGO, *in his normal tone*] I trust you, lad, but you have to be realistic. If I make an exception of you today, tomorrow they will ask me to do it again, with the result that one fine day a guy will come along and kill us all because they neglected to look in his pockets. Suppose they ask you politely, now you're friends, would you let them have a look around?

HUGO: I'm afraid—not.

HŒDERER: Ah! [*He looks at him.*] And if I were the one to ask you? [*A pause.*] I see: you have principles. I could make this a question of principle too. But principles and I— [*A pause.*] Look at me. You have no weapons?

HUGO: No.

HŒDERER: And your wife?

HUGO: No.

HŒDERER: Good. I trust you. Get out, you two.

JESSICA: Wait. [*They come back.*] Hugo, it would be wrong not to answer trust with trust.

HUGO: What do you mean?

JESSICA: You can search anywhere you like.

HUGO: But, Jessica—

JESSICA: Well, why not? You're going to make them think you have a revolver hidden here.

HUGO: You're mad!

JESSICA: Well, then let them look. Your pride is saved, since we're doing the asking.

[GEORGE *and* SLICK *remain hesitant on the threshold.*]

HŒDERER: Well, what are you waiting for? You heard what she said?

SLICK: I thought—

HŒDERER: I don't care what you thought; do as you're told.

SLICK: O.K., O.K., O.K.

GEORGE: It wasn't worth all this fuss.

[*While they begin to search the place, slowly,* HUGO *looks at* JESSICA *with stupefaction.*]

HŒDERER [*to* SLICK *and* GEORGE]: This will teach you to trust people. I am always trustful. I trust everybody. [*They search.*] Look carefully! There's no point in doing it if you don't do it right. Slick, look in the wardrobe. Good. Take that suit out. Run through the pockets.

SLICK: Already did it.

HŒDERER: Do it again. Look under the mattress too. Good. Slick, keep it up. And you, George, come here. [*Pointing to* HUGO] Frisk him. Just look in his coat pockets. And the inside pocket. There. Now his trousers. Good. And the hip pockets. Fine.

JESSICA: What about me?

HŒDERER: If you ask for it. George. [GEORGE *doesn't budge.*] Well? You're not afraid of her?

GEORGE: Oh, O.K. [*He goes up to* JESSICA, *very red, and glides his fingertips over her.* JESSICA *laughs.*]

JESSICA: He has the touch of a lady's maid.

[SLICK *approaches the suitcase that contained the revolver.*]

SLICK: Suitcases empty?

HUGO [*taut*]: Yes. [HŒDERER *looks him over carefully.*]

HŒDERER: That one too?

HUGO: Yes. [SLICK *lifts it.*]

SLICK: No.

HUGO: Oh, no, not that one. I was going to unpack it when you came in.

HŒDERER: Open it. [SLICK *opens and rummages through it.*]

SLICK: Nothing there.

HŒDERER: Good. That's settled. You can beat it now.

SLICK [*to* HUGO]: No hard feelings.

HUGO: No hard feelings.

JESSICA [*while they are going out*]: I'll come to see you in your hallway.

HŒDERER: If I were you, I wouldn't go to see them too often.

JESSICA: And why not? They're so cute, George particularly; he's like a young girl.

HŒDERER: Hmm! [*He approaches her.*] You're pretty, that's a fact. No use regretting it. Only, things being the way they are, I can see but two solutions. The first would be this: if your heart were big enough, you could make us all happy.

JESSICA: I have a very tiny heart.

HŒDERER: I thought as much. Besides, they would manage to fight just the same. The second solution: when your husband is out, you are to lock yourself in and open to nobody—not even to me.

JESSICA: Very well, but if you let me I'll choose a third course.

HŒDERER: As you will. [*He leans over her and breathes deeply.*] You smell nice. Don't use this perfume when you go to see them.

JESSICA: I'm not wearing any perfume.

HŒDERER: That makes it worse. [*He moves away from her, walks slowly to the center of the room, then stops. All the while his glance sweeps over the place. He is looking for something. From time to time his glance falls on* HUGO, *whom he watches very carefully.*] Very well. We'll let it go at that. [*A pause.*] Hugo, you're to see me tomorrow morning at ten o'clock.

HUGO: I know.

HŒDERER [*absent-mindedly, while his eyes search around the room*]: Fine, fine, fine. Settled. Everything is fine. All's well that ends well. Yet, you look kind of funny. Everything is fine. Everybody is reconciled, we all love each other. . . . [*Suddenly*] You're fagged out, son.

HUGO: It's nothing. [HŒDERER *watches him attentively.* HUGO, *very uneasy, evidently has to make an effort to speak.*] About what happened just now—please forgive me.

HŒDERER [*without taking his eyes from him*]: I've forgotten all about it.

HUGO: In the future you'll have no cause to complain of me. I'll accept discipline.

HŒDERER: You already told me that. Are you sure you're not ill? [HUGO *doesn't reply.*] If you're sick, there's still time to tell me and I will ask the Central Committee to send someone to take your place.

HUGO: I'm not sick.

HŒDERER: Excellent. Well, I shall leave you. I suppose you want to be alone. [*He goes to the table and looks at the books on it.*] Hegel, Marx, excellent. Lorca, Eliot: never heard of them. [*He leafs through the books.*]

HUGO: They are poets.

HŒDERER [*picking up some other books*]: Poetry—poetry. A lot of poetry. Do you write poems?

HUGO: N—no.

HŒDERER: Well, you used to, eh? [*He moves away from the table, stops by the bed.*] A dressing-gown, you're well set up. You took it with you when you left your father?

HUGO: Yes.

HŒDERER: The two suits also, I suppose. [*He offers him a cigarette.*]

HUGO [*declining*]: Thanks.

HŒDERER: You don't smoke? [*A negative gesture from* HUGO.] Good. The Central Committee gave me to understand that you've never taken part in any direct action. Is that true?

HUGO: Yes, it's true.

HŒDERER: That must have driven you mad. All intellectuals dream of doing something.

HUGO: I put out the paper.

HŒDERER: That's what they told me. I haven't received a copy for two months. Were you in charge of the earlier issues?

HUGO: Yes.

HŒDERER: You did a good job. And they deprived themselves of such a good editor in order to send you to me?

HUGO: They thought I was just the man you needed.

HŒDERER: They're so kind. And what about you? Don't you object to giving up your work?

HUGO: I—

HŒDERER: The paper was made to order for you. There were risks, responsibilities. In a certain sense that kind of work could even be called action. [*He looks at him.*] And now you are a secretary. [*A pause.*] Why did you drop your other job? Why?

HUGO: I believe in discipline.

HŒDERER: Don't talk so much about discipline. I distrust people who always have that word on their lips.

HUGO: I *need* discipline.

HŒDERER: Why?

HUGO [*wearily*]: There are too many ideas in my head. I must get rid of them.

HŒDERER: What sort of ideas?

HUGO: "What am I doing here? Am I right to want what I want? Am I really just kidding myself?" Ideas like that.

HŒDERER [*slowly*]: I see. Ideas like that, eh? And at this moment your head is full of them?

HUGO [*uneasily*]: No.—No, not at this moment. [*A pause.*] But they might come back. I have to protect myself. By installing other thoughts in my head. Assignments: "Do this. Go. Stop. Say such and such." I need to obey. To obey, just like that. To eat, sleep, obey.

HŒDERER: Very good. If you are obedient we'll get along. [*He puts his hand on* HUGO's *shoulder.*] Now listen to me— [HUGO *disengages himself and steps back.* HŒDERER *regards him with increasing interest. His voice becomes harsh and cutting.*] Aha? [*A pause.*] Ha ha ha!

HUGO: I—I don't like to have anyone touch me.

HŒDERER [*in a harsh and rapid tone*]: When they searched this suitcase, you were afraid. Why?

HUGO: I wasn't afraid.

HŒDERER: Yes. You were afraid. What's in it?

HUGO: They searched and found nothing.

HŒDERER: Nothing? Well, we'll see. [*He goes to the suitcase and opens it.*] They were looking for a weapon. One can hide weapons in a suitcase, but one might also hide papers.

HUGO: Or strictly personal effects.

HŒDERER: From the moment you start to work under me, you're to understand that nothing concerning you is any longer strictly personal. [*He searches the suitcase.*] Shirts, shorts, all new. Do you have any money?

HUGO: My wife has some.

HŒDERER: What are these snapshots? [*He takes them out and looks at them. A moment of silence.*] So that was it! That was it! [*He looks at one of the snapshots.*] A velvet jacket. [*He looks at another.*] A sailor collar with a beret. What a well-dressed little man!

HUGO: Give me back those pictures.

HŒDERER: Quiet! [*He pushes him back.*] So these, then, are the strictly personal effects. You were afraid they would find them.

HUGO: If they had put their dirty paws on them, if they had so much as snickered when they saw them, I—

HŒDERER: Now we have it! The mystery is solved. That's what it is to carry your crime on your face; I would have sworn you were hiding a hand-grenade at least. [*He looks at the snapshots.*] Well, you haven't changed. These thin little legs— You sure didn't have much appetite. You were so small that they had you stand on a chair, and you crossed your arms and surveyed your world like a Napoleon. Nothing lighthearted about you. No—it mustn't be much fun to be a rich kid day in, day out. It's a bad way to begin life. Why do you lug your past around with you in that suitcase if you want to bury it? [*A vague gesture from* HUGO.] At any rate, you pay a great deal of attention to yourself.

HUGO: I am in the party to forget myself.

HŒDERER: And you think of yourself at the very moment that you should forget about yourself. Oh, well. Each one gets by the best way he can. [*He returns the snap-*

shots.] Hide them well. [HUGO *takes them and puts them in the inside pocket of his coat.*] Till tomorrow, Hugo.

HUGO: Till tomorrow.

HŒDERER: Good night, Jessica.

JESSICA: Good night.

[*On the threshold* HŒDERER *turns back again.*]

HŒDERER: Pull down the shades and lock the door. You never know who might be hanging around the garden. That's an order. [*He goes out.*]

[HUGO *goes to the door and turns the key twice.*]

JESSICA: He really is vulgar. But he doesn't wear a polka-dot tie.

HUGO: Where's the revolver?

JESSICA: What fun I had! This is the first time I've seen you at grips with real men.

HUGO: Jessica, where is that gun?

JESSICA: Hugo, don't you know the rules of this game: what about the window? We can be seen from outside. [HUGO *goes to pull down the shades and then comes back to her.*]

HUGO: Well?

JESSICA [*producing the revolver, which she has tucked inside her dress*]: Hœderer would do well to hire a woman too, when he goes frisking. I shall offer him my services.

HUGO: When did you take it?

JESSICA: When you let the two watchdogs in.

HUGO: You had the laugh on all of us. I thought he had caught you in his trap.

JESSICA: Me? I just about laughed in his face: "I trust you! I trust everybody. This will teach you to be trusting. . . ." What did he think? The trick of trusting works on men only.

HUGO: Go on!

JESSICA: Calm yourself, my darling. You were really upset.

HUGO: I? When?

JESSICA: When he said he trusted you.

HUGO: No, I wasn't upset.

JESSICA: Yes.

HUGO: No.

JESSICA: In any case, if you ever leave me with a good-looking young man, don't tell me that you trust me, because I warn you: it wouldn't prevent me from deceiving you if I had a mind to. Quite the contrary.

HUGO: I am not at all disturbed. I would leave you with my eyes shut.

JESSICA: Do you suppose that I could be touched by emotion?

HUGO: No, my little snow-woman; I believe in that coldness of snow. The most passionate seducer would freeze his fingers. He would caress you to warm you a bit, and you would melt in his hands.

JESSICA: Idiot! I'm not playing now. [*A very brief silence.*] You were really frightened?

HUGO: Just now? No. I didn't believe it was happening. I watched them search the place, and I told myself: "We're in a play." Nothing seems to me to be entirely real.

JESSICA: Not even me?

HUGO: You? [*He looks at her for a moment and then turns his head away.*] Tell me, weren't you frightened too?

JESSICA: When I saw that they were going to search me. It was touch and go. I was sure that George would scarcely touch me, but Slick would have held me tight. I wasn't afraid he would find the gun: I was afraid of his hands.

HUGO: I shouldn't have dragged you into all this.

JESSICA: On the contrary, I always dreamed of being an adventuress.

HUGO: Jessica, this isn't a game. The man is dangerous.

JESSICA: Dangerous? To whom?

HUGO: To the party.

JESSICA: To the party? I thought he was its leader.

HUGO: He is *one* of the leaders; but that's just it; he—

JESSICA: Don't explain it to me. I believe what you said.

HUGO: What do you believe?

JESSICA [*as if reciting a lesson*]: I believe that this man is dangerous, that he should be removed, and that you are going to ki—

HUGO: Quiet! [*A pause.*] Look at me. Sometimes I tell myself that you only pretend to believe in me and that you really don't, and other times I tell myself that you really believe in me but that you pretend not to. Which is true?

JESSICA [*laughing*]: There is no truth.

HUGO: What would you do if I needed your help?

JESSICA: Haven't I just helped you?

HUGO: Yes, dear, but it's not that help that I want.

JESSICA: Ingrate.

HUGO [*looking at her*]: If I could only read your thoughts—

JESSICA: Ask me.

HUGO [*shrugging his shoulders*]: What's the use! [*A pause.*] Good God, when you're going to kill a man, you should be able to feel as heavy as stone. There should be silence in my head. [*Shouting*] Silence! [*A pause.*] Did you see how big he is? How alive? [*A pause.*] It's true! It's true! It's true that I'm going to kill him: in a week he'll be stretched out dead on the ground with five holes in him. [*A pause.*] What a comedy!

JESSICA [*begins to laugh*]: My poor little darling, if you want to convince me that you're going to become a murderer, you should start by convincing yourself.

HUGO: I don't seem to be convinced, do I?

JESSICA: Not at all: you're playing your part very badly

HUGO: But I'm not playing, Jessica.

JESSICA: Yes, you are.

HUGO: No, it's you who are playing. It's always you.

JESSICA: No, it's you. Besides, how could you kill him when I have the revolver?

HUGO: Give me that gun.

JESSICA: Not on your life: I've won it. If it hadn't been for me, you would have had it taken from you.

HUGO: Give me that gun.

JESSICA: No, I shall never give it back to you. I shall go
find Hœderer and tell him: "I have come to make you
happy," and when he embraces me— [HUGO, *who
pretends to be resigned to letting her keep the revolver,
suddenly springs on her and, as before, they fall on the
bed, struggling, shouting, and laughing.* HUGO *finally
seizes the gun while the curtain falls and she cries:*]
Careful! Careful! It'll go off!

ACT IV

HŒDERER'S OFFICE

An austere but comfortable room. To the right, a desk; in the center, a table covered with books and papers, with a scarf that extends down to the floor. To the left, a window through which one can see the trees of the garden. To the right rear, a door; to the left of the door, a kitchen table with a gas burner. On the burner a coffee pot. Chairs of various sorts. It is afternoon.

HUGO is alone. He approaches the desk, picks up HŒDERER's penholder, and plays with it. Then he goes back to the burner, picks up the coffee pot, and looks at it, whistling. JESSICA enters softly.

JESSICA: What are you doing with that coffee pot? [HUGO *hastily sets it down.*]

HUGO: Jessica, you were forbidden to enter this office.

JESSICA: What are you doing with that coffee pot?

HUGO: And what are *you* doing in here?

JESSICA: I came to see you, my love.

HUGO: Well, you've had a good look. Get out of here now. Hœderer is coming down.

JESSICA: How miserable I was without you, my little lamb!

HUGO: I have no time to play, Jessica.

JESSICA .[*looking about her*]: Of course you couldn't describe anything to me. This room smells of stale tobacco, like my father's office when I was a girl. Yet it would have been so easy to talk about odors.

HUGO: Look here—

JESSICA: Wait! [*She reaches into the pocket of her jacket.*] I came to bring you this.

HUGO: What?

JESSICA [*taking the revolver from her pocket and presenting it to* HUGO *on the palm of her hand*]: There! You forgot it.

HUGO: I didn't forget it; I never carry it.

JESSICA: Exactly: you should always have it with you.

HUGO: Jessica, since you don't seem to understand, I must tell you outright that I forbid you to set foot here. If you want to play, you have the garden and the summerhouse.

JESSICA: Hugo, you're talking to me as if I were a child of six.

HUGO: And whose fault is that? It's become unendurable; you can scarcely look at me now without laughing. It's going to be just dandy when we are fifty. We must get out of it; it's only a habit, you know, a filthy habit we formed together. Do you understand me?

JESSICA: Very well.

HUGO: Will you make an effort?

JESSICA: Yes.

HUGO: Good. Then begin by putting the gun back where you found it.

JESSICA: I can't.

HUGO: Jessica!

JESSICA: It's yours, you have to take it.

HUGO: But I tell you I have no use for it.

JESSICA: And what do you want me to do with it?

HUGO: Whatever you like, it's no concern of mine.

JESSICA: You wouldn't force your wife to go around all day with a gun in her pocket?

HUGO: Go back to our room and put it in my suitcase.

JESSICA: But I don't want to go there; you're being horrible!

HUGO: You had no business to bring it here in the first place.

JESSICA: And you shouldn't have forgotten it.

HUGO: I tell you, I didn't forget it.

JESSICA: No? Then, Hugo, you must have changed your plans.

HUGO: Be quiet.

JESSICA: Hugo, look me in the eyes. Have you changed your plans or haven't you?

HUGO: No, I haven't.

JESSICA: Yes or no, do you intend to—

HUGO: Yes! Yes! Yes! But not today.

JESSICA: Oh, Hugo, my little Hugo, why not today? I'm so bored, I've read all the novels you gave me and I don't fancy spending the whole day in bed like an odalisque; it makes me fat. What are you waiting for?

HUGO: Jessica, you're still playing.

JESSICA: You're the one who's playing. For ten days now you've put on grand airs to impress me, but he's still living. If this is a game, it's taking much too long: we have to talk in whispers all the time for fear of being heard, and I have to put up with all your whims as if you were a pregnant woman.

HUGO: You know perfectly well that this is not a game.

JESSICA [*dryly*]: Then it's much worse: I loathe people who can't finish what they set out to do. If you want me to believe in you, you'll have to get it done with today.

HUGO: Today would be inopportune.

JESSICA [*in her normal voice*]: You see!

HUGO: You drive me mad! He's expecting visitors today.

JESSICA: How many?

HUGO: Two.

JESSICA: Kill them too.

HUGO: There's no one who is a worse pest than somebody who insists on playing when nobody else wants to. I'm not asking you to help me. Not at all! I simply want you not to bother me.

JESSICA: Very well, very well! Do as you like, since you insist on keeping me outside your life. But take this gun, because if I keep it it'll make my pocket sag.

HUGO: If I take it will you go?

JESSICA: Take it first.

[HUGO *takes the revolver and puts it in his pocket.*]

HUGO: Now beat it.

JESSICA: One moment! I have a right to look at the office where my husband works. [*She goes behind* HOEDERER'S *desk. Indicating the desk*] Who sits here? He or you?

HUGO [*ill-humoredly*]: He does. [*Pointing to the table*] I work at this table.

JESSICA [*without hearing him*]: Is this his handwriting? [*She takes a sheet of paper off the desk.*]

HUGO: Yes.

JESSICA [*with lively interest*]: Ha, ha, ha!

HUGO: Put that down.

JESSICA: Did you notice those flourishes? And that he prints his letters without connecting them?

HUGO: So what?

JESSICA: What do you mean, so what? It's very important.

HUGO: For whom?

JESSICA: To know his character. It's just as well to know the man you are going to kill. Look at the spaces he leaves between the words! Each letter is like a little island; the words are like archipelagoes. That certainly means something.

HUGO: What?

JESSICA: I don't know. It's so provoking: his childhood memories, the women he's had, his way of loving, all that is right there in his handwriting, and I don't know how to read it. Hugo, you must buy me a book on graphology, I feel I have a talent for it.

HUGO: I'll buy you one if you get out of here right now.

JESSICA: This looks just like a piano stool.

HUGO: That's just what it is.

JESSICA [*seating herself on the stool and spinning on it*]: What fun! When he sits down, he smokes, he talks, and spins on his piano stool.

HUGO: Yes. [JESSICA *uncorks a flask that is on the desk and sniffs it.*]

JESSICA: He drinks?

HUGO: Like a fish.

JESSICA: While he's working?

HUGO: Yes.

JESSICA: And he's never drunk?

HUGO: Never.

JESSICA: I hope that you never touch alcohol, even if he offers you a drink; you can't hold it.

HUGO: Don't big-sister me; I know perfectly well that I can't stand alcohol, nor tobacco, nor heat, nor cold, nor humidity, nor the smell of hay. I can't stand anything.

JESSICA [*slowly*]: Here he sits, he talks, he smokes, he drinks, he turns on his pedestal—

HUGO: Yes, and I, I—

JESSICA [*spying the gas burner*]: What's that doing here? Does he do his own cooking?

HUGO: Yes.

JESSICA [*bursting into laughter*]: But why? I could do it for him, since I do it for you. He could come and eat with us.

HUGO: You can't cook as well as he does; and anyway, I think he enjoys it. In the morning he makes coffee for us. Very good coffee, from the black market.

JESSICA [*pointing to the coffee pot*]: In that?

HUGO: Yes.

JESSICA: That's the coffee pot you were holding when I came in, isn't it?

HUGO: Yes.

JESSICA: What were you doing with it? What were you trying to find out?

HUGO: I don't know. [*A pause.*] It seems real when he touches it. [*He picks it up.*] Everything he touches seems real. He pours the coffee in the cups. I drink. I watch him drinking and I feel that the taste of the coffee in his mouth is real. [*A pause.*] That it's the real flavor of coffee, real warmth, the real essence that is going to vanish. Only this will be left. [*He picks up the coffee pot.*]

JESSICA: Just that?

HUGO [*taking in the whole room with a sweep of his arm*]: All that is here: lies. [*He sets down the coffee pot.*] I live in a stage set. [*He is absorbed in his thoughts.*]

JESSICA: Hugo!

HUGO [*starting*]: Yes?

JESSICA: The smell of tobacco will go when he is dead. [*Suddenly*] Don't kill him.

HUGO: Then you do believe I'm going to kill him? Answer me. Do you believe it?

JESSICA: I don't know. Everything here seems so peaceful. It all seems to remind me of my childhood. Nothing will happen! Nothing can happen, you're just teasing me.

HUGO: Here he is. Out through the window. [*He tries to force her.*]

JESSICA [*resisting*]: I should like to watch you when you are alone.

HUGO [*dragging her*]: Out, and quick.

JESSICA: At my father's place I would get under the table and watch him work for hours.

[HUGO *opens the window with his left hand.* JESSICA *frees herself and slips under the table.* HŒDERER *enters.*]

HŒDERER: What are you doing under there?

JESSICA: I'm hiding.

HŒDERER: Hiding? From what?

JESSICA: I want to see what you're like when I'm not here.

HŒDERER: It's no go. [*To* HUGO] Who let her in?

HUGO: I don't know.

HŒDERER: She's your wife. Can't you control her any better than that?

JESSICA: My poor lamb, he takes you for my husband.

HŒDERER: Isn't he your husband?

JESSICA: He's my younger brother.

HŒDERER [*to* HUGO]: She doesn't respect you.

HUGO: No.

HŒDERER: Why did you marry her?

HUGO: Because she didn't respect me.

HŒDERER: When you're in the party, you marry someone from the party.

JESSICA: Why?

HŒDERER: It's simpler.

JESSICA: How do you know that I'm not a party member?

HŒDERER: That's evident. [_He looks at her._] You're not good at anything, except love.

JESSICA: Not even at love. [_A pause._] Do you think I ought to join the party?

HŒDERER: You can do as you please. The case is hopeless.

JESSICA: Is that my fault?

HŒDERER: How do I know? I suppose that you're half victim and half accomplice, like everybody else.

JESSICA [_with sudden violence_]: I'm no one's accomplice. Things were decided for me without asking my opinion.

HŒDERER: That's very possible. In any case, the emancipation of women doesn't interest me.

JESSICA [_indicating_ HUGO]: Do you think I'm bad for him?

HŒDERER: Did you come here to ask me that?

JESSICA: Why not?

HŒDERER: I suppose you're his luxury. The sons of the bourgeoisie who come to us have a mania for bringing along with them a bit of the luxury they knew, like a souvenir. With some it's their freedom to think, with others a stickpin. With him, it's his wife.

JESSICA: Yes. And you, of course, have no need for luxury.

HŒDERER: Naturally. [_They face each other._] Go on, now, beat it, and never set foot in here again.

JESSICA: Very well. I leave you to your masculine friendship. [_She goes out with dignity._]

HŒDERER: You are fond of her?

HUGO: Naturally.

HŒDERER: Then forbid her to set foot in here. When I have to choose between a man and a woman, I choose the man. But you mustn't make the task too difficult for me.

HUGO: Who asks you to choose?

HŒDERER: No matter. Anyway, I chose you.

HUGO [_laughing_]: You don't know Jessica.

HŒDERER: That's very possible. And so much the better. [_A pause._] Just the same, tell her not to come back. [_Sharply_] What time is it?

HUGO: Ten after four.

HŒDERER: They're late. [*He goes to the window, looks outside, and then turns around.*]

HUGO: Do you want me to take dictation?

HŒDERER: Not today. [HUGO *makes a move.*] No. Stay. Ten after four?

HUGO: Yes.

HŒDERER: If they don't come, they'll regret it.

HUGO: Who's coming?

HŒDERER: You'll see. People from your world. [*He paces back and forth.*] I don't like to wait. [*Approaching* HUGO] If they come, the matter is as good as settled; but if they are afraid at the last moment, we'll have to start all over again. And I believe I shan't have the time for that. How old are you?

HUGO: Twenty-one.

HŒDERER: You, you've got time.

HUGO: You're not so old either.

HŒDERER: I'm not old, but I'm on the spot. [*He shows* HUGO *the garden.*] On the other side of those walls, there are men who think night and day of getting me; and since I don't think all the time of protecting myself, sooner or later they're sure to succeed.

HUGO: How do you know they think of it night and day?

HŒDERER: Because I know them. They're always logical.

HUGO: You know who they are?

HŒDERER: Yes. Did you hear the sound of a car?

HUGO: No. [*They listen.*] No.

HŒDERER: This would be the moment for one of them to jump over the wall. He'd have a chance a pull a good job.

HUGO [*slowly*]: This would be the moment—

HŒDERER [*watching him*]: You understand, it would be better for them if I were unable to receive these visitors. [*He goes to the desk and pours a drink.*] Will you have one?

HUGO: No. [*A pause.*] Are you afraid?

HŒDERER: Of what?

HUGO: Of dying.

HŒDERER: No, but I'm in a hurry. I'm always in a hurry. Once I could wait. Now I can't.

HUGO: How you must hate them!

HŒDERER: Why? In principle, I have no objection to political assassination. All parties do it.

HUGO: Give me a drink.

HŒDERER [*surprised*]: Well! [*He takes the bottle and pours a drink.* HUGO *drinks without taking his eyes from him.*] What are you looking at? Haven't you ever seen me before?

HUGO: No. I've never seen you before.

HŒDERER: For you I am only a stopping-off place. That's natural. You can look at me from the perspective of your future. You say to yourself: "I'll spend two or three years with this guy, and when he's dead I'll go somewhere else and do something else."

HUGO: I don't know if I'll ever do anything else.

HŒDERER: Twenty years from now you'll say to your pals: "That was the time when I was Hœderer's secretary." Twenty years from now. That's rich!

HUGO: In twenty years—

HŒDERER: Well?

HUGO: It's far off.

HŒDERER: Why? Are you a lunger?

HUGO: No. Give me another drink. [HŒDERER *pours him a drink.*] I always felt I'd never make old age. I'm too much in a hurry, too.

HŒDERER: It's not the same thing.

HUGO: No. [*A pause.*] Sometimes I would cut off my hand to grow up all at once, and at other times I feel that I don't want to survive my youth.

HŒDERER: I don't know what it is.

HUGO: What?

HŒDERER: Youth, I don't know what it is: I went directly from childhood to maturity.

HUGO: Yes. It's a bourgeois malady. [*He laughs.*] And many people die of it.

HŒDERER: Would you like me to help you?

HUGO: How?

HŒDERER: You seem off to a bad start. Do you want me to help you?

HUGO [*with a start*]: Not you! [*He collects himself quickly.*] No one can help me.

HŒDERER [*going up to him*]: Look here, son. [*He stops and listens.*] Here they are. [*He goes to the window.* HUGO *follows him.*] The tall one is Karsky, the secretary of the Pentagon. The fat one is Prince Paul.

HUGO: The Regent's son?

HŒDERER: Yes. [*His expression has changed; he has an air of indifference now, hardness, and self-assurance.*] You've had enough to drink. Give me your glass. [*He empties it out the window.*] Go and sit down; listen to everything that is said, and if I give you a sign, take notes. [*He shuts the window and seats himself at his desk.*]

[KARSKY *and* PRINCE PAUL *enter, followed by* SLICK *and* GEORGE, *who cover them with their machine guns.*]

KARSKY: I'm Karsky.

HŒDERER [*without getting up*]: I recognized you.

KARSKY: You know this gentleman?

HŒDERER: Yes.

KARSKY: Then send away your watchdogs.

HŒDERER: That'll do. Beat it. [SLICK *and* GEORGE *leave.*]

KARSKY [*ironically*]: You are well protected.

HŒDERER: If I hadn't taken precautions recently, I wouldn't have the pleasure of receiving you.

KARSKY [*turning toward* HUGO]: And this one?

HŒDERER: My secretary. He's staying.

KARSKY [*going up to* HUGO]: You are Hugo Barine? [HUGO *doesn't reply.*] Are you with these people?

HUGO: Yes.

KARSKY: I saw your father last week. Would you still be interested in any news of him?

HUGO: No.

KARSKY: It is very likely that you will bear the responsibility for his death.

HUGO: It is practically certain that he bears the responsibility for my life, so we are even.

KARSKY [without raising his voice]: You are a little wretch.

HUGO: Tell me—

HŒDERER: Be quiet. [To KARSKY]: You didn't come here to insult my secretary? Please be seated. [They sit down.] Cognac?

KARSKY: Thank you.

THE PRINCE: Delighted. [HŒDERER serves him.]

KARSKY: So this is the famous Hœderer. [He looks at him.] The other day your men fired on ours again.

HŒDERER: Why?

KARSKY: We have a cache of arms in a garage and your men wanted them: it's as simple as that.

HŒDERER: Did they get them?

KARSKY: Yes.

HŒDERER: Nicely done.

KARSKY: There's nothing to be proud of: they outnumbered us ten to one.

HŒDERER: When the point is to win, ten to one is the right proportion. That way it's surer.

KARSKY: Let's drop the subject; I don't think we could ever come to an understanding. We just don't belong to the same race of men.

HŒDERER: We're the same race, but not the same class.

THE PRINCE: Gentlemen, let's get down to business.

HŒDERER: Good. I'm listening to you.

KARSKY: But we are the ones who want to hear from you.

HŒDERER: There must be some misunderstanding.

KARSKY: Very likely. If I hadn't thought you had a definite offer to make us, I wouldn't have troubled to come to see you.

HŒDERER: I have nothing to propose.

KARSKY: That's perfect. [He gets to his feet.]

THE PRINCE: Please, please, gentlemen. Sit down, Karsky. This is a bad way to begin. Shouldn't we introduce a little plain dealing into the discussion?

KARSKY [*to the* PRINCE]: Plain dealing? Did you see his
eyes when his two watchdogs shoved us in here with
their machine guns? These people hate us. I consented
to the interview only because of your insistence, but
I'm convinced that no good·will come of it.

THE PRINCE: Karsky, last year you organized two attempts
against my father, yet I was willing to meet you. We
haven't perhaps many reasons to like each other, but
our personal feelings don't enter into it when the
national interest is at stake. [*A pause.*] This interest,
of course, we don't always interpret in the same way.
You, Hœderer, think of it perhaps somewhat too
exclusively in terms of the legitimate claims of the
working class. My father and I, who have always been
favorable to these claims, have been obliged, because
of the threatening attitude of Germany, to relegate
them to a secondary plane, because we recognized that
our first duty was to safeguard the independence of our
territories, even at the price of unpopular measures.

HŒDERER: You mean by declaring war on the U.S.S.R.

THE PRINCE [*continuing*]: On the other hand, Karsky
and his friends, who do not share our point of view
on foreign policy, have perhaps underestimated the
need for Illyria to present a strong and united front
to the outside world, one people behind a single
leader, and they have formed an underground resistance movement. Thus it happens that men equally
honest, equally devoted to their fatherland, are mo-
mentarily separated by different conceptions of their
duty. [HŒDERER *laughs rudely.*] I beg your pardon?

HŒDERER: Nothing. Go on.

THE PRINCE: Fortunately today our positions are not so
far apart, and it seems that each of us has a keener
understanding of the point of view of the others. My
father does not wish to continue this useless and costly
war. Naturally we are not in a position to conclude
a separate peace, but I can assure you that military
operations will be conducted in the future without un-
due zeal. As for Karsky, he realizes now that internal

divisions can only be a disservice to the cause of our
country, and wants both of us to prepare for the
imminent peace by bringing about a national front.
Naturally this united front cannot come into the open
without stirring the suspicions of the Germans, but
the framework for it can be worked out in the underground organizations that already exist.

HŒDERER: And then?

THE PRINCE: Well, that's about all. Karsky and I want
you to announce the good news that we agree in
principle.

HŒDERER: Why should that interest me?

KARSKY: That's enough; we are wasting our time.

THE PRINCE [*continuing*]: It goes without saying that
this front should be as broad as possible. If the Proletarian Party expresses a desire to join us—

HŒDERER: What do you offer?

KARSKY: Two votes for your party in the national underground committee we shall set up.

HŒDERER: Two votes out of how many?

KARSKY: Out of twelve.

HŒDERER [*pretending to be politely surprised*]: Two votes
out of twelve?

KARSKY: The Regent will send four of his advisers as
delegates, and six other votes will go to the Pentagon.
The chairman is to be elected.

HŒDERER [*chuckling*]: Two votes out of twelve.

KARSKY: The Pentagon includes the major part of the
peasantry—that is to say, fifty-seven per cent of the
population—plus almost the whole of the middle class.
The workers scarcely represent twenty per cent of the
population, and you don't even have all of them behind
you.

HŒDERER: Right. Go on.

KARSKY: We shall reorganize and fuse the structure of
our two underground organizations. Your men will
enter our echelons.

HŒDERER: You mean that the Pentagon will absorb our
troops.

KARSKY: That's the best formula for reconciliation.

HŒDERER: How right you are: reconciliation by means of the annihilation of one of your opponents. That achieved, it's perfectly logical to grant us only two votes on the Central Committee. Even that's too many: the two votes would represent nothing.

KARSKY: No one is forcing you to accept.

THE PRINCE [*hastily*]: But if you accept, of course, the government would be ready to set aside the laws of '39 controlling the press, union organization, and labor legislation.

HŒDERER: Very tempting! [*He raps on the table.*] Excellent. Well, we have become acquainted; now let's get to work. Here are my conditions: a steering committee reduced to six members. The Proletarian Party is to have three votes; you can divide the other three as you see fit. The underground organizations are to remain distinct and separate and will undertake joint action only on the decision of the Central Committee. Take it or leave it.

KARSKY: Do you take us for fools?

HŒDERER: No one is forcing you to accept.

KARSKY [*to* THE PRINCE]: I told you that you can't deal with these people. We have two thirds of the country, money, arms, trained military groups, not to speak of the moral superiority given us by our martyrs. Here is a handful of men without a penny who calmly claim a majority of the Central Committee.

HŒDERER: Then the answer is no?

KARSKY: Definitely. We'll manage without you.

HŒDERER: Very well, then; you may leave. [KARSKY *hesitates for a moment, then makes for the door.* THE PRINCE *doesn't budge.*] Look at the Prince, Karsky; he's sharper than you. He already understands.

THE PRINCE [*to* KARSKY, *smoothly*]: We can't reject these proposals without a discussion.

KARSKY [*violently*]: These are not proposals. These are absurd ultimatums, which I refuse to discuss. [*But he makes no move to withdraw.*]

HŒDERER: In '42 the police hunted your men and ours. You organized attempts on the life of the Regent and we sabotaged war production. When a man from the Pentagon met one of our boys, one of the two was killed on the spot. And today, suddenly, you want us all to embrace. Why?

THE PRINCE: For the good of the fatherland.

HŒDERER: Why isn't it the same good as in '42? [*A silence.*] Isn't it because the Russians beat Paulus at Stalingrad, and because the German troops are about to lose the war?

THE PRINCE: It's obvious that the general tendency of the conflict has created a new situation. But I don't see—

HŒDERER: On the contrary, I am sure that your vision is perfectly good. You want to save Illyria, of that I'm convinced. But you want to save it as it stands, with its regime of social inequality and its class privileges. When the Germans seemed on the point of victory, your father supported them. Today the tables are turned, and he seeks the favor of the Russians. But this is more difficult.

KARSKY: Hœderer, too many of our men fell in struggling against Germany for me to let you say that we compromised with the enemy to preserve our privileges.

HŒDERER: I know, Karsky: the Pentagon was anti-German. You had the perfect set-up: the Regent paid off Hitler to prevent the invasion of Illyria. But you were also anti-Russian, because the Russians were far off. "Illyria, and Illyria alone": I know the song well. You sang it for two years to the nationalist bourgeoisie. But the Russians are approaching; in a year they will be with us; Illyria won't be utterly alone. And so? You'll have to make compromises. What a stroke of luck if you could say to them: the Pentagon worked for you, and the Regent played a double game! There's just this difficulty: they don't have to believe you. What will they do, eh? What will they do? After all, we declared war on them.

THE PRINCE: My dear Hœderer, when the U.S.S.R. understands that we sincerely—

HŒDERER: When it understands that a fascist dictator and a conservative party flew sincerely to its side when its victory was assured, I doubt whether it will be very grateful. [*A pause.*] A single party has the confidence of the U.S.S.R., a single party has remained in contact with it throughout the war, a single party can send emissaries to it through the lines; only one party can guarantee your little scheme; and that is our party. When the Russians are here, they shall see through our eyes. [*A pause.*] Gentlemen, I'm afraid you'll have to do it our way.

KARSKY: I should have refused to come here.

THE PRINCE: Karsky!

KARSKY: I should have foreseen that you would reply to honest proposals with a contemptible piece of blackmail.

HŒDERER: Squeal if you like: I'm not susceptible. Squeal like a stuck pig. But remember this: when the Soviet armies are on our soil, we can take power together, your people and mine, if in the meantime we work together. But if we don't come to an understanding, at the end of the war, my party will govern *alone*. You must decide now.

KARSKY: I—

THE PRINCE [*to* KARSKY]: Violence will get us nowhere. We must take a realistic view of the situation.

KARSKY [*to* THE PRINCE]: You're a coward. You brought me into a trap to save your neck.

HŒDERER: What trap? Go if you wish to. The Prince and I can come to an agreement without you.

KARSKY [*to* THE PRINCE]: You wouldn't—

THE PRINCE: Why not? If the arrangement doesn't suit you, you don't have to accept; but my decision doesn't depend on yours.

HŒDERER: It goes without saying that my party's support of the Regent's government would put the Pentagon in a difficult situation during the last months of the war. It is also evident that we shall proceed to liquidate it completely when the Germans are defeated. But if you insist on remaining above—

KARSKY: We fought for three years for the independence of our country. Thousands of young men died for our cause. We've won the respect of the whole world. And now all of this is to go for nothing so that the pro-German party can join with the pro-Russian party and shoot us down in some dark corner.

HŒDERER: Don't be sentimental, Karsky. You've lost because you played a losing game. "Illyria, and Illyria alone"—in that slogan there's small protection for a tiny country surrounded by powerful neighbors. [*A pause.*] Do you accept my conditions?

KARSKY: I don't have the authority to accept: I'm not the only one who has to decide.

HŒDERER: I'm pressed for time, Karsky.

THE PRINCE: My dear Hœderer, perhaps we should give him time to think it over: the war isn't over and isn't likely to be in the next week.

HŒDERER: I may be finished in a week. Karsky, I trust you. I always trust people on principle. I know that you will have to consult your friends, but I also know that you can convince them. If you accept on principle today, I will speak tomorrow to my party comrades.

HUGO [*suddenly jumping to his feet*]: Hœderer!

HŒDERER: What now?

HUGO: How dare you—?

HŒDERER: Shut up.

HUGO: You have no right. They are—my God, they are the same ones! The same ones who used to come to my father's home. The same sneering and frivolous mouths, and—and they seek me out even here. You have no right, they'll slide in every place and ruin everything. They are the strongest—

HŒDERER: Will you be quiet!

HUGO: Look here, you two: the party won't support him in this scheme! Don't count on him to whitewash you; the party isn't with him.

HŒDERER [*calmly to the two others*]: It's of no importance. A strictly personal reaction.

THE PRINCE: Yes, but this outburst annoys me. Couldn't we have your guards make the young man leave?

HŒDERER: No need for that. He'll go himself. [*He gets up and goes toward* HUGO.]

HUGO [*stepping back*]: Don't touch me. [*He puts his hand in the pocket that holds his revolver.*] Won't you listen to me? Won't you listen to me? [*At this moment a loud explosion is heard. The windowpanes are shattered, and the sashes of the window are torn off.*]

HŒDERER: Hit the ground! Duck! [*He seizes* HUGO *by the shoulders and throws him to the ground. The other two flatten out also.*]

[LEON, SLICK, GEORGE *enter on the run.*]

SLICK: You hurt?

HŒDERER [*getting up*]: No. Anyone wounded? [*To* KARSKY, *who has got to his feet*] You're bleeding!

KARSKY: It's nothing. Some splinters of glass.

GEORGE: A grenade?

HŒDERER: A grenade or a bomb. Their aim was short. Search the garden.

HUGO [*who is already by the window*]: The bastards! The dirty bastards!

[LEON *and* GEORGE *leap through the window.*]

HŒDERER [*to* THE PRINCE]: I expected something like this. But I'm sorry that they picked this moment.

THE PRINCE: Pooh! It reminds me of my father's palace. Karsky! Are your men responsible for this?

KARSKY: Are you mad?

HŒDERER: I am the one they wanted to get. They were after me and nobody else. [*To* KARSKY] You see? It's best to take precautions. [*He looks at him.*] You're still bleeding.

[JESSICA *enters, out of breath.*]

JESSICA: Was Hœderer killed?

HŒDERER: Your husband is all right. [*To* KARSKY] Leon will take you up to my room and bandage that for you. Then we'll be able to go on with the discussion.

SLICK: You better all go up there; they might try again. You can talk while Leon patches him up.

HŒDERER: Fine.

[GEORGE *and* LEON *return through the window.*]

GEORGE: A bomb! Someone threw it from the garden and then scrammed. The wall took most of it.

HUGO: The dirty bastards.

HŒDERER: Let's go. [*He motions them toward the door.* HUGO *is about to follow them.*] Not you. [*They look at each other, then* HŒDERER *turns away and goes out.*]

HUGO [*between his teeth*]: The dirty bastards.

SLICK: What?

HUGO: The ones who threw that firecracker, they're dirty bastards. [*He goes to pour himself a drink.*]

SLICK: You're a little nervous, huh?

HUGO: Bah!

SLICK: Don't be ashamed. This is the first time, eh? You'll get used to it.

GEORGE: I really ought to tell you, eventually it's a welcome distraction. Right, Slick?

SLICK: It's a change—puts you on your toes again, takes the stiffness out of your joints.

HUGO: I'm not nervous. I'm furious. [*He takes a drink.*]

JESSICA: At whom, my little lamb?

HUGO: At the bastards who let off that blast.

SLICK: Don't let it get you down; it's a long time since we got so excited.

GEORGE: It's our business; if it weren't for them, we wouldn't be here.

HUGO: That's the way it is: everyone is calm, everyone smiles, everyone is happy. He bleeds like a pig, wipes his cheek, smiling, and says: "It's nothing." They have guts. They're the greatest sons of bitches on earth, and they've got guts, if only to keep you from despising them utterly. [*Sadly*] It's a problem. [*He drinks.*] Virtues and vices are not equitably distributed.

JESSICA: You're not a coward, my love.

HUGO: I'm not cowardly, but I'm not courageous either.

Too many nerves. I should like to go to sleep and dream that I'm Slick. Look at him: two hundred and twenty pounds of meat and a peanut for a brain. He's a real whale. The peanut up above sends out signals of fear and rage, but they're lost in all that mass. It tickles him, that's all.

SLICK [*laughing*]: You hear that?

GEORGE [*laughing*]: He's not so wrong.

[HUGO *drinks*.]

JESSICA: Hugo!

HUGO: What?

JESSICA: Don't drink any more.

HUGO: Why not? There's nothing more for me to do. I've been relieved of my duties.

JESSICA: Hœderer relieved you of your duties?

HUGO: Hœderer? Who's talking about Hœderer? You can think what you like of Hœderer, but he's a man who trusted me. You can't say as much for everybody. [*He drinks, then goes up to* SLICK.] Some guys entrust you with a confidential mission, and you work your ass off to carry it out. And then, at the very moment you might have done it, you see that they don't give a damn for you, and that they had the job pulled off by somebody else.

JESSICA: Will you be quiet? You're not going to tell them all about our married life.

HUGO: Our married life? Ha! [*Cheering up*] Isn't she wonderful?

JESSICA: He's talking about me. For two years he's been reproaching me for not trusting him.

HUGO [*to* SLICK]: What a character, eh? [*To* JESSICA] No, you don't trust me. Or do you?

JESSICA: Certainly not at this moment.

HUGO: Nobody trusts me. There must be something wrong with my face. Tell me you love me.

JESSICA: Not in front of them.

SLICK: Don't mind us.

HUGO: She doesn't love me. She doesn't know what love is. She's an angel. A statue of salt.

SLICK: A statue of salt?

HUGO: No, I mean a statue of snow. When you caress her, she melts.

GEORGE: No kidding.

JESSICA: Come along, Hugo.

HUGO: Wait a minute, I want to give Slick some advice. I like Slick very much, I have a soft spot for him, because he's strong and never thinks. Do you want some advice, Slick?

SLICK: If I can't get out of it.

HUGO: Listen: don't marry too young.

SLICK: No danger of that.

HUGO [*beginning to show he is drunk*]: No, but listen anyway: don't marry too young. You understand what I mean? Don't marry too young. Don't take up a burden that you can't bear. Later on you'll find it's too heavy. Everything is so heavy. I don't know if you've noticed, but it's no fun being young. [*He laughs.*] A confidential mission. Well, where's the confidence?

GEORGE: What mission?

HUGO: I've been entrusted with a mission.

GEORGE: What mission?

HUGO: They would like to get me to talk, but seeing it's me, they're wasting their time. I am impenetrable. [*He looks in the mirror.*] Impenetrable! An absolute poker face. A mug like everyone else's. Anyone could see that. Good God, anyone could see that!

GEORGE: What?

HUGO: That I've been entrusted with a confidential mission.

GEORGE: Slick?

SLICK: Hmmm.

JESSICA [*calmly*]: Don't puzzle your heads: he means I'm going to have a child. He's consulting the mirror to see if he looks like the head of a family.

HUGO: By God! The head of a family. That's it. That's just what I am. The head of a family. She and I understand each other so well. Impenetrable! By which you can recognize the—head of a family. A something.

A certain expression. A taste in the mouth. A thorn in the heart. [*He drinks.*] I'm sorry about Hœderer. Because, I tell you, he could have helped me. [*He laughs.*] Tell me: they're upstairs, aren't they, talking, while Leon is washing Karsky's dirty snout? What are you? Bumps on logs? Shoot me!

SLICK [*to* JESSICA]: This kid shouldn't drink.

GEORGE: He can't take it.

HUGO: Shoot me, I tell you. That's your trade. Listen closely: the head of a family is never really the head of a family. An assassin is never really an assassin. They play at it, you understand. While a dead man is really dead. To be or not to be, eh? You see what I mean. There's nothing I can be but a corpse under six feet of earth. The rest, I tell you, is clowning. [*He breaks off suddenly.*] And this too is clowning. All of it! All that I said here. Maybe you think that I'm desperate? Not at all: I'm acting out the comedy of despair. Will it ever end?

JESSICA: Do you want to go to our room?

HUGO: Wait. No. I don't know. How can I tell whether I want to or I don't want to?

JESSICA [*filling his glass*]: Then drink.

HUGO: Good. [*He drinks.*]

SLICK: You're crazy to give him any more to drink.

JESSICA: It's just to get this over with. Now all we have to do is wait.

[HUGO *empties the glass.* JESSICA *fills it again.*]

HUGO [*drunk*]: What did I say to you? I talked about assassins? Jessica and I know what that means. The truth is that there's too much talk in here. [*He taps his forehead.*] I would like it to be quiet. [*To* SLICK] It must be so nice inside your head: not a sound, just darkness. Why do you spin around so? Don't laugh; I know I'm drunk, I know I'm ridiculous. I'll tell you: I wouldn't want to be in my own shoes. Oh no. That's not a good spot. Hold still! The whole point is to light the fuse. It seems little enough, but I wouldn't want you to have to do it. The fuse, that's what it comes down to. Light the fuse. Then everybody is blown up and I along with them: no need for an alibi. Silence. Night. Unless the dead too play comedies. What if we die and discover that the dead are alive and are simply playing at being dead? We'll see. We'll see. The thing is to light the fuse. That's the psychological moment. [*He laughs.*] But don't turn so, good God, or I'll start spinning around too. [*He tries to spin around and falls across a chair.*] Such are the benefits of a bourgeois education. [*His head droops. *JESSICA *stands over him and looks at him.*]

JESSICA: Good. It's finished. Will you help me carry him to bed?

[SLICK *looks at him and scratches his head.*]

SLICK: He talks too much, your husband.

JESSICA [*laughing*]: You don't know him. Nothing he says really means anything.

[SLICK *and* GEORGE *lift him off the chair.*]

CURTAIN

ACT V

IN THE SUMMERHOUSE

HUGO *is stretched out on the bed, fully dressed, but un-der a cover. He is sleeping. He tosses and groans in his sleep.* JESSICA *sits motionless at the bedside. He continues to groan; she gets up and goes into the bathroom. There is the sound of water being drawn.* OLGA· *is hiding behind the window curtains. She parts the curtains and looks into the room. She makes a quick decision and approaches* HUGO. *She looks him over.* HUGO *groans.* OLGA *smooths his forehead and arranges his pillow. In the meantime* JESSICA *returns and observes this scene.* JESSICA *is holding a wet com-press.*

JESSICA: How touching! How do you do, madame?

OLGA: Don't scream. I am—

JESSICA: I have no intention of screaming. But please sit down. I have more of a mind to laugh.

OLGA: I am Olga Lorame.

JESSICA: I thought as much.

OLGA: Hugo told you about me?

JESSICA: Yes.

OLGA: Is he wounded?

JESSICA: No, he's drunk. [*Walking in front of* OLGA] Allow me. [*She puts the compress on* HUGO's *fore-head.*]

OLGA: Not like that. [*She rearranges the compress.*]

JESSICA: Excuse me.

OLGA: And Hœderer?

JESSICA: Hœderer? Do sit down please. [OLGA *sits down.*] It·was you, madame, who threw the bomb?

OLGA: Yes.

JESSICA: No one dead; better luck next time. How did you get in here?

OLGA: By the door. You left it open while you were gone. You should never leave doors open.

JESSICA [*pointing to* HUGO]: You knew that he was in the office?

OLGA: No.

JESSICA: But you knew that he might be there?

OLGA: The risk had to be taken.

JESSICA: With a bit of luck, you would have killed him.

OLGA: That's the best thing that could have happened to him.

JESSICA: Really?

OLGA: The party doesn't like traitors.

JESSICA: Hugo is no traitor.

OLGA: I believe it, but I can't make the others believe it. [*A pause.*] This business is taking much too long: the job should have been finished a week ago.

JESSICA: You have to wait for the right moment.

OLGA: You have to *make* the right moment.

JESSICA: Did the party send you?

OLGA: The party doesn't know I'm here. I came on my own account.

JESSICA: I see. You put a bomb in your handbag and kindly came to throw it at Hugo to save his reputation.

OLGA: If I had succeeded, they would have thought that he had given his life to kill Hœderer.

JESSICA: Yes, but he would be dead.

OLGA: However he goes about it, he hasn't much chance of getting out of it now.

JESSICA: Good friend, you are!

OLGA: Surely my friendship is better than your love. [*They face each other.*] You are the one who prevented him from doing his work?

JESSICA: I didn't hinder him in the least.

OLGA: But you didn't help him either.

JESSICA: Why should I have helped him? Did he consult me before he entered the party? And when he decided he had nothing better to do with his life than to go and assassinate a man he didn't know, did he consult me then?

OLGA: Why should he have consulted you? Could you
have advised him?

JESSICA: Evidently not.

OLGA: He chose this party; he requested this mission.
That ought to have been enough for you.

JESSICA: It's not enough for me.

[HUGO *groans*.]

OLGA: He's in bad shape. You shouldn't have let him
drink.

JESSICA: He would be in even worse shape if he had a
sliver of your bomb in his face. [*A pause*.] What a
shame he didn't marry you! He needs a resolute
woman. He could have stayed in your room ironing
your underwear while you went out throwing bombs
in the square. Then we should all have been very
happy. [*She looks her over*.] I thought you were big
and bony.

OLGA: With a mustache?

JESSICA: Not with a mustache, but with a wart under
your nose. He always had such an air of importance
when he came from seeing you. He would say: "We
talked politics."

OLGA: Naturally he never talked about politics with you.

JESSICA: You may be sure he didn't marry me for that.
[*A pause*.] You're in love with him, aren't you?

OLGA: What's love got to do with this? You read too
many novels.

JESSICA: You've got to do something when you're not in
politics.

OLGA: Set your mind at rest: love doesn't much bother
women of resolution. We don't live by it.

JESSICA: Whereas I, I suppose, do?

OLGA: Like all emotional women.

JESSICA: The emotional woman is all right with me. I
like my heart better than your head.

OLGA: Poor Hugo!

JESSICA: Yes. Poor Hugo! How you must detest me,
madame!

OLGA: I? I haven't the time to lose. [*A pause.*] Wake
him up. I have to talk to him.

JESSICA [*goes to the bed and shakes* HUGO]: Hugo! Hugo!
You have a visitor.

HUGO: What? [*He sits upright.*] Olga! Olga, you came!
I'm so glad to see you; you have to help me. [*He sits
on the edge of the bed.*] Good God, what a headache!
What are we? I'm really glad to see. you, you know.
Wait: something just struck me—a big annoyance. No,
I guess you can't help me any more. As things stand,
you can't help me any more. You threw the bomb,
didn't you?

OLGA: Yes.

HUGO: Why didn't you trust me?

OLGA: Hugo, in a quarter of an hour someone will throw
a rope over the wall and I'll have to go. I'm in a hurry
and you've got to listen.

HUGO: Why didn't you trust me?

OLGA: Jessica, give me that glass and that carafe.
[JESSICA *hands them to her. She fills the glass and
throws the water in* HUGO's *face.*]

HUGO: Phew!

OLGA: Are you listening?

HUGO: Yes. [*He wipes his face.*] What a headache! Is
there some more water in the carafe?

JESSICA: Yes.

HUGO: Pour me a drink, will you? [*She hands him the
glass and he drinks.*] What do the comrades think?

OLGA: They think you're a traitor.

HUGO: That's pretty strong.

OLGA: You haven't a day to lose. The matter must be
closed before tomorrow night.

HUGO: You shouldn't have thrown the bomb.

OLGA: Hugo, you wanted to take on a difficult task and
to take it on alone. I was the first to have confidence
in you when there were a hundred reasons to refuse,
and I passed my confidence on to the others. But
we're not Boy Scouts, and the party was not meant

to furnish you with occasions to play the hero. There's work to do and it has to be done; no matter who does it. If in twenty-four hours you haven't finished your job, we'll get someone else to do it instead.

HUGO: If I am replaced I'll leave the party.

OLGA: What kind of talk is that? Do you imagine that you can *leave* the party? We are at war, Hugo, and the comrades aren't fooling. One only leaves the party feet first.

HUGO: I'm not afraid to die.

OLGA: It's nothing at all to die. But to die so stupidly after fouling everything up; to be kicked around like a sucker; worse yet, to be disposed of like a little imbecile got rid of for fear he'll spoil everything— is that what you want? Was that what you wanted the first time you came to see me, when you seemed so happy and so proud? Why don't you say something to him! If you love him a little you can't want to have him shot like a dog.

JESSICA: You know perfectly well, Miss Lorame, that I don't understand politics.

OLGA: What have you decided?

HUGO: You shouldn't have thrown the bomb.

OLGA: What is your decision?

HUGO: You'll know tomorrow.

OLGA: Very well. Good-by, Hugo.

HUGO: Good-by, Olga.

JESSICA: See you again, madame.

OLGA: Turn off the lights. I mustn't be seen going out.
   [JESSICA *turns off the lights.* OLGA *opens the door and goes out.*]

JESSICA: Should I turn on the lights again?

HUGO: Wait. She may have to come back.
   [*They wait in the dark.*]

JESSICA: We could peek out of the windows and see what's happening.

HUGO: No. [*A silence.*]

JESSICA: You feel sick? [HUGO *doesn't answer.*] Answer while it's dark.

HUGO: I have a headache, that's all. [A *pause*.] Trust isn't so much, when it can't wait a week.

JESSICA: No, not much.

HUGO: How can you want to live when nobody believes in you?

JESSICA: Nobody ever believed in me, you least of all. Just the same, I got along.

HUGO: She was the only one who had a little trust in me.

JESSICA: Hugo—

HUGO: The only one, you know perfectly well. [A *pause*.] She must be safe now. I think we can put on the lights. [*He switches on the lights.* JESSICA *turns away abruptly.*] What's wrong?

JESSICA: It upsets me to see you again in the light.

HUGO: Do you want me to turn it off?

JESSICA: No. [*She turns toward him.*] You. You're going to kill a man.

HUGO: Do I know what I'm going to do?

JESSICA: Show me the revolver.

HUGO: Why?

JESSICA: I want to see how it works.

HUGO: You had it with you all afternoon.

JESSICA: It was just a toy then.

HUGO [*handing it to her*]: Careful.

JESSICA: Yes. [*She looks at it.*] It's funny.

HUGO: What's funny?

JESSICA: At this point it frightens me. Take it back. [A *pause*.] You are going to kill a man. [HUGO *begins to laugh.*] Why are you laughing?

HUGO: You believe that now! You decided to believe it?

JESSICA: Yes.

HUGO: You certainly picked the right moment; nobody else believes it now. [A *pause*.] Last week it might have helped me—

JESSICA: It's not my fault: I only believe what I see. Just this morning I couldn't even imagine him dead. [A *pause*.] I went into the office just now, and there was that fellow bleeding and you were all dead. Hœderer

was dead; I saw it on his face! If you don't kill him
they'll send someone else.

HUGO: I'll do it. [*A pause.*] The guy who was bleeding,
that was messy, wasn't it?

JESSICA: Yes, it was messy.

HUGO: Hœderer will bleed too.

JESSICA: Be quiet.

HUGO: He'll be stretched out on the ground with an
idiotic expression and he'll bleed into his clothes.

JESSICA [*slowly and in an undertone*]: Will you be quiet?

HUGO: She threw a bomb over the wall. Certainly nothing to be proud of; she didn't even see us. Anybody
can kill who isn't forced to see what he's doing. I was
going to shoot him. I was in the office, I looked them
in the eye and I was going to shoot. She's the one
who made me miss my chance.

JESSICA: You were really going to shoot him?

HUGO: I had my hand in my pocket and my finger on
the trigger.

JESSICA: And you were going to fire! Are you sure you
would have fired?

HUGO: I—I was lucky enough to be mad. Of course I was
going to shoot. Now we have to start from scratch.
[*He laughs.*] You heard her; they say I'm a traitor.
They've got it easy. Up there, when they decide that
a man's to die, it's as if they scratched a name off a
list; it's neat, and elegant. Here death is a chore.
The slaughterhouses are here. [*A pause.*] He drinks,
he smokes, he speaks to me of the party, he makes
plans, and I—I think only of the corpse he is going
to be; it's obscene. Did you notice his eyes?

JESSICA: Yes.

HUGO: You noticed how hard and brilliant his eyes are?
And how alive?

JESSICA: Yes.

HUGO: Maybe I'll hit him in the eyes when I shoot. You
aim at the belly, you know, but the gun jerks upward.

JESSICA: I like his eyes.

HUGO [*abruptly*]: It's so abstract.

JESSICA: What?

HUGO: A murder. I say, it's so abstract. You pull the trigger and after that you no longer know what goes on. [*A pause.*] If only you could shoot with your head turned away. [*A pause.*] I wonder why I'm saying all this to you.

JESSICA: So do I.

HUGO: Forgive me. [*A pause.*] And yet, if I were lying in this bed, about to die, you wouldn't abandon me, would you?

JESSICA: No.

HUGO: It's the same thing—killing and dying; it's just the same: you're just as alone. Now he has luck, he'll die only once. But I have had to kill him every minute for ten days. [*Abruptly*] What would you do, Jessica?

JESSICA: What do you mean?

HUGO: Look here, if I haven't killed him by tomorrow, I'll either have to disappear or go to them and say: do with me what you will. If I kill—[*He covers his face with his hand for a moment.*] What ought I to do? What would you do?

JESSICA: Me? You're asking me what I would do in your place?

HUGO: Whom do you want me to ask? I have no one but you in all the world.

JESSICA [*slowly*]: That's true. You have only me. No one but me. Poor Hugo. [*A pause.*] I would go to Hœderer and say to him: "It's like this. I was sent here to kill you, but I've changed my mind and I want to work with you."

HUGO: Poor Jessica!

JESSICA: Couldn't you do that?

HUGO: That's exactly what's called treason.

JESSICA [*sadly*]: You see? I can't advise you. [*A pause.*] But why couldn't you do it? Because he doesn't think like you?

HUGO: If you like. Because he doesn't think like me.

JESSICA: And you have to kill the people who don't think your way?

HUGO: Sometimes.

JESSICA: But why did you choose the ideas of Louis and Olga?

HUGO: Because their ideas are correct.

JESSICA: But, Hugo, suppose you had met Hœderer last year, instead of Louis. It's his ideas that would have seemed to you to be the right ones.

HUGO: You're crazy.

JESSICA: Why?

HUGO: To hear you, one would think that all opinions have the same weight, that one catches them like a disease.

JESSICA: I didn't mean that; I—I don't know what I mean. Hugo, he is so strong that he just has to open his mouth and you're sure that he's right. And then, it seemed to me he was sincere when he said that he wanted the good of the party.

HUGO: I don't care what he thinks or what he wants. What counts is what he does.

JESSICA: But—

HUGO: *Objectively*, he's acting like a class traitor.

JESSICA [*not understanding*]: Objectively?

HUGO: Yes.

JESSICA: Ah! [*A pause.*] And he, if he knew what you are up to, wouldn't he consider you a class traitor?

HUGO: I have no idea.

JESSICA: But isn't that what he would think?

HUGO: What of it? Yes, probably.

JESSICA: But who is right?

HUGO: I'm right.

JESSICA: How do you know?

HUGO: Politics is a science. You can demonstrate that you are right and that others are wrong.

JESSICA: So in this case why do you hesitate?

HUGO: That would take too long to explain.

JESSICA: We have all night.

HUGO: It would take months and years.

JESSICA: Oh. [*She goes to the books on the table.*] Is it all written in here?

HUGO: In a way, yes. If you know how to read them.

JESSICA: Good Lord! [*She takes one up, opens it, looks at it fascinated, and sets it down sighing.*] Good heavens!

HUGO: Now let me be. Sleep or do whatever you like.

JESSICA: What's wrong? What have I said?

HUGO: Nothing. You didn't say anything. I'm the guilty party: it was mad to ask your help. Your advice comes from another world.

JESSICA: Whose fault is that? Why was I never taught anything? Why didn't you explain anything to me? You heard what he said: that I was your luxury. For nineteen years now I've been in your man's world, with signs everywhere saying: "Do not touch," made to believe that everything was going very well, that there was nothing for me to do except to arrange flowers in vases. Why did you lie to me? Why did you leave me in ignorance if it was only to confess to me one fine day that the world is falling to pieces and that you're not up to your responsibilities, forcing me to choose between a suicide and an assassination. I don't want to choose: I don't want you to get yourself killed, and I don't want you to kill him. Why have you thrust the burden on my shoulders? I don't understand this whole business and I wash my hands of it. I am neither an oppressor nor a class traitor nor a revolutionary. I've done nothing. I am innocent of everything.

HUGO: I won't ask you anything any more, Jessica.

JESSICA: It's too late, Hugo; you've got me into it, and now I have to choose. For both of us: it's my life that I'm choosing with yours, and I— Oh my God! I can't.

HUGO: Now you understand.

[*A pause.* HUGO *sits on the bed and stares into space.* JESSICA *sits near him and puts her arms around his neck.*]

JESSICA: Don't say a word. Don't bother about me. I won't speak to you; I won't disturb your thinking.

But I'll be here. It'll be cold in the morning: you'll be
glad to have a little of my warmth, since I have nothing
else to give you. Your head still hurts?

HUGO: Yes.

JESSICA: Here, rest it on my shoulder. Your forehead is
burning up. [*She caresses his hair.*] Poor head.

HUGO [*suddenly straightening up*]: That's enough!

JESSICA [*tenderly*]: Hugo.

HUGO: You're playing mother.

JESSICA: I'm not playing, I'll never pretend any more.

HUGO: Your body is cold and you have no warmth to
give me. It's not difficult to lean over a man with a
maternal air and run your hand through his hair. Any
girl in her teens would like to be in your place. But
when I took you in my arms and asked you to be my
wife, you weren't up to it.

JESSICA: Be quiet.

HUGO: Why should I be quiet? Don't you know that our
love was just a game?

JESSICA: What counts tonight is not our love; it's what
you must do tomorrow.

HUGO: Everything makes sense. If I had been certain—
[*Abruptly*] Jessica, look at me. Can you tell me that
you love me? [*He looks at her. Silence.*] There you
are. I shan't even have had that.

JESSICA: And you, Hugo? Do you believe you loved me?
[*He doesn't answer.*] So you see how it is. [*A pause.
Abruptly*] Why don't you try to convince him?

HUGO: To convince him? Who? Hœderer?

JESSICA: Since he's wrong, you ought to be able to prove
it to him.

HUGO: What an idea! He's too shrewd.

JESSICA: Why do you keep maintaining your ideas are
right if you can't prove them? Hugo, it would be so
wonderful if you could reconcile everybody. Everyone
would be happy; you could all work together. Try,
Hugo, I beg you. Try at least once before you kill him.
[*A knock on the door.* HUGO *gets to his feet, his eyes
shining.*]

HUGO: It's Olga; she's come back. I was sure she'd come back. Turn off the light and open the door.

JESSICA: How you need her! [*She goes to turn off the light and opens the door.* HŒDERER *enters.* HUGO *turns on the light again when the door is shut.* JESSICA, *recognizing* HŒDERER] You!

HŒDERER: I frightened you?

JESSICA: I'm nervous tonight. That bomb—

HŒDERER: Yes, of course. Do you usually sit in the dark?

JESSICA: I had to. My eyes are very tired.

HŒDERER: Oh! [*A pause.*] May I sit down a minute? [*He sits in the easy chair.*] Don't bother about me.

HUGO: You have something to tell me?

HŒDERER: No, nothing. You made me laugh awhile ago: you were red with anger.

HUGO: I—

HŒDERER: Don't apologize; I anticipated that. I think I would have been disturbed if you hadn't protested. There are many things I must explain to you. But to-morrow. Tomorrow we'll both say what's on our minds. But now your day is over. Mine too. A funny day, eh? Why don't you hang up some prints on the walls? That would make the place less bare. There are some in the attic. Slick will get them for you.

JESSICA: What are they like?

HŒDERER: All sorts. You can take your pick.

JESSICA: That's very nice of you. But I don't like prints.

HŒDERER: As you wish. You don't have anything to drink?

JESSICA: Nothing. I'm sorry.

HŒDERER: Too bad, too bad! What were you doing just before I came?

JESSICA: We were talking.

HŒDERER: Very well. Go on and talk. Talk! Don't bother about me. [*He fills his pipe and lights it. A very heavy silence. He smiles.*] Yes, evidently.

JESSICA: It's not very easy to pretend that you're not here.

HŒDERER: You can put me out. [*To* HUGO] You don't have to receive your boss when he has little whims.

[*A pause.*] I don't know why I came. I couldn't sleep.
I tried to work. [*Shrugging his shoulders*] You can't
be working all the time.

JESSICA: No.

HŒDERER: We'll wind up this affair.

HUGO [*interested*]: What affair?

HŒDERER: This business with Karsky. He wants to be
coaxed, but it'll go through quicker than I thought.

HUGO [*violently*]: You—

HŒDERER: Sh, sh! Tomorrow! [*A pause.*] When some
business like this is about to be concluded, you feel
lost. You had your lights on just a moment ago?

JESSICA: Yes.

HŒDERER: I was at the window. In the dark, so as not
to be a target. You saw how calm and overcast the
night is? The light slipped between the shutters of
your blinds. [*A pause.*] We were close to death.

JESSICA: Yes.

HŒDERER [*with a chuckle*]: Very close. [*A pause.*] I left
my room very softly. Slick was sleeping in the corridor.
George was sleeping in the office. Leon was sleeping
in the foyer. I wanted to wake them, and then— Bah!
[*A pause.*] Then I came here. [*To* JESSICA] What's
wrong? You seemed less frightened this afternoon.

JESSICA: It's because of the way you act.

HŒDERER: What do you mean?

JESSICA: I thought you didn't need anyone.

HŒDERER: I don't need anyone. [*A pause.*] Slick told me
you were pregnant.

JESSICA [*sharply*]: It's not true.

HUGO: See here, Jessica, if you told Slick so, why hide it
from Hœderer?

JESSICA: I was kidding Slick.

HŒDERER [*looks at her for a long time*]: Good. [*A
pause.*] When I was deputy to the Landstag, I lived
with a mechanic. In the evening I used to smoke my
pipe in their dining-room. They had a radio, the
children were playing. [*A pause.*] I think I'll go to bed.
It was a mirage.

JESSICA: What was a mirage?

HŒDERER [*with a gesture*]: All that. You, too. A man must work, that's all he can do. You'll telephone the village and get the carpenter to come and repair the office window. [*He looks at him.*] You look fagged out. It seems you got drunk. Sleep tonight. You don't have to come before nine o'clock. [*He gets up.* HUGO *takes a step forward.* JESSICA *throws herself between them.*]

JESSICA: Hugo, now is the time.

HUGO: What's that?

JESSICA: You promised me you would try to convince him.

HŒDERER: To convince me?

HUGO: Be quiet. [*He tries to disengage himself. She gets in front of him.*]

JESSICA: He doesn't agree with you.

HŒDERER [*amused*]: I noticed that.

JESSICA: He would like to explain.

HŒDERER: Tomorrow! Tomorrow!

JESSICA: Tomorrow will be too late.

HŒDERER: Why?

JESSICA [*remaining in front of* HUGO]: He—he says he doesn't want to be your secretary if you don't hear him out. Neither of you is sleepy and you have the whole night before you and—and you both had a narrow escape; that should make you feel closer.

HUGO: Drop it, I tell you.

JESSICA: Hugo, you promised me! [*To* HŒDERER] He says you are a class traitor.

HŒDERER: A class traitor! No less?

JESSICA: Objectively. He said objectively.

HŒDERER [*changing his tone and expression*]: All right. Well then, my boy, tell me what's on your mind, since we can't prevent it. I suppose I have to settle this matter before going to bed. Why am I a class traitor?

HUGO: Because you have no right to involve the party in your schemes.

HŒDERER: Why not?

HUGO: It's a revolutionary organization and you are going to make it a government party.

HŒDERER: Revolutionary parties are organized to take power.

HUGO: To take it. Yes. To seize power, arms in hand. Not to get it through some swindle.

HŒDERER: Is it the lack of bloodshed you regret? Too bad, but you ought to know that we can't get power through an armed struggle. In case of a civil war the Pentagon has the arms and the military leaders. It would serve as a perfect framework for counter-revolutionary troops.

HUGO: Who's talking about civil war? Hœderer, I don't understand you; all we need is a little patience. You yourself said that the Red Army will chase out the Regent and we'll have power alone.

HŒDERER: And what will we do to keep it? [*A pause.*] When the Red Army has crossed our frontiers, I can promise you some nasty moments.

HUGO: The Red Army—

HŒDERER: Yes, yes, I know. I too await its coming. And impatiently. But let me tell you this: all armies at war, whether they come as liberators or not, are alike. They live off the occupied country. Our peasants will detest the Russians, that's sure. How do you suppose they will feel about us, since the Russians will have forced us on them? They'll call us the party of foreigners and maybe worse. The Pentagon will go underground again; it won't have to change its slogans.

HUGO: The Pentagon, I—

HŒDERER: And besides, there's something else: the country is ruined; it may even serve as a battlefield. Any government that succeeds the Regent's will have to take terrible measures, which will make it hated. The morning after the Red Army's departure we would be swept out by an insurrection.

HUGO: An insurrection can be put down. We shall hold the country in an iron grip.

HŒDERER: An iron grip? Who will support us? Even after the revolution the proletariat will be the weakest class for a long time to come. An iron grip! With a bourgeois party that will sabotage industry and a peasant population that will burn the crops to starve us out?

HUGO: What of that? The Bolshevik Party survived worse in 1917.

HŒDERER: It wasn't imposed by a foreign power. Listen to me, son, and try to understand. We can take power with Karsky's liberals and the Regent's conservatives. No fuss, nobody hurt, a united front. No one can accuse us of having been put in by a foreign power. I demanded half the votes on the resistance committee, but I wouldn't be foolish enough to ask for half the ministries. A minority, that's what we must be. A minority, leaving to the other parties the responsibility for unpopular measures and thus able to win support by opposing these measures inside the government. They're cornered: in two years you'll see the bankruptcy of the liberals, and the whole country will ask us to take a try.

HUGO: But at that moment the party will be done for.

HŒDERER: Done for? Why?

HUGO: The party has one program: the realization of a socialist economy, and one method of achieving it: the class struggle. You are going to use it to pursue a policy of class collaboration in the framework of a capitalist economy. For years you will have to cheat, trick, and maneuver; we'll go from compromise to compromise. Before your comrades, you will have to defend the reactionary measures taken by the government in which you participate. No one will understand: the hardened ones will leave us, the others will lose whatever political faith they have just acquired. We shall be contaminated, weakened, disoriented; we shall become reformists and nationalists; in the end the bourgeois parties won't even have to go to the trouble of liquidating us. Hœderer! This party is yours, you cannot have forgotten the hardships you endured to forge it, the sacrifices that were required, the discipline you had to impose. I beg you: don't sacrifice it with your own hands.

HŒDERER: What babbling! If you don't want to take chances you shouldn't be in politics.

HUGO: I don't want to run these particular risks.

HŒDERER: Excellent. Then how would you stay in power?

HUGO: Why take it?

HŒDERER: Are you mad? A socialist army is going to occupy the country; would you let it go without profiting by its aid? Such a chance never comes twice. I tell you we are not strong enough to swing the revolution alone.

HUGO: You should not take power at such a price.

HŒDERER: What do you think the party is, a racing stable? Why polish a knife every day if you don't intend to cut something with it? A party is always only a tool. It has only one goal: power.

HUGO: It has only one goal: to make our ideas, all our ideas, and only these victorious.

HŒDERER: That's true. Now you—you have ideas. You'll get over them.

HUGO: You think I'm the only one who has these ideas? Wasn't it for these ideas that our comrades were killed by the Regent's police? Don't you see that we'll betray them if we use the party to whitewash their assassins?

HŒDERER: I don't give a damn for the dead. They died for the party, and the party can decide as it sees fit about them. I pursue a policy of the living for the living.

HUGO: And do you think that the living will agree to your schemes?

HŒDERER: We'll get them to swallow them little by little.

HUGO: By lying to them?

HŒDERER: By lying to them sometimes.

HUGO: You—you seem so real, so solid! How can you stand it to lie to your comrades?

HŒDERER: Why not? We're at war, and it's not customary to keep each individual soldier posted hour by hour on operations.

HUGO: Hœderer, I—I know better than you what lies are like. In my father's home everybody lied to himself, everybody lied to me. I couldn't breathe until I joined the party. Then for the first time I saw men who didn't lie to other men. Everyone could have confidence in everyone else, the humblest militant had the feeling that the orders of the leaders revealed to him his own secret will, and if things got tough, each one knew why he was ready to die. You're not going to—

HŒDERER: What are you talking about?

HUGO: Our party.

HŒDERER: Our party? But we have always told lies, just like any other party. And you, Hugo, are you sure that you've never lied, never lied to yourself, that you are not even lying to me this very moment?

HUGO: I never lie to my comrades. I— Why should you fight for the liberation of men, if you think no more of them than to stuff their heads with falsehoods?

HŒDERER: I'll lie when I must, and I have contempt for no one. I wasn't the one who invented lying. It grew out of a society divided into classes, and each one of us has inherited it from birth. We shall not abolish lying by refusing to tell lies, but by using every means at hand to abolish classes.

HUGO: All means are not good.

HŒDERER: All means are good when they're effective.

HUGO: Then what right have you to condemn the policy of the Regent? He declared war on the U.S.S.R. because this was the most effective way of safeguarding national independence.

HŒDERER: Do you imagine I condemn him? He did what any fellow of his class would have done in his place. We're not fighting against men nor against a policy, but against the class that produces this policy and these men.

HUGO: And the best means you've found to fight that class is to ask it to share power with you?

HŒDERER: Right! Today it's the best means. [*A pause.*] How you cling to your purity, young man! How afraid you are to soil your hands! All right, stay pure! What good will it do? Why did you join us? Purity is an idea for a yogi or a monk. You intellectuals and bourgeois anarchists use it as a pretext for doing nothing. To do nothing, to remain motionless, arms at your sides, wearing kid gloves. Well, I have dirty hands. Right up to the elbows. I've plunged them in filth and blood. But what do you hope? Do you think you can govern innocently?

HUGO: You'll see some day that I'm not afraid of blood.

HŒDERER: Really! Red gloves, that's elegant. It's the rest that scares you. That's what stinks to your little aristocratic nose.

HUGO: So we're back to that! I'm an aristocrat, a guy who has never gone hungry. Unfortunately for you, I'm not alone in my opinion.

HŒDERER: Not alone? Then you knew something of these negotiations before you came here?

HUGO: N—no. There was some vague talk in the party, and most of the fellows didn't agree. And I swear to ~~you that they weren't aristocrats.~~

HŒDERER: My boy, you misunderstand something; I know these people of the party who disagree with my policy, and I can tell you that they belong to my tribe and not to yours—as you'll soon discover. If they oppose these negotiations, it's simply because they believe them to be inopportune; under other circumstances they would be the first to launch them. But you are making this a matter of principle.

HUGO: Who spoke of principles?

HŒDERER: Aren't you trying to make this into a matter of principle? Good. Then here is something that ought to convince you: if we deal with the Regent, he'll stop the war; the Illyrian troops will wait very patiently for the Russians to come and disarm them. If we break off these parleys, they'll know the game is off and they'll assail us like mad dogs. Hundreds of thousands of men will lose their hides. What do you say to that? [*A pause.*] Now what do you say? Can you scratch out a hundred thousand men with the stroke of a pen?

HUGO [*with difficulty*]: You can't make a revolution with flowers. If there's no other way—

HŒDERER: Then?

HUGO: Why then, so much the worse!

HŒDERER: There you are! You can see for yourself! You don't love men, Hugo. You love only principles.

HUGO: Men? Why should I love them? Do they love me?

HŒDERER: Then why did you come to us? If you don't love men, you can't fight for them.

HUGO: I joined the party because its cause is just, and I shall leave it when that cause ceases to be just. As for men, it's not what they are that interests me, but what they can become.

HŒDERER: And I, I love them for what they are. With all their filth and all their vices. I love their voices and their warm grasping hands, and their skin, the nudest skin of all, and their uneasy glances, and the desperate struggle each has to pursue against anguish and against death. For me, one man more or less in the world is something that counts. It's something precious. You, I know you now, you are a destroyer. You detest men because you detest yourself. Your purity resembles death. The revolution you dream of is not ours. You don't want to change the world, you want to blow it up.

HUGO [*excited*]: Hœderer:

HŒDERER: It's not your fault; you're all alike. An intellectual is never a real revolutionary; just good enough to make an assassin.

HUGO: An assassin. Yes!

JESSICA: Hugo! [*She slips between them.*]

[*The sound of a key in the lock. Enter* SLICK *and* GEORGE.]

GEORGE: So here you are. We've been looking all over for you.

HUGO: Who gave you my key?

SLICK: We have keys to all the doors. Remember—we're bodyguards.

GEORGE [*to* HŒDERER]: You gave us a scare. It was Slick

who woke: no Hœderer. You ought to warn us when you want to go out for a breath of air.

HŒDERER: You were sleeping.

SLICK [*flustered*]: What of it? Since when do you let us sleep when you want to wake us?

HŒDERER [*laughing*]: That's right: What's got into me? [*A pause.*] I'll go along with you. Till tomorrow, son. At nine o'clock. We can talk some more then. [HUGO *does not answer.*] Good-by, Jessica.

JESSICA: Till tomorrow, Hœderer. [*They go out. A long silence.*]

JESSICA: Well?

HUGO: Well, you were here. You heard.

JESSICA: What are you thinking?

HUGO: What do you want me to think? I told you he was shrewd.

JESSICA: Hugo! He was right.

HUGO: My poor Jessica, what could you know about it?

JESSICA: And you, what do you know about it? You didn't look so big in front of him.

HUGO: Oh, for heaven's sake! With me, he had it lucky. I should like to see how he would make out with Louis. He wouldn't have come out so well.

JESSICA: Perhaps he would have put him in his pocket.

HUGO [*laughing*]: What? Louis? You don't know him. Louis can't be wrong.

JESSICA: Why?

HUGO: Because. Because he's Louis.

JESSICA: Hugo! You don't mean what you're saying. I watched you while you were arguing with Hœderer: he convinced you.

HUGO: He didn't convince me. No one can convince me that one should lie to one's comrades. But if he had convinced me, that would be one more reason to kill him, because that would prove that he's capable of convincing others. Tomorrow morning I'll finish the job.

CURTAIN

ACT VI

HŒDERER'S OFFICE

The two torn-off sashes of the window have been leaned against the wall. The fragments of glass have been carefully swept up and the window is covered with a drape, which hangs to the floor.

At the beginning of the scene, HŒDERER *is standing in front of the gas burner, making coffee and smoking his pipe. There is a knock and* SLICK *sticks his head through the partly open door.*

SLICK: It's the dame. She wants to see you.

HŒDERER: No.

SLICK: She says it's very important.

HŒDERER: Very well. Tell her to come in.

[JESSICA *enters.* SLICK *withdraws.*]

Well? [*She is silent.*] Come here. [*She remains standing by the door, her hair falling across her face. He goes up to her.*] I suppose you have something to tell me? [*She nods.*] Very well, out with it, and then make yourself scarce.

JESSICA: You're always in such a hurry.

HŒDERER: I'm working.

JESSICA: You weren't working: you're making yourself coffee. May I have a cup?

HŒDERER: Yes. [*A pause.*] Well?

JESSICA: You must give me a little time. It's so hard to talk to you. You're waiting for Hugo and he hasn't even begun to shave.

HŒDERER: All right. You have five minutes to collect yourself. Here's your coffee.

JESSICA: Talk to me.

HŒDERER: Why?

JESSICA: So I can pull myself together. Talk to me.

HŒDERER: I have nothing to say to you. I don't know how to talk to women.

JESSICA: Yes you do. And very well.

HŒDERER: Oh! [*A pause.*]

JESSICA: Last night—

HŒDERER: What about last night?

JESSICA: I discovered that you're the one who's right.

HŒDERER: Right? Oh! [*A pause.*] Thank you, I feel encouraged.

JESSICA: You are making fun of me.

HŒDERER: Yes. [*A pause.*]

JESSICA: What would they do with me if I joined the party?

HŒDERER: They would first have to let you in.

JESSICA: But if they let me in, what would they do with me?

HŒDERER: I wonder. [*A pause.*] Is that what you came to tell me?

JESSICA: No.

HŒDERER: Well then? What's wrong? Did you quarrel with Hugo and decide to walk out?

JESSICA: No. Would you be annoyed if I left?

HŒDERER: I should be delighted. I could work in peace.

JESSICA: You don't really mean that.

HŒDERER: No?

JESSICA: No. [*A pause.*] Last night when you came in, you seemed so alone in the world.

HŒDERER: And?

JESSICA: It's wonderful to see a man who stands alone.

HŒDERER: So wonderful that you at once want to keep him company. And so, just like that, he's no longer alone. The world is made badly.

JESSICA: With me you'd be quite alone. I wouldn't get in your way.

HŒDERER: With you?

JESSICA: That's a manner of speaking. [*A pause.*] Were you ever married?

HŒDERER: Yes.

JESSICA: To a woman in the party?

HŒDERER: No.

JESSICA: You said one should always marry a woman in the party.

HŒDERER: Exactly.

JESSICA: Was she beautiful?

HŒDERER: That depended on the hour and the point of view.

JESSICA: And do you think I'm beautiful?

HŒDERER: Are you making an ass of me?

JESSICA [*laughing*]: Yes.

HŒDERER: The five minutes are up. Talk or be off with you.

JESSICA: You won't hurt him.

HŒDERER: Whom?

JESSICA: Hugo! You like him, don't you?

HŒDERER: Please don't get sentimental. He means to kill me, eh? Isn't that what's on your mind?

JESSICA: Don't harm him.

HŒDERER: Of course I shan't hurt him.

JESSICA: You—you've known?

HŒDERER: Since yesterday. How does he intend to kill me?

JESSICA: How?

HŒDERER: With what weapon? Hand-grenade, revolver, pickax, dagger, or poison?

JESSICA: Revolver.

HŒDERER: I prefer that.

JESSICA: When he comes in this morning he'll have his revolver on him.

HŒDERER: Good. Good, good. But why do you betray him? Are you angry with him?

JESSICA: No. But—

HŒDERER: Well?

JESSICA: He asked me to help him.

HŒDERER: And this is how you go about helping him? You surprise me.

JESSICA: He doesn't want to kill you. Not in the least. He thinks too much of you for that. It's just that he

has his assignment. He won t admit it, but I know that
at the bottom of his heart he would be happy if he
were prevented from carrying it out.

HŒDERER: That remains to be seen.

JESSICA: What are you going to do?

HŒDERER: I don't know yet.

JESSICA: Have him disarmed gently by Slick. He has just
that gun. Once the gun is gone, it will be all over.

HŒDERER: No. That would humiliate him. One shouldn't
humiliate a man. I'll talk to him.

JESSICA: You are going to let him come in here armed?

HŒDERER: Why not? I want to win him over. It will be
risky for five minutes, but not after that. If he doesn't
go through with it this morning, he'll never do it.

JESSICA [abruptly]: I don't want him to kill you.

HŒDERER: Would you care if I got killed?

JESSICA: I? I should be delighted.

[A knock.]

SLICK: It's Hugo.

HŒDERER: Just a minute. [SLICK closes the door.] Go out
by the window.

JESSICA: I don't want to leave you.

HŒDERER: If you stay he's certain to shoot. In front
of you he wouldn't back down. Come on, get out!
[She goes out through the window, and the drape falls
back into place.]

HŒDERER: Let him in.

[HUGO enters. HŒDERER goes to the door and follows
HUGO to the table. He stays close to him, observing all
his gestures while they talk, ready to seize his wrists if
HUGO should reach for the gun in his pocket.]

HŒDERER: Did you sleep well?

HUGO: All right.

HŒDERER: Hangover?

HUGO: Awful.

HŒDERER: Did you make up your mind?

HUGO [startled]: To do what?

HŒDERER: You told me yesterday you would leave me if
you were unable to make me change your views.

HUGO: I still feel the same way.

HŒDERER: Good. But we'll talk about that later. Meantime let's do some work. Sit down. [HUGO *sits at the work-table.*] Where were we?

HUGO [*reading his notes*]: "According to official figures the number of agricultural workers fell in 1906 from 8,771,000 to—"

HŒDERER: Tell me: did you know that it was a woman who threw the bomb?

HUGO: A woman?

HŒDERER: Slick saw footprints in a flowerbed. Did you know her?

HUGO: How should I know her? [*A pause.*]

HŒDERER: It's strange, isn't it?

HUGO: Very.

HŒDERER: But you don't really seem to think it's strange. What's the matter with you?

HUGO: I'm sick.

HŒDERER: Would you like to take the morning off?

HUGO: No. Let's work.

HŒDERER: Then finish that sentence.

HUGO [*takes up his notes and begins again to read*]: "According to official statistics—" [HŒDERER *begins to laugh.* HUGO *raises his head sharply.*]

HŒDERER: Do you know why she missed us? I'll bet she shut her eyes when she threw the bomb.

HUGO [*absent-mindedly*]: Why?

HŒDERER: Because of the noise. They close their eyes so as not to hear it; explain it any way you like. Women are all afraid of loud noises, the little mice, otherwise they'd make remarkable killers. They're pigheaded, you know. They get their ideas ready-made, and then they believe in them as in God. With us others, it's not so easy for us to shoot some chap for the sake of a theory, because we're the ones who cook up the theories and we know how they are made. We can never be entirely certain that we're right. Take you: are you sure you're right?

HUGO: Yes.

HŒDERER: In any case, you'll never make a killer; it's a vocation.

HUGO: Anyone can kill if the party orders him to.

HŒDERER: If the party ordered you to dance on a tight-rope, do you think you would succeed? One has to be born a killer. Take you, you think too much; you couldn't do it.

HUGO: I could if I made up my mind.

HŒDERER: You could coldly put a bullet between my eyes because I don't agree with your political views?

HUGO: Yes, if I had decided to or if the party had ordered it.

HŒDERER: You surprise me. [HUGO *is about to reach into his pocket, but* HŒDERER *grabs his arm and lifts it lightly above the table.*] Suppose this arm were clasping a gun and the finger rested on the trigger.

HUGO: Let go of my hand.

HŒDERER [*not releasing it*]: Suppose I were facing you, just as now, and you took aim.

HUGO: Let me go and let's get to work.

HŒDERER: You would look at me and just as you were all set to fire, this is what would come into your mind: "What if he were right?" Don't you see?

HUGO: I wouldn't think of that. I would only think of killing.

HŒDERER: You would think of that. Being an intellectual, you can't keep from thinking. Before pulling the trigger you would have already seen all the possible conse-quences of your act: the work of a lifetime in ruins, a policy gone to pot, nobody to replace me, the party condemned, maybe, never to take power—

HUGO: I tell you I would think no such thing!

HŒDERER: You couldn't help yourself. And rightly so, for if you didn't think of it beforehand, a whole lifetime of thinking would not be enough for you afterwards. [A *pause.*] What's this mania that you all have to play the assassin? Your killer is a guy without imagination: he doesn't give a damn for death because he has no idea of what life is. I prefer people who fear the death of others: it shows they know how to live.

HUGO: I'm not built for living, I don't know what life is and I don't need to know. I'm in the way, I haven't found the right place for myself and I get on everyone's nerves. Nobody loves me, nobody trusts me.

HŒDERER: *I* trust you.

HUGO: You?

HŒDERER: Certainly. You're a kid for whom the passage to maturity is not easy, but you'll make a fair enough man if somebody helps you over the hump. If I escape their bombs I'll keep you with me and help you.

HUGO: Why do you tell me this? Why tell it to me today?

HŒDERER [*releasing him*]: Simply to prove to you that you can't drop a man in cold blood unless you're a specialist.

HUGO: If I decided to, I should be able to do it. [*To himself, with a kind of desperation*] I should be able to do it.

HŒDERER: Could you face me and fire? [*They face each other.* HUGO *backs his chair away from the table.*] Your real killer has no notion of what the other one is thinking. But you have a very good notion. Could you bear to know what I would be thinking as I saw you take aim? [*A pause.* HŒDERER *keeps watching* HUGO.] Would you like some coffee? [HUGO *doesn't answer.*] It's ready; I'll get you a cup. [*He turns his back on* HUGO *and pours a cup of coffee.* HUGO *gets up from his chair and reaches into the pocket that holds his revolver. It is clear that he is struggling with himself. After a moment* HŒDERER *turns around and calmly approaches* HUGO, *carrying a full cup. He offers it to him.*] Take it. [HUGO *takes the cup.*] And now give me your gun. Give it to me! I gave you your chance and you didn't take it. [*He reaches into* HUGO's *pocket and takes out the revolver.*] Why, it's a plaything! [*He goes to his desk and deposits the gun.*]

HUGO: I hate you. [HŒDERER *comes up to him.*]

HŒDERER: No, you don't hate me. What reason have you to hate me?

HUGO: You take me for a coward.

HŒDERER: Why? You don't know how to kill, but that
doesn't mean that you don't know how to die. On
the contrary.

HUGO: I had my finger on the trigger.

HŒDERER: Yes.

HUGO: And I— [*with a gesture of helplessness*].

HŒDERER: Yes. I told you: it's harder than you think.

HUGO: I knew that you were deliberately turning your
back. That was why—

HŒDERER: Oh! In any case—

HUGO: I'm not a traitor!

HŒDERER: Who said anything about that? Treachery,
too, is a vocation.

HUGO: They'll think I'm a traitor because I didn't do as
I was instructed.

HŒDERER: Who? They? [*Silence.*] It's Louis who sent
you? [*Silence.*] You won't say. That's as it should be.
[*A pause.*] Listen to me: your fate is linked with mine.
Since yesterday I have some trump cards, and I'm
going to try to save both our necks. Tomorrow I'll
go to the city and talk to Louis. He's tough, but
then so am I. We can square it with your pals easily
enough. The difficult thing for you will be to square
it with yourself.

HUGO: Not so difficult. Just give me back the gun.

HŒDERER: No.

HUGO: What's it to you if I put a bullet in my head?
I'm your enemy.

HŒDERER: First of all you're not my enemy. And then,
too, you can still be of use.

HUGO: You know that I'm washed up!

HŒDERER: Nonsense! You wanted to prove that you were
capable of acting and you chose the hard way, as if
you wanted to gather up credit in heaven; that's youth.
You didn't succeed. Well, what of that? There's nothing to prove, you know, and the revolution's not a
question of virtue but of effectiveness. There is no
heaven. There's work to be done, that's all. And you

must do what you're cut out for; all the better if it comes easy to you. The best work is not the work that takes the most sacrifices. It's the work in which you can best succeed.

HUGO: I have no gift for anything.

HŒDERER: You have a gift for writing.

HUGO: For writing! Words! Always words!

HŒDERER: And why not? The point is to succeed. Better a good journalist than a poor assassin.

HUGO [*hesitating, but with a kind of confidence*]: Hœderer, when you were my age—

HŒDERER: Yes?

HUGO: What would you have done in my place?

HŒDERER: I? I should have killed my man. But that doesn't mean I should have done the best thing. But then, we are not of the same tribe.

HUGO: I would rather belong to your tribe; you must feel right inside.

HŒDERER: You think so? [*He laughs dryly.*] Some day I'll tell you about me.

HUGO: Some day? [*A pause.*] Hœderer, I missed my chance, and I know now that I could never shoot you because—because I like you. But make no mistake about it: on the question we discussed yesterday I shall never agree with you, I shall never be on your side and I don't want you to defend me. Not tomorrow nor any other day.

HŒDERER: As you like.

HUGO: And now may I have your permission to leave? I'd like to think this whole thing over.

HŒDERER: Will you give me your word that you won't do anything foolish until you have talked with me again?

HUGO: If you like.

HŒDERER: Then go on. Get some fresh air and come back as soon as you can. And don't forget that you're still my secretary. So long as you don't shoot me and I don't fire you, you'll work for me.

[HUGO *goes out.* HŒDERER *goes to the door.*]

HŒDERER: Slick!

SLICK: Yes?

HŒDERER: The kid's unhappy. Keep an eye on him from a distance, and if necessary, keep him from doing himself any mischief. But be nice about it. And if he wants to come back here in a little while, don't stop him on the pretext that you have to announce him. Let him go and come as he pleases. The important thing is not to excite him.

[*He shuts the door and goes to the table on which the gas burner is sitting. He pours himself a cup of coffee.* JESSICA *lifts the hanging that covers the window and comes in.*]

HŒDERER: You again, you poison? What do you want now?

JESSICA: I was sitting on the window-ledge and I heard everything.

HŒDERER: Well?

JESSICA: I was frightened.

HŒDERER: You didn't have to stay.

JESSICA: I couldn't leave you.

HŒDERER: You wouldn't have been much help.

JESSICA: I know. [*A pause.*] Maybe I would have thrown myself in between you and got the bullets meant for you.

HŒDERER: You're a romantic.

JESSICA: So are you.

HŒDERER: What?

JESSICA: You are romantic too: you risked your life rather than humiliate him.

HŒDERER: To know what life is worth you have to risk it once in a while.

JESSICA: You offered to help him and he refused and yet you were not discouraged. You actually seemed to be fond of him.

HŒDERER: What of it?

JESSICA: Nothing. That's how it was, that's all. [*They look at each other.*]

HŒDERER: Now beat it! [*She doesn't budge.*] Jessica, I'm

not in the habit of refusing what is offered me, and it's six months since I've touched a woman. You still have time to go, but in five minutes it will be too late. Do you understand what I mean? [*She doesn't budge.*] The boy has only you in the world and he has all sorts of trouble ahead of him. He needs someone to give him courage.

JESSICA: You're the one who can give him courage. Not me. We can only harm each other.

HŒDERER: You love each other.

JESSICA: Not even. We're too much alike. [*A pause.*]

HŒDERER: When did this start?

JESSICA: What?

HŒDERER [*with a gesture*]: All this. All this in your head.

JESSICA: I don't know. Yesterday, I think when you looked at me and seemed so alone.

HŒDERER: If I had known—

JESSICA: You wouldn't have come?

HŒDERER: I— [*He looks at her and shrugs his shoulders. A pause.*] But good God! If you're restless, there are Slick and George to distract you. Why pick me?

JESSICA: I'm not restless and I didn't pick anyone. I didn't have to pick.

HŒDERER: You bother me. [*A pause.*] What did you expect? I don't have the time to worry with you. You don't expect me to give you a toss on that sofa and then abandon you afterwards, do you?

JESSICA: Make up your mind.

HŒDERER: Just the same, you ought to know—

JESSICA: I don't know anything. I'm not a girl, but I'm not a woman either. I've lived in a dream, and when I was kissed I always wanted to laugh. And now that I am standing here in front of you, it seems to me that the morning has come and that I just woke up. You are real. A real man of flesh and bone. I am actually afraid of you and I think I really love you. Do whatever you like with me. No matter what happens, I'll not complain.

HŒDERER: You felt like laughing when you were kissed?

[JESSICA, *embarrassed, lowers her head.*] Eh?

JESSICA: Yes.

HŒDERER: Why? Are you cold?

JESSICA: That's what they say.

HŒDERER: And you, what's your opinion?

JESSICA: I don't know.

HŒDERER: Well, let's just see. [*He kisses her.*] Well?

JESSICA: I didn't feel like laughing. [*The door opens.* HUGO *enters.*]

HUGO: So that's the way it is!

HŒDERER: Hugo—

HUGO: That's enough. [*A pause.*] So that's why you spared me. I wondered why you didn't have your men beat me up and throw me out. I said to myself: he can't be so mad or so generous. But it's all clear now: it was on account of my wife. I like it better this way.

JESSICA: Listen to me.

HUGO: Never mind, Jessica, forget it. I'm not sore at you and I'm not jealous; we weren't really in love. But he, he almost took me in: "I'll help you, I'll help make a man of you." What a fool I was! He didn't give a damn for me.

HŒDERER: Hugo, do you want me to swear that—

HUGO: Above all, don't apologize. On the contrary, I should thank you. At least once I've had the pleasure of catching you in a bad moment. And besides—besides — [*He rushes to the desk, snatches up the revolver, and covers* HŒDERER.] And besides, you have freed me.

JESSICA [*shouting*]: Hugo!

HUGO: You see, Hœderer, I am looking you straight in the eyes and I'm aiming and my hand's not shaking and I don't give a bloody damn for what's going on in your head.

HŒDERER: Wait, kid! Don't be stupid. Not for a woman! [HUGO *fires three shots.* JESSICA *screams.* SLICK *and* GEORGE *rush in.*] You imbecile! You've ruined everything.

SLICK: You bastard! [*He draws his revolver.*]

HŒDERER: Don't hurt him. [*He sinks into a chair.*] He was jealous. That's why he shot me.

SLICK: What's that mean?

HŒDERER: I've been sleeping with his wife. [*A pause.*] What a god-damn waste!

[*He dies.*]

CURTAIN

ACT VII

IN OLGA'S ROOM

OLGA *and* HUGO *talking in the dark. First their voices are heard, and then gradually the room is lighted.*

OLGA: Was it true? Did you really kill him over Jessica?

HUGO: I—I killed him because I opened the door. That's all I know. If I hadn't opened that door— He was there, he held Jessica in his arms, he had lipstick on his chin. It was all so trivial. But I had been living for so long in tragedy. It was to save the tragedy that I fired.

OLGA: But weren't you jealous?

HUGO: Jealous? Perhaps. But not about Jessica.

OLGA: Look at me and answer me frankly, for what I am going to ask now is very important. Are you proud of your deed? Do you claim it as your own? Would you do it again if necessary?

HUGO: Did I even do it? It wasn't I who killed—it was chance. If I had opened the door two minutes sooner or two minutes later, I wouldn't have surprised them in each other's arms, and I wouldn't have fired. [*A pause.*] I was coming to tell him that I would let him help me.

OLGA: Yes.

HUGO: Chance fired three shots, just as in cheap detective stories. Chance lets you do a lot of "iffing": "*If* I had stayed a bit longer by the chestnut trees, *if* I had walked to the end of the garden, *if* I had gone back into the summerhouse. . . ." But me? *Me?* Where does that put me in the thing? It was an assassination without an assassin. [*A pause.*] I often asked myself in prison: what would Olga say if she were here? What would she want me to think?

OLGA [*dryly*]: Well?

HUGO: Oh, I know perfectly well what you would have said to me. You would have said: "Be modest, Hugo. Nobody cares about your motives or reasons. We asked you to kill this man and you killed him. What counts is the result." But I—well, I'm not modest, Olga. I can't separate the murder from the motive for it.

OLGA: I like that better.

HUGO: What do you mean, you like that better? Is that really you talking, Olga? The Olga who always told me that—

OLGA: I'll explain. What time is it?

HUGO [*looking at his wrist watch*]: Twenty minutes to twelve.

OLGA: Good. We have time. What were you saying? That you do not understand your deed.

HUGO: Rather, that I understand it too well. It's a door that any key can open. I could tell myself, if I had a mind to, that I shot him out of political passion and that the rage that came over me when I opened the door was merely the little jolt I needed to make my task easier.

OLGA [*observing him with uneasiness*]: Do you believe that, Hugo? Do you really believe that you fired for the right reasons?

HUGO: Olga, I believe everything. And at the same time I wonder whether I really killed him at all.

OLGA: What do you mean—at all?

HUGO: What if it were all a comedy?

OLGA: You really pulled the trigger.

HUGO: Yes. I really drew my finger back. Actors do that too, on the stage. Look here: I cock my forefinger, I aim at you. [*He aims at her with his right hand, his forefinger coiled back.*] It's the same gesture. Perhaps I wasn't real. Perhaps only the bullet was. Why do you smile?

OLGA: Because you make many things easy for me.

HUGO: I thought I was too young. I wanted to hang a crime round my neck, like a stone. And I feared it would be too heavy for me to carry. How wrong I was! It's light, horribly light. It has no weight at all. Look at me: I've grown older, I spent two years in the cooler, I've been separated from Jessica, and I shall lead this life of senseless puzzlement until your pals take it upon themselves to rid me of it. And all this comes from my crime, isn't that right? And yet it has no weight, I don't feel that it's there. It's not around my neck, nor on my shoulders, nor in my heart. It has become my destiny, do you understand? It controls my life from outside, but I can't see it or touch it, it's not mine, it's a fatal disease that kills painlessly. Where is my crime? Does it exist? And yet I fired. The door was open. I loved Hœderer, Olga. I loved him more than I ever loved anyone in the world. I loved to watch him and to hear him talk, I loved his hands and his face, and when I was with him all my fears were calmed. It's not my crime that tortures me but the fact that he's dead. [*A pause.*] So there you are. Nothing happened. Nothing. I spent ten days in the country and two years in jail; I haven't changed; I'm still the same old chatterbox. Assassins should wear something by which they can be recognized. A poppy in their lapels. [*A pause.*] Well, then? What's the conclusion?

OLGA: You're coming back to the party.

HUGO: Good.

OLGA: At midnight Louis and Charles will return to kill you. But I won't let them in. I'll tell them you are salvageable.

HUGO [*laughs*]: Salvageable! What an odd word! That's a word you use for scrap, isn't it?

OLGA: Do you agree?

HUGO: Why not?

OLGA: Tomorrow you'll get new instructions.

HUGO: Good.

OLGA: Thank heaven! [*She sinks into a chair.*]

HUGO: What's wrong with you?

OLGA: I'm so glad. [*A pause.*] You talked for three hours and I was frightened all that time.

HUGO: What were you afraid of?

OLGA: Of what I might have had to tell them. But everything is all right now. You'll come back with us now and do a man's work.

HUGO: Will you help me, as before?

OLGA: Yes, Hugo, I'll help you.

HUGO: I do like you, Olga. You are just as you always were. So pure, so clear. It was you who taught me purity.

OLGA: Have I aged?

HUGO: No. [*He takes her hand.*]

OLGA: I thought of you every day.

HUGO: Tell me, Olga—

OLGA: Yes?

HUGO: About those packages. Did you send them?

OLGA: What packages?

HUGO: The chocolates.

OLGA: No. It wasn't I. But I knew they were going to send them.

HUGO: And you let them?

OLGA: Yes.

HUGO: But what did you think about it?

OLGA [*showing her hair*]: Look.

HUGO: What's this? White hairs?

OLGA: They came in one night. You must never leave me again. And if there are rough times we'll manage them together.

HUGO [*smiling*]: You remember: Raskolnikov.

OLGA [*leaping to her feet*]: Raskolnikov?

HUGO: It's the name you chose for me in the underground. Oh, Olga, you don't remember!

OLGA: Yes. I remember.

HUGO: I'll use it again.

OLGA: No.

HUGO: Why? I liked it. You said it fitted me like a glove.

OLGA: You're too well known under that name.

HUGO: Known? By whom?

OLGA [*suddenly limp*]: What time is it?

HUGO: Five minutes to.

OLGA: Listen carefully, Hugo. And don't interrupt. I have something to tell you. It isn't much. You mustn't attach any importance to it. You—you'll be surprised at first, but you'll come to understand after a while.

HUGO: Well?

OLGA: I'm happy about what you told me, about your —about your deed. If you had taken pride in it or spoken of it with satisfaction, it would have been more difficult for you.

HUGO: Difficult? Difficult to do what?

OLGA: To forget it.

HUGO: To forget it? But, Olga—

OLGA: Hugo! You must forget it. I'm not asking much of you; you said yourself that you didn't know what you were doing or why you did it. You're not even sure that you killed Hœderer. Very good, you're on the right track. You've got to go just a bit farther, that's all. Forget it; it was a nightmare. Never mention it again; not even to me. The man who killed Hœderer is dead. He was known as Raskolnikov, and he died of eating some poisoned brandy-chocolates. [*She strokes his hair.*] I'll choose another name for you.

HUGO: What's going on here, Olga? What have you done?

OLGA: The party has changed its policy. [HUGO *regards her fixedly.*] Don't look at me like that. Try to understand. When we sent you to Hœderer's our communications with the Soviet Union were severed. We had to decide our line by ourselves. Don't look at me that way, Hugo. Don't look at me like that.

HUGO: Then what?

OLGA: Then the contact was renewed. Last winter the U.S.S.R. informed us that for purely military reasons it favored a policy of conciliation with the Regent.

HUGO: And you—did you obey?

OLGA: Yes. We set up a secret committee of six members with the government people and the Pentagon.

HUGO: Six members? And you have three votes?

OLGA: Yes. How did you know?

HUGO: It came into my head, somehow. Go on.

OLGA: Since then our troops have been practically out of the war. We've probably saved a hundred thousand lives. Except that the Germans immediately invaded the country.

HUGO: Just perfect. I suppose the Russians also gave you to understand that they didn't want to give sole power to the Proletarian Party; that they would have trouble with the Allies and that, what's more, you would soon be swept out by an insurrection?

OLGA: But—

HUGO: I seem to have heard all that once before. What about Hœderer?

OLGA: His attempt was premature and he was not the right man to direct such a policy.

HUGO: So he had to be killed; that's clear. But I suppose you have rehabilitated his reputation?

OLGA: We had to.

HUGO: He'll have a statue to him at the end of the war, and streets named after him in all our cities, and his name in the history books. That makes me happy for him. And who was his assassin? What was he? Some character in the pay of Germany?

OLGA: Hugo—

HUGO: Answer me.

OLGA: The comrades know that you were one of us. They never believed it was a crime of passion. Then it was explained to them—as best it could be.

HUGO: You've lied to your comrades.

OLGA: Lied, no. But we—we are at war, Hugo. You can't tell the whole truth to troops. [HUGO *bursts into laughter.*] What is the matter? Hugo! Hugo!
[HUGO *sinks into a chair, laughing to the point of tears.*]

HUGO: That's just what he said! Just what he said! Oh, this is a farce.

OLGA: Hugo!

HUGO: Wait, Olga, let me have my laugh. It's been ten years since I've been able to laugh like this. Here's an embarrassing crime: nobody wants to claim it. I don't know why I committed it and you don't know what to do with it. [*He looks at her.*] You're all alike.

OLGA: Hugo, I beg you—

HUGO: Alike. Hœderer, Louis, and you yourself, all belong to the same tribe. The right tribe. You're the tough ones, the conquerors, the leaders. I am the only one who got in by the wrong door.

OLGA: Hugo, you loved Hœderer.

HUGO: I believe I never before loved him as much as I do at this moment.

OLGA: Then you must help us complete his work. [*She recoils under his glance.*] Hugo!

HUGO [*softly*]: Don't be afraid, Olga. I'll not harm you. But you must be quiet. For one minute, just for one minute more, while I put my thoughts in order. Good. So I am salvageable. Excellent. But all alone, naked, without bag or baggage. On condition that I change my skin—if I could develop amnesia, that would be better still. The crime itself cannot be salvaged, isn't that so? It was an error of no significance. To be left in the ash-can. As for me, I'll change my name tomorrow, call myself Julien Sorel or Rastignac or Muishkin, and I'll work hand in hand with the guys of the Pentagon.

OLGA: I'm going—

HUGO: Quiet, Olga. I beg you, don't say a word. [*He reflects a moment.*] The answer is no.

OLGA: What?

HUGO: My answer is no. I won't work with you.

OLGA: Then you can't have understood, Hugo. They're coming with their revolvers—

HUGO: I understand perfectly well. They're even a little late.

OLGA: You're not going to let them kill you like a dog. You can't be willing to die for nothing! We will trust you, Hugo. You'll see, you'll be our comrade for good, you have proved yourself. . . . [*A car. The sound of a motor.*]

HUGO: Here they are.

OLGA: Hugo, it would be criminal. The party—

HUGO: No big words, Olga. There are too many big words in this story already and they've done much harm. [*The car passes on.*] It's not their car. I have time to explain it to you. Listen: I don't know why I killed Hœderer, but I know why it was right to kill him: because his policy was wrong, because he lied to the rank and file and jeopardized the life of the party. If I had had the courage to shoot when I was alone with him in his office, he would be dead for these reasons and I could think of myself without shame. But I am ashamed because I killed him—afterwards. And now you want me to dishonor myself even more and to agree that I killed him for nothing. Olga, what I thought about Hœderer's line I continue to think. When I was in prison I believed that you agreed with me, and that's what kept me going. I know now that I'm alone in my opinion, but I won't change. [*The sound of a motor.*]

OLGA: This time they're here. Listen, I can't—take this revolver, go out through my bedroom and make a try.

HUGO [*not taking the gun*]: You have made Hœderer a great man. But I loved him more than you could ever love him. If I renounced my deed he would become a nameless corpse, a throw-off of the party. [*The car stops.*] Killed by accident. Killed over a woman.

OLGA: Get out of here.

HUGO: A man like Hœderer doesn't die by accident. He dies for his ideas, for his political program; he's responsible for his death. If I openly claim my crime and declare myself Raskolnikov and am willing to pay the necessary price, then he will have the death he deserves. [*A rap on the door.*]

OLGA: Hugo, I—

HUGO [*going to the door*]: I have not yet killed Hœderer, Olga. Not yet. But I am going to kill him now, along with myself. [*More knocking.*]

OLGA [*shouting*]: Go on! Get out!

[HUGO *kicks open the door.*]

HUGO [*shouting*]: Unsalvageable!

CURTAIN

THE RESPECTFUL
PROSTITUTE

(*La Putain respectueuse*)

TO MICHEL AND ZETTE LEIRIS

A PLAY IN ONE ACT AND TWO SCENES

CHARACTERS IN THE PLAY

LIZZIE

THE NEGRO

FRED

JOHN

JAMES

THE SENATOR

SEVERAL MEN

La Putain respectueuse (*The Respectful Prostitute*) was presented for the first time at the Théâtre Antoine, Paris, on November 8, 1946.

SCENE ONE

A room in a Southern town of the United States. White walls. A couch. To the right, a window; to the left, a bathroom door. In the background, a small ante-chamber leading to the street.

Before the curtain rises, a roaring noise from the stage. LIZZIE is alone, half dressed, running the vacuum cleaner. The bell rings. She hesitates, looks toward the door leading to the bathroom. The bell rings again. She turns off the vacuum cleaner, goes to the bathroom door, and half opens it.

LIZZIE [*in a low voice*]: Someone is ringing, don't come out. [*She goes to open the door leading to the street. THE NEGRO appears in the doorway. He is a tall, strapping Negro with white hair. He stands stiffly.*] What is it? You must have the wrong address. [*A pause.*] What do you want? Speak up.

THE NEGRO [*pleading*]: Please, ma'am, please.

LIZZIE: Please what? [*She looks him over.*] Wait a minute. That was you on the train, wasn't it? So you got away from them, eh? How did you find my place?

THE NEGRO: I looked, ma'am, I looked for it everywhere. [*He motions for permission to enter the room.*] Please!

LIZZIE: Don't come in. I have somebody here. What do you want, anyway?

THE NEGRO: Please.

LIZZIE: Please what? What? Do you want money?

THE NEGRO: No, ma'am. [*A pause.*] Please tell them that I didn't do anything.

LIZZIE: Tell who?

THE NEGRO: The judge. Tell him, ma'am, please tell him.

LIZZIE: I'll tell him nothing.

THE NEGRO: Please.

LIZZIE: Nothing doing. I'm not buying anybody else's troubles, I got enough of my own. Beat it.

THE NEGRO: You know I didn't do anything. Did I do something?

LIZZIE: Nothing. But I'm not going to the judge. Judges and cops make me sick.

THE NEGRO: I left my wife and children. I've been running and dodging all night. I'm dead beat.

LIZZIE: Get out of town.

THE NEGRO: They're watching all the stations.

LIZZIE: Who's watching?

THE NEGRO: The white folks.

LIZZIE: Which white folks?

THE NEGRO: All of them. Were you out this morning?

LIZZIE: No.

THE NEGRO: The streets are full of all kinds of white folks. Old ones, young ones; they talk without even knowing each other.

LIZZIE: What does that mean?

THE NEGRO: It means all I can do is run around until they get me. When white folk who have never met before, start to talk to each other, friendly like, it means some nigger's goin' to die. [A *pause*.] Say I haven't done anything, ma'am. Tell the judge; tell the newspaper people. Maybe they'll print it. Tell them, ma'am, tell them, tell them!

LIZZIE: Don't shout. I got somebody here. [A *pause*.] Newspapers are out of the question. I can't afford to call attention to myself right now. [A *pause*.] If they force me to testify, I promise to tell the truth.

THE NEGRO: Are you gonna tell them I haven't done anything?

LIZZIE: I'll tell them.

THE NEGRO: You swear, ma'am?

LIZZIE: Yes, yes.

THE NEGRO: By our Lord, who sees us all?

LIZZIE: Oh, get the hell out of here. I promise, that ought to be enough. [A *pause*.] But get going. Get out!

THE NEGRO [*suddenly*]: Please, won't you hide me?

LIZZIE: Hide you?

THE NEGRO: Won't you, ma'am? Won't you?

LIZZIE: Hide you! Me? I'll show you! [*She slams the door in his face.*] And that's that! [*She turns toward the bathroom.*] You can come out.

[*FRED emerges in shirt sleeves, without collar or tie.*]

FRED: Who was that?

LIZZIE: Nobody.

FRED: I thought it was the police.

LIZZIE: The police? Are you mixed up with the police?

FRED: Me? No. I thought they came for you.

LIZZIE [*offended*]: You got a nerve! I never took a cent off anyone!

FRED: Weren't you ever in trouble with the police?

LIZZIE: Not for stealing, anyway. [*She busies herself with the vacuum cleaner.*]

FRED [*irritated by the noise*]: Hey!

LIZZIE [*shouting to make herself heard*]: What's the matter, honey?

FRED [*shouting*]: You're busting my eardrums.

LIZZIE [*shouting*]: I'll soon be finished. [*A pause.*] That's the way I am.

FRED [*shouting*]: What?

LIZZIE [*shouting*]: I tell you I'm like that.

FRED [*shouting*]: Like what?

LIZZIE [*shouting*]: Like that. I can't help it, the next morning I have to take a bath and run the vacuum cleaner. [*She leaves the vacuum cleaner.*]

FRED [*pointing toward the bed*]: Cover that, while you're at it.

LIZZIE: What?

FRED: The bed. I said you should cover the bed. It smells of sin.

LIZZIE: Sin? How come you talk like that? Are you a preacher?

FRED: No. Why?

LIZZIE: You sound like the Bible. [*She looks at him.*] No, you're not a preacher: you're too well dressed. Let's see your rings. [*Admiringly*] Say—look at that! Are you rich?

FRED: Yes.

LIZZIE: Very rich?

FRED: Yes, very.

LIZZIE: So much the better. [*She puts her arms around his neck and holds up her lips to be kissed.*] It's better when a man is rich; you feel more secure that way. [*He is about to embrace her, then turns away.*]

FRED: Cover the bed.

LIZZIE: All right, all right. I'll cover it. [*She covers the bed and laughs to herself.*] "It smells of sin!" What do you know about that? You know, it's *your* sin, honey. [FRED *shakes his head.*] Yes, of course, it's mine too. But then, I've got so many on my conscience — [*She sits down on the bed and forces* FRED *to sit beside her.*] Come on. Sit on *our* sin. A pretty nice sin, wasn't it? [*She laughs.*] But don't lower your eyes like that. Do I frighten you? [FRED *crushes her against him brutally.*] You're hurting me! You're hurting me! [*He releases her.*] You're a funny guy. You seem to be in a bad mood. [*After a while*] Tell me your first name. You don't want to? That bothers me, not to know your first name. Really, it would be the first time. They don't usually tell me their last names, and I can understand that. But the first name! How do you expect me to know one of you from another if I don't know your first names? Tell me, honey, go on.

FRED: No.

LIZZIE: Well, then, you can be the nameless gentleman. [*She gets up.*] Wait. I'm going to finish straightening things up. [*She puts a few things in order.*] There we are. Everything's in place. The chairs around the table: that's more refined. Do you know anyone who sells prints? I'd like some pictures on the wall. I have a lovely one in my trunk. *The Broken Pitcher*, it's called. It shows a young girl; she's broken her pitcher, poor thing. It's French.

FRED: What pitcher?

LIZZIE: How should I know? Her pitcher. She must have had a pitcher. I'd like to have an old grandmother to match. She could be knitting, or telling her grand-

children a story. I think I'll pull up the shades and
open the window. [*She does.*] How nice it is outside!
It's going to be a fine day. [*She stretches.*] Oh, I feel
good; it's a beautiful day, I've taken a bath, I've had
good loving; gee, I feel swell! How good I do feel!
Come look at the view I have. Look! I have a lovely
view. Nothing but trees, it makes you feel rich. I
certainly had luck: right off I found a room in a nice
place. Aren't you coming? Don't you like your own
town?

FRED: I like it from my own window.

LIZZIE [*suddenly*]: It doesn't bring bad luck, to see a
nigger just after waking up, does it?

FRED: Why?

LIZZIE: I—there's one going past down there, on the
other side of the street.

FRED: It's always bad luck when you see a nigger. Niggers
are the Devil. [*A pause.*] Close the window.

LIZZIE: Don't you want me to air the place?

FRED: I told you to close the window. O.K. And pull
down the shade. Put the lights on again.

LIZZIE: Why? Because of the niggers?

FRED: Don't be stupid!

LIZZIE: It's so nice and sunny.

FRED: I don't want any sunshine in here. I want it to
be like it was last night. Close the window, I said. I'll
find the sunshine again when I go out. [*He gets up,
goes toward her, and looks at her.*]

LIZZIE [*vaguely uneasy*]: What's the matter?

FRED: Nothing. Give me my tie.

LIZZIE: It's in the bathroom. [*She goes out.* FRED *hastily
opens the drawers of the table and rummages through
them.* LIZZIE *comes back with his tie.*] Here you are!
Wait. [*She ties it for him.*] You know, I don't usually
take one-night stands because then I have to see too
many new faces. What I'd like would be to have three
or four older men, one for Tuesday, one for Thursday,
one for the week end. I'm telling you this: you're rather
young, but you are a serious fellow, and should you

ever feel the urge— Well, well, I won't insist. Think it
over. My, my! You're as pretty as a picture. Kiss me,
good-looking; kiss me just for the hell of it. What's the
matter? Don't you want to kiss me? [*He kisses her
suddenly and brutally, then pushes her away.*] Oof!

FRED: You're the Devil.

LIZZIE: What?

FRED: You're the Devil.

LIZZIE: The Bible again! What's the matter with you?

FRED: Nothing. I was just kidding.

LIZZIE: Funny way to kid. [*A pause.*] Did you like it?

FRED: Like what?

LIZZIE [*she mimics him, smiling*]: Like what? My, but
you're stupid, my little lady.

FRED: Oh! Oh that? Yes, I liked it. I liked it fine. How
much do you want?

LIZZIE: Who said anything about that? I asked you if
you liked it. You might have answered me nicely.
What's the matter? You didn't really like it? Oh, that
would surprise me, you know, that would surprise me
very much.

FRED: Shut up.

LIZZIE: You held me tight, so tight. And then you whis-
pered that you loved me.

FRED: You were drunk.

LIZZIE: No, I was not drunk.

FRED: Yes, you were drunk.

LIZZIE: I tell you I wasn't.

FRED: In any case, I was. I don't remember anything.

LIZZIE: That's a pity. I got undressed in the bathroom,
and when I came back to you, you got all red and
flustered, don't you remember? I even said to you:
"There's my little lobster." Don't you remember how
you wanted to put out the light and how you loved
me in the dark? I thought that was nice and respectful.
Don't you remember?

FRED: No.

LIZZIE: And when we pretended we were two babies in
the same crib? Don't you remember that?

FRED: I tell you to shut up. What's done at night belongs to the night. In the daytime you don't talk about it.

LIZZIE: And if it gives me a kick to talk about it? I had a good time, you know.

FRED: Sure, you had a good time! [*He approaches her, gently kisses her shoulders, then takes her by the throat.*] You always enjoy yourself when you've got a man wrapped up. [*A pause.*] I've forgotten all about it, your wonderful night. Completely forgotten it. I remember the dance hall, that's all. If there was anything else, you're the only one who remembers it. [*He presses his hands to her throat.*]

LIZZIE: What are you doing?

FRED: Just holding your throat in my hands.

LIZZIE: You're hurting me.

FRED: You are the only one who remembers. If I were to squeeze a tiny bit harder, there would be no one in the world to remember last night. [*He releases her.*] How much do you want?

LIZZIE: If you don't remember, it must be because I didn't do my work well. I wouldn't charge for a bad job.

FRED: Cut the comedy. How much?

LIZZIE: Look here; I've been in this place since the day before yesterday. You were the first one to visit me. The first customer gets me free; it brings luck.

FRED: I don't need your presents. [*He puts a ten-dollar bill on the table.*]

LIZZIE: I don't want your dough, but I'd like to know how much you think I'm worth. Wait, let me guess! [*She picks up the bill with her eyes closed.*] Forty dollars? No, that's too much, and anyway there would be two bills. Twenty dollars? No? Then this must be more than forty dollars. Fifty. A hundred? [*All the while, FRED watches her, laughing silently.*] I hate to do this, but I'm going to look. [*She looks at the bill.*] Haven't you made a mistake?

FRED: I don't think so.

LIZZIE: You know what you gave me?

FRED: Yes.

LIZZIE: Take it back. Take it right back. [*He makes a gesture of refusal.*] Ten dollars! Ten dollars! That's what I call a good lay—a young girl like me for ten dollars? Did you see my legs? [*She shows him her legs.*] And my breasts? Did you see them? Are these ten-dollar breasts? Take your ten bucks and scram, before I get sore. Ten bucks. My lord kisses me all over, my lord keeps wanting to start all over again, my lord asks me to tell him about my childhood, and this morning my lord thinks he can crab, and complain, as if he paid me by the month; and all for how much? Not for forty, not for thirty, not for twenty: for ten dollars!

FRED: For pigging around, that's a lot.

LIZZIE: Pig yourself. Where do you come from, you hayseed? Your mother must have been a fine slut if she didn't teach you to respect women.

FRED: Will you shut up?

LIZZIE: A fine bitch! A fine bitch!

FRED [*with cold rage*]: My advice to you, young woman, is don't talk to the fellows around here about their mothers, if you don't want to get your neck twisted.

LIZZIE [*approaching him*]: Go on, strangle me! Strangle me! Let's see you do it!

FRED [*retreating*]: Don't get excited. [LIZZIE *takes a vase from the table, with the evident intention of throwing it at him.*] Here's ten dollars more, just don't get excited. Don't get excited or I'll have you run in.

LIZZIE: You, you're going to have me run in?

FRED: Yes. Me.

LIZZIE: You?

FRED: Me.

LIZZIE: That I'd like to see!

FRED: I'm Clarke's son.

LIZZIE: Which Clarke?

FRED: Senator Clarke.

LIZZIE: Yeah? And I'm Roosevelt's daughter.

FRED: Have you ever seen a picture of Senator Clarke in the papers?

LIZZIE: Yeah. So what?

FRED: Here it is. [*He shows her a photograph.*] I'm there next to him. He's got his arm around my shoulder.

LIZZIE [*suddenly calm*]: Look at that! Gosh, he's a good-looking man, your father. Let me see. [FRED *snatches the photograph out of her hands.*]

FRED: That's enough.

LIZZIE: He looks so nice—sorta kind and yet firm! Is it true that he's got a silver tongue? [*He doesn't answer.*] Is this your garden?

FRED: Yes.

LIZZIE: He looks so tall. And those little girls on the chairs—are they your sisters? [*He doesn't reply.*] Is your house on the hill?

FRED: Yes.

LIZZIE: Then, when you get your breakfast in the morning, you can see the whole town from your window?

FRED: Yes.

LIZZIE: Do they ring a bell at mealtime to call you? You might answer me.

FRED: We have a gong for that.

LIZZIE [*in ecstasy*]: A gong! I don't understand you. With such a family and such a house, you'd have to pay me to sleep out. [*A pause.*] I'm sorry I said that about your mother; I was mad. Is she in the picture too?

FRED: I've forbidden you to talk about her.

LIZZIE: All right, all right. [*A pause.*] Can I ask you a question? [*He doesn't answer.*] If it disgusts you to make love, why did you come here to me? [*He doesn't answer. She sighs.*] Well, as long as I'm here, I guess I'll have to get used to your ways.

[*A pause.* FRED *combs his hair in front of the mirror.*]

FRED: You're from up North?

LIZZIE: Yes.

FRED: From New York?

LIZZIE: What's it to you?

FRED: You spoke of New York, just before.

LIZZIE: Anyone can talk about New York. That doesn't prove a thing.

FRED: Why didn't you stay up there?

LIZZIE: I was fed up.

FRED: Trouble?

LIZZIE: Yes, sure. I attract trouble; some people are like that. You see this snake? [*She shows him her bracelet.*] It brings bad luck.

FRED: Why do you wear it?

LIZZIE: As long as I have it, I have to keep it. It's supposed to be pretty awful—a snake's revenge.

FRED: You were the one the nigger tried to rape?

LIZZIE: What's that?

FRED: You arrived the day before yesterday, on the six-o'clock express?

LIZZIE: Yes.

FRED: Then you must be the one.

LIZZIE: No one tried to rape me. [*She laughs, not without a trace of bitterness.*] Rape me! That's a good one!

FRED: It's you; Webster told me yesterday, on the dance floor.

LIZZIE: Webster? [*A pause.*] So that's it!

FRED: That's what?

LIZZIE: So that's what made your eyes shine. It excited you, huh? You bastard! With such a good father.

FRED: You little fool! [*A pause.*] If I thought you had slept with a nigger—

LIZZIE: Go on.

FRED: I have five colored servants. When they call me to the phone, they wipe it off before they hand it to me.

LIZZIE [*whistles admiringly*]: I see.

FRED [*calmly*]: We don't like niggers too much here, and we don't like white folk who play around with them.

LIZZIE: That'll do. I have nothing against them, but I don't like them to touch me.

FRED: How could anyone be sure? You are the Devil.

The nigger is the Devil too. [*Abruptly*] So he tried to rape you?

LIZZIE: What's it to you?

FRED: The two of them came over to your seat. Then after a while they jumped on you. You called for help and some white people came. One of the niggers flashed his razor, and a white man shot him. The other nigger got away.

LIZZIE: Is that what Webster told you?

FRED: Yes.

LIZZIE: Where did he get that story?

FRED: It's all over town.

LIZZIE: All over town? That's just my luck. Haven't you got anything else to talk about?

FRED: Did it happen the way I said?

LIZZIE: Not at all. The two niggers kept to themselves and didn't even look at me. Then four white men got on the train, and two of them made passes at me. They had just won a football game, and they were drunk. They said that they could smell nigger and wanted to throw them out of the window. The blacks fought back as well as they could, and one of the white men got punched in the eye. And that was when he pulled out a gun and fired. That was all. The other nigger jumped off the train as we were coming into the station.

FRED: We know who it is. He'll gain nothing by waiting. [*A pause.*] When you come up before the judge, are you going to tell him the story you just told me?

LIZZIE: What's it to you?

FRED: Answer me.

LIZZIE: I am not coming up before any judge. I told you I hate any trouble.

FRED: You'll have to appear in court.

LIZZIE: I won't go. I don't want anything more to do with the cops.

FRED: They'll come and get you.

LIZZIE: Then I'll tell them what I saw. [*A pause.*]

FRED: Do you realize what that means?

LIZZIE: What does that mean?

FRED: It means testifying against a white man in behalf of a nigger.

LIZZIE: But suppose the white man is guilty.

FRED: He isn't guilty.

LIZZIE: Since he killed, he's guilty.

FRED: Guilty of what?

LIZZIE: Of killing!

FRED: But it was a nigger he killed.

LIZZIE: So what?

FRED: If you were guilty every time you killed a nigger—

LIZZIE: He had no right.

FRED: What right?

LIZZIE: He had no right.

FRED: That right comes from up North. [*A pause.*] Guilty or not, you can't punish a fellow of your own race.

LIZZIE: I don't want to have anyone punished. They'll just ask me what I saw, and I'll tell them. [*A pause. FRED comes up to her.*]

FRED: What is there between you and this nigger? Why are you protecting him?

LIZZIE: I don't even know him.

FRED: Then what's the trouble?

LIZZIE: I just want to tell the truth.

FRED: The truth! A ten-dollar whore who wants to tell the truth! There is no truth; there's only whites and blacks, that's all. Seventeen · thousand white men, twenty thousand niggers. This isn't New York; we can't fool around down here. [*A pause.*] Thomas is my cousin.

LIZZIE: What?

FRED: Thomas, the one who killed the nigger; he's my cousin.

LIZZIE [*surprised*]: Oh!

FRED: He comes from a good family. That might not mean much to you, but he's from a good family all the same.

LIZZIE: Good! A guy who kept rubbing up against me and tried to put his hand under my skirt. I can do without such gentlemen. I'm not surprised that you both come from the same family.

FRED [*raising his hand*]: You dirty bitch! [*He controls himself.*] You are the Devil, and with the Devil you can't win. He put his hand under your skirt, he shot down a dirty nigger; so what? You do things like that without thinking; they don't count. Thomas is a leading citizen, that's what counts.

LIZZIE: Maybe so. But the nigger didn't do anything.

FRED: A nigger has always done something.

LIZZIE: I'd never rat on anyone.

FRED: If it's not on him, it'll be on Thomas. You'll have to give away one of them, whatever you do. You'll just have to choose.

LIZZIE: So there we are! Here's me in it up to my neck —just for a change. [*To her bracelet*] God damn you, can't you pick on anyone else? [*She throws the bracelet on the floor.*]

FRED: How much do you want?

LIZZIE: I don't want a cent.

FRED: Five hundred dollars.

LIZZIE: Not a cent.

FRED: It would take you much more than one night to earn five hundred dollars.

LIZZIE: Especially if all I get is tightwads like you. [*A pause.*] So that's why you picked me up last night?

FRED: Oh, hell.

LIZZIE: So that was why. You said to yourself: "There's the babe. I'll go home with her and arrange the whole thing." So that's what you wanted! You tickled my hand, but you were as cold as ice. You were thinking: "How'll I get her to do it?" [*A pause.*] But tell me this! Tell me this, my boy. If you came up here with me to talk business, did you have to sleep with me? Huh? Why did you sleep with me, you bastard? Why did you sleep with me?

FRED: Damned if I know.

LIZZIE [*sinks into a chair, weeping*]: Oh, you dirty, filthy bastard!

FRED: Five hundred dollars. Don't cry, for Christ's sake! Five hundred dollars! Stop bawling! Stop bawling! Look, Lizzie! Lizzie! Be reasonable! Five hundred dollars!

LIZZIE [*sobbing*]: I'm not reasonable, and I don't want your five hundred dollars. I just don't want to bear false witness. I want to go back to New York, I want to get out of here! I want to get out of here! [*The bell rings. Startled, she stops crying. The bell rings again. Whispering*] Who is it? Be quiet. [*A long ring.*] I won't open. Be still. [*Knocking on the door.*]

A VOICE: Open up. Police.

LIZZIE [*in a low voice*]: The cops. I knew it had to happen. [*She exhibits the bracelet.*] It's this thing's fault. [*She kisses it and puts it back on her arm.*] I guess I'd better keep it on me. Hide. [*Knocking on the door.*]

THE VOICE: Police!

LIZZIE: But why don't you go hide? Go in the toilet. [*He doesn't budge. She pushes him with all her strength.*] Well, go on! Get out!

THE VOICE: Are you there, Fred? Fred? Are you there?

FRED: Yes, I'm here. [*He brushes her aside. She looks at him with amazement.*]

LIZZIE: So that's what you were after!

[*FRED opens the door and admits* JOHN *and* JAMES. *The door to the street remains open.*]

JOHN: Police. Are you Lizzie MacKay?

LIZZIE [*without hearing him, continues to look at* FRED]: So that's why!

JOHN [*shaking her by the shoulder*]: Answer when you are spoken to.

LIZZIE: What? Yes, that's me.

JOHN: Your papers.

LIZZIE [*makes an effort to control herself*]: What right have you got to question me? What are you doing in my place? [*JOHN shows his badge.*] Anyone can

wear a star. You're buddies of my fine gentleman here
and you're ganging up on me to make me talk.

JOHN [*showing his police card*]: You know what that is?

LIZZIE [*indicating* JAMES]: How about him?

JOHN [*to* JAMES]: Show her your card.

[JAMES *shows it to her.* LIZZIE *looks at it, goes to the
table, without saying anything, pulls out some papers,
and gives them to the men.*]

JOHN [*pointing to* FRED]: You brought him here last
night, right? You know that prostitution is against the
law?

LIZZIE: Are you sure you can come in here without a
warrant? Aren't you afraid I'll make trouble for you?

JOHN: Don't you worry about us. [*A pause.*] I asked
if you brought him up here to your place?

LIZZIE [*since the police entered she has changed; she
has become more hard and vulgar*]: Don't crack your
skull. Sure, I brought him up to my place. I let him
have it for free. That burns you up, doesn't it?

FRED: You will find two ten-dollar bills on the table.
They are mine.

LIZZIE: Prove it!

FRED [*to the two others, without looking at her*]: I
picked them up at the bank yesterday morning with
twenty-eight others of the same series. You've only
got to check up on the serial numbers.

LIZZIE [*violently*]: I wouldn't take them. I refused his
filthy money. I threw it in his face.

JOHN: If you refused, why is it lying on the table?

LIZZIE [*after a pause*]: That does it. [*She looks at* FRED
in a kind of stupor and says, almost tenderly]: So
that's what you were up to? [*To the others*] Well, what
do you want?

JOHN: Sit down. [*To* FRED] You told her what's what?
[FRED *nods.*] I told you to sit down. [*He pushes her
into a chair.*] The judge agrees to let Thomas go if
he has a signed statement from you. The statement
has already been written for you; all you have to do
is sign it. Tomorrow there'll be a formal hearing. Can

you read? [LIZZIE *shrugs her shoulders, and he hands her a paper.*] Read it and sign.

LIZZIE: Lies from beginning to end.

JOHN: Maybe so. So what?

LIZZIE: I won't sign.

FRED: Take her along. [*To* LIZZIE] It's eighteen months, you know.

LIZZIE: Eighteen months, yes. But when I get out, I'll fry your hide.

FRED: Not if I can help it. [*They look at each other.*] You might telegraph New York; I think she's wanted up there for something.

LIZZIE [*admiringly*]: You're as bitchy as a woman. I never thought I'd meet a guy who could be such a bastard.

JOHN: Make up your mind. Either you sign or it's the cooler.

LIZZIE: I prefer the cooler. I don't want to lie.

FRED: Not lie, you slut! And what did you do all night? When you called me "honey baby," "lover man," I suppose you weren't lying. When you sighed to make me think I was giving you a thrill, weren't you lying?

LIZZIE [*defiantly*]: You'd like to think so, wouldn't you? No, I wasn't lying. [*They stare at each other.* FRED *looks away.*]

FRED: Let's get this over with. Here's my fountain pen. Sign.

LIZZIE: You can put it away.

[*A pause. The three men seem embarrassed.*]

FRED: So that's the way it is! The finest fellow in town, and his life depends on the whim of a floozy like this! [*He walks up and down, then comes abruptly up to* LIZZIE.] Look at him. [*He shows her a photograph.*] You've seen a man or two, in your filthy trade. Have you ever seen a face like that? Look at that forehead, look at that chin, look at the medals on his uniform. No, no, don't look away. There is no getting out of it: here's your victim, you have got to face him. See how young he is, how straight he stands. Isn't he handsome? But don't you worry, when he leaves prison, ten years from now, he will be bent like an old man, bald and toothless. But you'll be proud of your good work. You were just a little chiseler until now; but this time, you're dealing with a real man, and you want to take his life. What do you say to that? Are you rotten to the core? [*He forces her to her knees.*] On your knees, whore. On your knees before the picture of the man you want to dishonor!

[CLARKE *enters through the door they have left open.*]

THE SENATOR: Let her go. [*To* LIZZIE] Get up.

FRED: Hello!

JOHN: Hello!

THE SENATOR: Hello! Hello!

JOHN [*to* LIZZIE]: Meet Senator Clarke.

THE SENATOR [*to* LIZZIE]: Hello!

LIZZIE: Hello!

THE SENATOR: Fine! Now we've all been introduced. [*He looks at* LIZZIE.] So this is the young lady. She impresses me as a mighty nice girl.

FRED: She doesn't want to sign.

THE SENATOR: She is perfectly right. You break in on her without having the right to do so. [*Then, more forcefully, to forestall* JOHN] Without having the slightest right to do so. You are brutal to her, and you try to make her go against her own conscience. This is not the American way. Did the Negro rape you, my child?

LIZZIE: No.

THE SENATOR: Excellent. So that is clear. Look me in the eyes. [*He looks at her fixedly.*] I am sure she is telling the truth. [*A pause.*] Poor Mary! [*To the others*] Well, boys, let's go. There is nothing more to be done here. Let's make our apologies to the young lady and go.

LIZZIE: Who's Mary?

THE SENATOR: Mary? She is my sister, the mother of this unfortunate Thomas. A poor, dear old lady, who is going to be killed by all this. Good-by, my child.

LIZZIE [*in a choking voice*]: Senator!

THE SENATOR: My child?

LIZZIE: I'm sorry.

THE SENATOR: Why should you be sorry, when you have told the truth?

LIZZIE: I am sorry that—that that's the truth.

THE SENATOR: There is nothing either of us can do about that. And no one has the right to ask you to bear false witness. [*A pause.*] No. Don't think of her any more.

LIZZIE: Who?

THE SENATOR: Of my sister. Weren't you thinking about my sister?

LIZZIE: Yes.

THE SENATOR: I can read your mind, my child. Do you want me to tell you what's going on in your head? [*Imitating* LIZZIE] "If I signed, the Senator would go to her and say: 'Lizzie MacKay is a good girl, and she's the one who's giving your son back to you.' And she would smile through her tears. She would say: 'Lizzie Mackay? I shall not forget that name.' And I who have no family, relegated by cruel fate to social banishment, I would know that a dear little old lady was thinking of me in her great house; that an American mother had taken me to her heart." Poor Lizzie, think no more about it.

LIZZIE: Has she white hair?

THE SENATOR: Completely white. But her face has stayed young. And if you could see her smile— She'll never smile again. Good-by. Tomorrow you shall tell the judge the truth.

LIZZIE: Are you going?

THE SENATOR: Why, yes; I am going to her house. I shall have to tell her about our conversation.

LIZZIE: She knows you are here?

THE SENATOR: She begged me to come to you.

LIZZIE: My God! And she's waiting? And you're going to tell her that I refused to sign. How she will hate me!

THE SENATOR [*putting his hands on her shoulders*]: My poor child, I wouldn't want to be in your shoes.

LIZZIE: What a mess! [*Addressing her bracelet*] It's all your fault, you filthy thing.

THE SENATOR: What?

LIZZIE: Nothing. [*A pause.*] As things stand, it's too bad the nigger didn't really rape me.

THE SENATOR [*touched*]: My child.

LIZZIE [*sadly*]: It would have meant so much to you, and it would have been so little trouble for me.

THE SENATOR: Thank you. [*A pause.*] I should so like to help you. [*A pause.*] Alas, the truth is the truth.

LIZZIE [*sadly*]: Yeah, sure.

THE SENATOR: And the truth is that the Negro didn't rape you.

LIZZIE [*sadly still*]: Yeah, sure.

THE SENATOR: Yes. [*A pause.*] Of course, here we have a truth of the first degree.

LIZZIE [*not understanding*]: Of the first degree.

THE SENATOR: Yes. I mean—a common truth.

LIZZIE: Common? Isn't that the truth?

THE SENATOR: Yes, yes, it is the truth. It's just that—there are various kinds of truths.

LIZZIE: You think the nigger raped me?

THE SENATOR: No. No, he didn't rape you. From a certain point of view, he didn't rape you at all. But, you see, I am an old man, who has lived a long time, who has made many mistakes, but for some time now I have been a little less often mistaken. And my opinion about this is utterly different from yours.

LIZZIE: What opinion?

THE SENATOR: How can I explain it to you? Look: suppose Uncle Sam suddenly stood before you. What would he say?

LIZZIE [*frightened*]: I don't suppose he would have much of anything to say to me.

THE SENATOR: Are you a Communist?

LIZZIE: Good Lord, no!

THE SENATOR: Then Uncle Sam would have many things to tell you. He would say: "Lizzie, you have reached a point where you must choose between two of my boys. One of them must go. What can you do in a case like this? Well, you keep the better man. Well, then, let us try to see which is the better one. Will you?"

LIZZIE [*carried away*]: Yes, I want to. Oh, I am sorry, I thought it was you saying all that.

THE SENATOR: I was speaking in his name. [*He goes on, as before.*] "Lizzie, this Negro whom you are protecting, what good is he? Somehow or other he was born, God knows where. I nourished and raised him, and how does he pay me back? What does he do for me? nothing at all; he dawdles, he chisels, he sings, he buys pink and green suits. He is my son, and I love him as much as I do my other boys. But I ask you: does he live like a man? I would not even notice if he died."

LIZZIE: My, how fine you talk.

THE SENATOR [*in the same vein*]: "The other one, this Thomas, has killed a Negro, and that's very bad. But I need him. He is a hundred-per-cent American, comes from one of our oldest families, has studied at Harvard, is an officer—I need officers—he employs two thousand workers in his factory—two thousand unemployed if he happened to die. He's a leader, a firm bulwark against the Communists, labor unions, and the Jews. His duty is to live, and yours is to preserve his life. That's all. Now, choose."

LIZZIE: My, how well you talk!

THE SENATOR: Choose!

LIZZIE [*startled*]: How's that? Oh yes. [*A pause.*] You mixed me up, I don't know where I am.

THE SENATOR: Look at me, Lizzie. Do you have confidence in me?

LIZZIE: Yes, Senator.

THE SENATOR: Do you believe that I would urge you to do anything wrong?

LIZZIE: No, Senator.

THE SENATOR: Then I urge you to sign. Here is my pen.

LIZZIE: You think she'll be pleased with me?

THE SENATOR: Who?

LIZZIE: Your sister.

THE SENATOR: She will love you, from a distance, as her very own child.

LIZZIE: Perhaps she'll send me some flowers?

THE SENATOR: Very likely.

LIZZIE: Oi her picture with an inscription.

THE SENATOR: It's quite possible.

LIZZIE: I'd hang it on the wall. [*A pause. She walks up and down, much agitated.*] What a mess! [*Coming up to* THE SENATOR *again*] What will you do to the nigger if I sign?

THE SENATOR: To the nigger? Pooh! [*He takes her by the shoulders.*] If you sign, the whole town will adopt you. The whole town. All the mothers in it.

LIZZIE: But—

THE SENATOR: Do you suppose that a whole town could be mistaken? A whole town, with its ministers and its priests, its doctors, its lawyers, its artists, its mayor and his aides, with all its charities? Do you think that could happen?

LIZZIE: No, no, no.

THE SENATOR: Give me your hand. [*He forces her to sign.*] So now it's done. I thank you in the name of my sister and my nephew, in the name of the seventeen thousand white inhabitants of our town, in the name of the American people, whom I represent in these parts. Give me your forehead, my child. [*He kisses her on the forehead.*] Come along, boys. [*To* LIZZIE] I shall see you later in the evening; we still have something to talk about. [*He goes out.*]

FRED [*leaving*]: Good-by, Lizzie.

LIZZIE: Good-by. [*They all go out. She stands there overwhelmed, then rushes to the door.*] Senator! Senator! I don't want to sign! Tear up the paper! Senator! [*She comes back to the front of the stage and mechanically takes hold of the vacuum cleaner.*] Uncle Sam! [*She turns on the sweeper.*] Something tells me I've been had —but good! [*She pushes the vacuum cleaner furiously.*]

CURTAIN

SCENE TWO

*Same setting, twelve hours later. The lamps are lit, the
windows are open. In the night, a growing clamor
outside.* THE NEGRO *appears at the window, straddles
the window-sill, and jumps into the empty room. He
crosses to the middle of the stage. The bell rings. He
hides behind a curtain.* LIZZIE *emerges from the bathroom, crosses to the street door, and opens it.*

LIZZIE: Come in! [THE SENATOR *enters.*] Well?

THE SENATOR: Thomas is in the arms of his mother. I
have come to bring you their thanks.

LIZZIE: Is she happy?

THE SENATOR: Supremely happy.

LIZZIE: Did she cry?

THE SENATOR: Cry? Why should she cry? She is a woman
of character.

LIZZIE: But you said she would cry.

THE SENATOR: That was just a manner of speaking.

LIZZIE: She didn't expect this, did she? She thought I was
a bad woman and that I would testify for the nigger.

THE SENATOR: She put her trust in God.

LIZZIE: What does she think of me?

THE SENATOR: She thanks you.

LIZZIE: Didn't she ask what I looked like?

THE SENATOR: No.

LIZZIE: She thinks I'm a good girl?

THE SENATOR: She thinks you did your duty.

LIZZIE: She does?

THE SENATOR: She hopes that you will continue to do it.

LIZZIE: Oh yes, yes.

THE SENATOR: Lizzie, look me in the eyes. [*He takes her
by the shoulders.*] You will continue to do your duty?
You aren't going to disappoint her?

LIZZIE: Don't you worry. I can't go back on what I said; they'd throw me in the clink. [*A pause.*] What's all that shouting about?

THE SENATOR: Pay no attention.

LIZZIE: I can't stand it any more. [*She closes the window.*] Senator?

THE SENATOR: My child?

LIZZIE: You are sure that we haven't. made a mistake, that I really did what I should?

THE SENATOR: Absolutely sure.

LIZZIE: I don't know where I am any more; you've mixed me up; you're too quick for me. What time is it?

THE SENATOR: Eleven o'clock.

LIZZIE: Eight hours left until daylight. I know I won't be able to sleep a wink. [*A pause.*] It's just as hot at night here as when the sun is up. [*A pause.*] What about the nigger?

THE SENATOR: What Negro? Oh, yes, of course, they are looking for him.

LIZZIE: What will they do to him? [THE SENATOR *shrugs his shoulders. The shouting outside increases.* LIZZIE *goes to the window.*] What is all this shouting for? Men are running about with flashlights and dogs. Are they celebrating something? Or— Tell me what's up, Senator! Tell me what's going on!

THE SENATOR [*taking a letter out of his pocket*]: My sister asked me to give you this.

LIZZIE [*with interest*]: She's written me? [*She tears open the envelope, and takes from it a hundred-dollar bill, rummages in it to find a letter, finds none, crushes the envelope, and throws it on the floor. She takes a different tone now.*] A hundred dollars. You've done very well; your son promised me five hundred. You got a bargain.

THE SENATOR: My child.

LIZZIE: You can thank the lady. You can tell her that I'd rather've had a porcelain vase or some nylons, something she took the trouble to pick out for me herself. But it's the intention that counts, isn't it? [*A pause.*] You've had me good. [*They face each other.* THE SENATOR *moves closer to her.*]

THE SENATOR: I thank you, my child; we'll have a little talk—just the two of us. You're facing a moral crisis and need my help.

LIZZIE: What I particularly need is some dough, but I think we can make a deal, you and me. [*A pause.*] Until now I liked old men best, because they looked so respectable, but I'm beginning to wonder if they're not more crooked than the others.

THE SENATOR [*gaily*]: Crooked! I wish my colleagues could hear you. What wonderful frankness! There is something in you that your deplorable circumstances have not spoiled! [*He pats her.*] Yes indeed. Something. [*She submits to him, passive but scornful.*] I'll be back, don't bother to see me out.

[*He goes out.* LIZZIE *is immobile, as if paralyzed. She picks up the bill, crumples it, throws it on the floor, falls into a chair, and bursts into sobs. Outside, the yelling is closer and more intense. Pistol-shots in the distance.* THE NEGRO *emerges from his hiding-place. He plants himself in front of her. She raises her head and gives a startled cry.*]

LIZZIE: Ah! [*A pause. She rises.*] I knew you'd show up. I just knew it. How did you get in?

THE NEGRO: Through the window.

LIZZIE: What do you want?

THE NEGRO: Hide me.

LIZZIE: I told you, no.

THE NEGRO: You hear them out there, ma'am?

LIZZIE: Yes.

THE NEGRO: That's the beginning of the hunt.

LIZZIE: What hunt?

THE NEGRO: The nigger hunt.

LIZZIE: Oh! [*A long pause.*] Are you sure no one saw you come in?

THE NEGRO: Yes, I'm sure.

LIZZIE: What will they do to you if they get you?

THE NEGRO: Gasoline.

LIZZIE: What?

THE NEGRO: Gasoline. [*He makes an expressive gesture.*] They'll set me on fire.

LIZZIE: I see. [*She goes to the window and draws the curtain.*] Sit down. [THE NEGRO *falls into a chair.*] You just had to come here! Won't I ever get out of this? [*She approaches him almost threateningly.*] I hate trouble, don't you understand? [*Tapping her foot.*] I hate it! I hate it! I hate it!

THE NEGRO: They think I harmed you, ma'am.

LIZZIE: So what?

THE NEGRO: So they won't look for me here.

LIZZIE: Do you know why they are after you?

THE NEGRO: Because they suppose I wronged you, ma'am.

LIZZIE: Do you know who told them that?

THE NEGRO: No.

LIZZIE: I did. [*A long silence.* THE NEGRO *looks at her.*] What do you think of that?

THE NEGRO: Why did you do that, ma'am? Oh, why did you do that?

LIZZIE: That's what I keep asking myself.

THE NEGRO: They won't have any pity; they'll whip me across the eyes, they'll pour their cans of gas over me. Oh, why did you do it? I didn't harm you.

LIZZIE: Oh yes, you did too. You can't imagine how much you've harmed me. [*A pause.*] Don't you want to choke me?

THE NEGRO: Lots of times they force people to say things they don't mean.

LIZZIE: Yes, lots of times. And when they can't force them, they mix them up with their sweet talk. [*A pause.*] Well? No? You're not going to choke me? You're a good guy. [*A pause.*] I'll hide you until tomorrow night. [*He makes a move.*] Don't touch me; I don't like niggers. [*Shouts and pistol-shots outside.*] They're getting closer. [*She goes to the window, draws the curtains, and looks out into the street.*] We're cooked.

THE NEGRO: What are they doing?

LIZZIE: They've put guards at both ends of the block, and they are searching all the houses. You just had to come here. Someone must have seen you come down the street. [*She looks out again.*] This is it. It's our turn. They are coming up here.

THE NEGRO: How many?

LIZZIE: Five or six. The others are waiting outside. [*She turns toward him again.*] Don't shake so. Good God, don't shake so! [*A pause. To her bracelet*] It's all your fault! You pig of a snake! [*She tears it from her arm, throws it on the floor, and tramples on it.*] Trash! [*To* THE NEGRO] You just had to come here. [THE NEGRO *rises, as if about to leave.*] Stay put. If you go out you're done for.

THE NEGRO: What about the roof?

LIZZIE: With this moon? You can go on up if you feel like being a target. [*A pause.*] Wait a second. They have two floors to search before ours. I told you not to shake so. [*A long silence. She walks up and down.* THE NEGRO, *completely overcome, stays in the chair.*] Do you have a gun?

THE NEGRO: Oh, no!

LIZZIE: All right. [*She rummages in a drawer and brings out a revolver.*]

THE NEGRO: What's that for, ma'am?

LIZZIE: I am going to open the door and ask them to come in. For twenty-five years I have had to take their crap about old mothers with white hair, about war heroes, about Uncle Sam. But now I've caught on. They won't get away with it altogether. I'll open the door and say to them: "He's inside. He's here, but he's done nothing; I was forced to sign a false statement. I swear by Christ that he did nothing."

THE NEGRO: They won't believe you.

LIZZIE: Maybe not. Maybe they won't believe me; but then you'll cover them with the gun, and if they still come after you, you can shoot.

THE NEGRO: Others will come.

LIZZIE: Shoot them too! And if you see the Senator's son, try not to miss him; he's the one who cooked this whole thing up. We're cornered, aren't we? Anyhow, this is our last chance 'cause if they find you here with me I won't be worth a plugged nickel. So we might as well kick off in company. [*She offers him the revolver.*] Take it! I tell you to take it!

THE NEGRO: I can't, ma'am.

LIZZIE: Why not?

THE NEGRO: I can't shoot white folks.

LIZZIE: Really! That would bother them, wouldn't it?

THE NEGRO: They're white folks, ma'am.

LIZZIE: So what? Maybe they got a right to bleed you like a pig just because they're white?

THE NEGRO: But they're white folks.

LIZZIE: What a laugh! You know, you're like me; you're just as big a sucker as I am. Still, when they all get together—

THE NEGRO: Why don't you shoot, ma'am?

LIZZIE: I told you that I'm a sucker. [*There are steps on the stairway.*] Here they come. [*A sharp laugh.*] We're sure sitting pretty. [*A pause.*] Get in the toilet and don't budge. Hold your breath.

[THE NEGRO *obeys.* LIZZIE *waits. The bell rings. She crosses herself, picks up the bracelet, and goes to open the door. There are men with guns.*]

FIRST MAN: We're looking for the nigger.

LIZZIE: What nigger?

FIRST MAN: The one that raped the woman in the train and cut the Senator's nephew with a razor.

LIZZIE: Well, by God, you won't find him here! [*A pause.*] Don't you recognize me?

SECOND MAN: Yes, yes. I saw you get off the train the day before yesterday.

LIZZIE: That's right. Because I'm the one who was raped, you understand? [*Exclamations. They look at her with fascination, desire, and a kind of horror. They draw back a little.*] If he messes around here, he'll get a little of this. [*She flourishes the revolver. They laugh.*]

FIRST MAN: Don't you want to see him lynched?

LIZZIE: Come for me when you get him.

FIRST MAN: That won't be long, sugar; we know he's hiding in this block.

LIZZIE: Good luck. [*They go out. She shuts the door and puts the revolver on the table.*] You can come out. [THE NEGRO *emerges, kneels, and kisses the hem of her skirt.*] I told you not to touch me. [*She looks him over.*] Just the same, you must be a queer character, to have a whole town after you.

THE NEGRO: I didn't do anything, ma'am, you know I didn't do anything.

LIZZIE: They say a nigger's always done something.

THE NEGRO: Never did anything. Never, never.

LIZZIE [*wiping her brow with her hand*]: I don't know what's right any more. [*A pause.*] Just the same, a whole city can't be completely wrong. [*A pause.*] Oh, shit! I don't understand anything any more.

THE NEGRO: That's how it goes, ma'am. That's how it always goes with white folks.

LIZZIE: You too? You feel guilty?

THE NEGRO: Yes, ma'am.

LIZZIE: But you didn't do anything?

THE NEGRO: No, ma'am.

LIZZIE: What have they got anyhow, that everybody's on their side all the time?

THE NEGRO: They're white folks.

LIZZIE: I'm white too. [*A pause. Sound of steps outside.*] They're coming down again. [*Instinctively she steps closer to him. He trembles, but puts his arm around her shoulders. The sound of steps is fainter. Silence. She suddenly frees herself from his embrace.*] Well, look at us, now! Aren't we alone in the world? Like two orphans. [*The bell rings. They make no answer. The bell rings again.*] Get in the toilet.

[*There is a rapping on the front door.* THE NEGRO *hides.* LIZZIE *goes to open the door. Enter* FRED.]

LIZZIE: Are you crazy? Why come to my door? No, you can't come in, you've given me enough trouble. Get out, get out, you bastard, get out! Get the hell out of here! [*He pushes her aside, closes the door, and takes her by the shoulder. A long pause.*] Well?

FRED: You are the Devil!

LIZZIE: And so you try to break down my door just to tell me that? What a mess! Where have you been? [*A pause.*] Answer me.

FRED: They caught a nigger. It wasn't the right one. But they lynched him just the same.

LIZZIE: So?

FRED: I was with them.

LIZZIE [*whistles*]: I see. [*A pause.*] It begins to look as if seeing a nigger lynched does something to you.

FRED: I want you.

LIZZIE: What?

FRED: You are the Devil. You've bewitched me. I was with them, I had my revolver in my hand, and the nigger was swinging from a branch. I looked at him, and I thought: "I want her." It's not natural.

LIZZIE: Let go of me! I tell you let go of me.

FRED: What have you done to me, what have you got, you witch? I looked at the nigger and I saw you. I saw you swaying above the flames. I fired.

LIZZIE: You filthy bastard! Let me go, let me go. You're a murderer!

FRED: What have you done to me. You stick to me like the teeth in my gums. I see your belly, your dirty whorish belly, I feel your heat in my hands, your smell in my nostrils. I came running here, and I didn't even know whether I wanted to kill you or rape you. Now I know. [*He releases her abruptly.*] I am not going to damn my soul to hell for a whore. [*He comes up to her again.*] Was it true what you told me this morning?

LIZZIE: What?

FRED: That I gave you a thrill?

LIZZIE: Let me alone.

FRED: Swear that it's true. Swear it! [*He twists her wrist. There is a noise of someone moving in the bathroom.*] What's that? [*He listens.*] Someone's in there.

LIZZIE: You're out of your mind. There's nobody.

FRED: Yes, in the toilet. [*He goes toward the bathroom.*]

LIZZIE: You can't go in.

FRED: You see, there is someone.

LIZZIE: It's today's customer. A guy who pays. There. Are you satisfied?

FRED: A customer? No more customers for you. Never any more. You belong to me. [*A pause.*] I must see what he looks like. [*He shouts*] Come out of there!

LIZZIE [*shouting*]: Don't come out. It's a trap.

FRED: You filthy little whore! [*He shoves her out of the way, goes toward the door, and opens it.* THE NEGRO *comes out.*] So that's your customer?

LIZZIE: I hid him because they wanted to hurt him. Don't shoot; you know very well that he's innocent. [FRED *draws his revolver.* THE NEGRO *gets set, pushes* FRED *out of the way, and dashes out.* FRED *runs after him.* LIZZIE *runs to the door, through which the two men have disappeared, and begins to shout.*]

LIZZIE: He's innocent! He's innocent! [*Two pistol-shots. She comes back into the room, her face hard. She goes to the table and takes the gun.* FRED *comes back. She turns toward him, her back to the audience, holding her gun behind her back.* FRED *puts his gun on the table.*] So you got him? [FRED *doesn't answer.*] Well, now it's your turn. [*She covers him with the revolver.*]

FRED: Lizzie! I have a mother!

LIZZIE: Shut your face! They pulled that on me before.

FRED [*approaching her slowly*]: The first Clarke cleared a whole forest, just by himself; he killed seventeen Indians with his bare hands before dying in an ambush; his son practically built this town; he was friends with George Washington, and died at Yorktown, for American independence; my great-grandfather was chief of the Vigilantes in San Francisco, he saved the lives of twenty-two persons in the great fire; my grandfather came back to settle down here, he dug the Mississippi Canal, and was elected Governor. My father is a Senator. I shall be senator after him. I am the last one to carry the family name. We have made this country, and its history is ours. There have been Clarkes in Alaska, in the Philippines, in New Mexico. Can you dare to shoot all of America?

LIZZIE: You come closer, and I'll let you have it.

FRED: Go ahead! Shoot! You see, you can't. A girl like you *can't* shoot a man like me. Who are you? What do you do in this world? Do you even know who your grandfather was? I have a right to live; there are things to be done, and I am expected to do them. Give me the revolver. [*She gives him the revolver, he puts it in his pocket.*] About the nigger, he was running too fast. I missed him. [*A pause. He puts his arms around her.*] I'll put you in a beautiful house, with a garden, on the hill across the river. You'll walk in the garden, but I forbid you to go out; I am very jealous. I'll come to see you after dark, three times a week—on Tuesday, Thursday, and for the week end. You'll have nigger servants, and more money than you ever dreamed of; but you will have to put up with all my whims, and I'll have plenty! [*She yields a bit to his embrace.*] Is it true that I gave you a thrill? Answer me. Is it true?

LIZZIE [*wearily*]: Yes, it's true.

FRED [*patting her on the cheek*]: Then everything is back to normal again. [*A pause.*] My name is Fred.

CURTAIN